RECOLLECTION

OF

MEN AND THINGS

AT

WASHINGTON,

DURING THE THIRD OF A CENTURY.

BY

L. A. GOBRIGHT.

PHILADELPHIA:
CLAXTON, REMSEN & HAFFELFINGER,
WASHINGTON: W. H. & O. H. MORRISON.
1869.

Entered according to Act of Congress, in the year 1869, by
L. A. GOBRIGHT,
In the Clerk's Office of the Supreme Court of the District of Columbia.

PRINTED BY MOORE BROTHERS.

INTRODUCTION.

THE undersigned has resided in the city of Washington for more than the third of a century. Owing to his continuous connection with the press, either as editor, or correspondent and Congressional reporter, he was a witness of many of the things related in this book. He is aware there are omissions of not a few interesting facts; but to carefully prepare them would require more time than he could spare from his regular business pursuits, and to print them would extend this work beyond the limits of a single volume.

When the author first came to this city, the travel between Baltimore and Washington was by stage, the journey occupying all the hours from the rising to the setting of the sun of the longest summer-day. But toward the close of that year—1834—the railroad connecting the two cities was completed.

The population of Washington was then about thirty thousand; now, it is at least one hundred and ten thousand souls. With the increase of inhabitants, there have been not only such improvements as their necessities required, but those which the increasing business of the General Government demanded; therefore, we can all point with pride to our grand public buildings, while the permanent dwellers in Washington can congratulate themselves that the designation of "the city of magnificent distances" will soon be no longer applicable to this locality.

L. A. GOBRIGHT.

WASHINGTON, Dec., 1868.

CONTENTS.

CHAPTER III.

CHAPTER IV.

CHAPTER V.

CHAPTER VI.

CHAPTER VII.

CHAPTER VIII.

CHAPTER IX.

CHAPTER X.

CHAPTER XI.

CHAPTER XII.

CHAPTER XIII.

CHAPTER XIV.

CHAPTER XV.

CHAPTER XVI.

CHAPTER XVII.

CHAPTER XVIII.

CHAPTER XIX.

CHAPTER XX.

CHAPTER XXI.

CHAPTER XXII.

RECOLLECTION OF MEN AND THINGS.

CHAPTER I.

JACKSON'S ADMINISTRATION — THE PANIC SESSION — THE POLITICAL FURNACE — FONDNESS FOR TALKING — EXHIBITIONS OF VIOLENCE — REUBEN M. WHITNEY — HOW HE WAS TREATED BY BAILIE PEYTON AND HENRY A. WISE — HARMLESS DUELS — "HONORABLES" — FISTICUFFS IN THE "BEAR GARDEN" — THE ATTEMPT TO SHOOT JACKSON — A PRINTERS' COLLEGE — PRINTERS' RIOT — RAT KILLING! — PULLING JACKSON'S NOSE — EARTHQUAKE — A FEW WORDS ABOUT THE "OLD HERO."

IT was during the excitement in 1834, growing out of the United States Bank question, that I came to Washington. The political furnace was in full blast. The friends of President Jackson regarded the Bank of the United States as a political means by which to overthrow our liberties, while his enemies neglected no opportunity to stigmatize him as a tyrant.

At that time there was no "hour rule" in the House of Representatives. The period of sixty minutes was not considered sufficiently long for a member to vent his views about any question which might be open to debate. Therefore, it was not unusual for a member to speak during two or three days, especially on the financial question. It seemed to be necessary that the constituency should have a surfeit of words from the representative, as if to establish the fact that his lungs were in a sound condition, and that he was not a silent member! Now, there is an "hour rule" in the House, which gives to all the members a share of the time, excepting when a majority choose to apply the garrote of "the previous question," and thus choke off all discussion, as frequently happens, even on important measures.

The violence of Congressional politicians was often exhibited in committee-rooms.

In February, 1837, Reuben M. Whitney was arraigned before the House of Representatives for contempt, in refusing to attend, when required, before a committee of investigation into the administration of the Executive office. His excuse was that he could not obey the summons without exposing himself thereby to outrage and violence in the committee-room. On examination at the bar of the House, Mr. Fairfield, of Maine, a member of the committee, afterward a Senator from, and Governor of that State, testified to the actual facts. It appeared that Mr. Bailie Peyton, of Tennessee, a member of the committee, regarding a certain answer in writing by Mr. Whitney to an interrogatory propounded by him as offensive, broke out in the words, "Mr. Chairman, I wish you would inform this witness that he is not to insult me in his answers; if he does, I will take his life on the spot." The witness, rising, claimed the protection of the committee; on which Mr. Peyton exclaimed, "You sha'n't speak; you sha'n't say one word while you are in this room; if you do, I will put you to death." Mr. Henry A. Wise, the chairman of the committee, then intervened, saying, "Yes, this insolence is insufferable." Soon after, Mr. Peyton, observing that the witness was looking at him, cried out, "His eyes are on me; he is looking at me — he sha'n't do it — he sha'n't look at me!" These exclamations were accompanied by repeated curses and other profane language.

Mr. Wise himself, in a speech, made the admission that he was armed with deadly weapons, saying: "I watched the motion of that right arm, (of the witness,) the elbow of which could be seen by me, and had it moved one inch he had died on the spot. This was my determination."

Mr. Whitney came to Washington by invitation of the Jackson politicians, and was an efficient co-worker with them in overthrowing the Bank of the United States; furnishing much data from its books, (he having previously been a director of that institution,) in order to show its alleged corruptions; and contributing editorial articles to the "Globe" newspaper to the same end.

Many of the members were exceedingly bitter in their resentments; and, as a consequence, challenges were passed to engage in the duello. It was seldom that any of the parties were hurt, as, not unfrequently, the rifles contained only powder and wad!

There was a difference between members of Congress, as between all other human-kind in the matter of "satisfaction." They were, by compliment, or courtesy, styled "honorable," or "Hon.," and this prefix was never omitted by those who wished to obtain or preserve their friendship. Owing to this difference, not a few were too impatient to await the slow process of "arrangement;" and therefore they followed offensive *words* with *blows*. Such scenes, a third of a century ago, were frequent, but it is not remembered that anything more formidable than a cane or an honorable fist was used in these diversions; although occasionally a pistol was exhibited as an intimidator! The House acquired the name of "Bear Garden," owing to the frequent disgraceful exhibitions.

On the twenty-ninth of January, 1835, an occurrence took place which produced, naturally, a great sensation. As President Jackson, at the ceremony of the funeral of the Hon. Warren R. Davis, of South Carolina, came to the portico of the Capitol, from the rotunda, a person stepped forward from the crowd into the space in front of the President, and snapped a pistol at him, the percussion-cap of which exploded without igniting the charge. This person was struck down by a blow from Lieutenant Gedney, of the Navy, who happened to be near. He also received a blow promptly aimed at him by Secretary Woodbury; but before he met this one, he snapped a second pistol at the President, the cap of which likewise exploded without igniting the charge. The perpetrator of this daring outrage was, of course, immediately secured, and taken into custody by the Marshal for the District of Columbia, by whom he was carried to the City Hall, where he underwent an examination before Chief Justice Cranch. His name was Richard Lawrence, by trade a painter, and a resident of Washington. The witnesses who appeared before the judge, were Secretaries Woodbury and Dickerson; Mr. Burd, a representative from Pennsylvania; Mr. Randolph, Sergeant-at-arms of the House of Representatives; Mr. Kingman, one of the reporters of the National Intelligencer, and Lieutenant Gedney. The pistols, which had been secured by Mr. Burd, were of brass, and on examination in court were found to be well loaded with powder and ball.

Lawrence declined making any explanation of his conduct. Bail was demanded in the sum of one thousand dollars; for want of which, the prisoner was committed to jail.

While on his way from the Capitol to the Marshal's office, in answer to the question as to his motive, he said, he intended to kill President Jackson, because Jackson had killed his father. When asked how, he made no response. His acquaintances said, that he thought himself entitled to be king or governor of this country, and that he brooded over the notion that Jackson stood in his way. It was also asserted that he had declared he was Richard the Third, King of England and America. The boys, therefore, gave him the nickname of "Richard the Third." He said to his sister, who called at the jail to see him, that it was all right, and that General Jackson was his servant, but had not done as he wished, and for this reason he ought to be punished.

The editor of the "Globe," and other Democratic editors, sought to make political capital out of the occurrence. Senator Poindexter, a prominent Whig from Mississippi, was accused of stimulating the attack; but the report of a Congressional committee dispelled all imputation.

Lawrence was tried for the offence; but it appearing that he was insane, he was sent to the asylum for such unfortunates, where, several years ago, he died.

During General Jackson's second term, he laid the corner-stone of "Jackson City," on the Virginia side of the Potomac River, opposite to Washington. There was a great parade on the occasion. The dealers in "corner-lots" appeared in large numbers, among the thousands of spectators.

Although a third of a century has passed since that day, no improvements are apparent — not even in the small tavern for "man and horse." The low flat is still the abode of the aborigines — the frogs. It would be difficult even to find the corner-stone of the *City*.

In the fall of 1834, Duff Green, the editor and publisher of "The Telegraph," issued a circular, addressed to the Southern public, proposing to establish a "Printers' College," in which apprentices were to be educated at "the case," for the editorial and medical professions; the principal feature being to rear nullification editors, subject to his command. Duff Green was the organ of Mr. Calhoun, and the exponent of the nullification doctrine. He set forth, in a plausible way, the advantages of his proposed institution, and urgently appealed to his party-friends for assistance. The printers in his office, however, did not appreciate his scheme; apprehensive that, if carried into execution, it would damage the craft, they unanimously "turned out," or "struck," against his enterprise. They returned to work on his announcement that he had surrendered the undertaking. But he again put forth his views in another form, and for a similar purpose; and the printers again applied to him a dose of his own nullification *physic.* Some accommodation was effected, when the malcontents returned to their work.

Mr. Green, or Duff Green, as he was generally called, carried on his printing operations, including "The Telegraph" and the public work, on E Street, north, between Ninth and Tenth Streets, west; but removed in the fall of 1834, to what is now known as Carroll Place; which was, during the late war, a part of the old Capitol prison. And there, another "turn out" disturbed the operations of the printing establishment; not on account of the "Printers' College," but because of an attempt to introduce the "two-thirds" system of compensation. There was, in this case, no reconciliation between the strikers and the proprietor.

This last strike has almost been forgotten; but

some of the incidents of it may here be revived, as a matter of industrial, as well as political history. Francis P. Blair, Sr., was the editor of the "Daily Globe," and Gales & Seaton were the editors of the "National Intelligencer;" the former paper, the organ of General Jackson; the latter, the Whig exponent; and "The Telegraph" was in the interest of Mr. Calhoun.

Accordingly, a triangular editorial fight was constantly in progress. The Globe and the Intelligencer, while opposed in politics, joined forces, as if by common consent, to make war on Duff Green. Therefore, it was no wonder that both of them should advocate the cause of the strikers. They opened their columns to the insurgents, and editorially assisted them to damage the proprietor of the "Telegraph." The files of that day show that the printers, in well-written documents, opposed the Printers' College, and sent forth their views and warnings against its alleged iniquity. Frequent meetings with reference to the last strike were held by the printers, who were consolidated in their movements; and so furious was the opposition to Duff Green, that the public peace was disturbed by the earnest workings of the craft. A fight between the regulars and the "rats" occurred; and the result was the arrest of the ringleaders of the "regular" printers, who were lodged in jail. There they remained for perhaps a week. After trial, they were pardoned by President Jackson; whether from motives of kindness, or from opposition to Duff Green, is a question not material to the history of those times.

The "rats" were men who had taken the "regulars'" places. Many of them were importations from South Carolina and other parts of the South.

The printers appointed "Rat-Killing Committees," whose business it was to damage those who had taken their places in the "Telegraph" establishment. Some of the regulars who were designated members of these committees, were not enthusiastic, had no heart in the work, were not impatient to crack crowns with big sticks, and avoided collisions; and even those who had "a mind to business," won no laurels and took no scalps in that campaign!

In the course of a very few years the "Telegraph" newspaper deceased.

A friend has related to me the following incidents, about the "nose-pulling," and in relation to "an earthquake."

During the month of May, 1833, General Jackson was invited to lay the corner-stone of the monument to Mary, the mother of Washington, at Fredericksburg, Virginia. The steamboat *Sidney* was chartered to convey thither a large and distinguished company, including President Jackson and several members of the Cabinet. While the boat was stopping at Alexandria, to receive additional passengers, among those who came on board was Lieutenant R. B. Randolph, late of the Navy. He made his way into the cabin, where the President was sitting reading a newspaper, and advanced as if to address him, beginning to draw off his gloves. The President, not knowing him, and supposing it was some person about to salute him, and seeing the difficulty in getting off his gloves, stretched forth his hand, saying, "Never mind your glove, sir." Randolph had then disengaged his gloves, and thrust one hand violently in his face, saying, "I came to pull your nose;" but before he could make use of the other, he received a blow from S. Chesley Potter, of Pennsylvania, a clerk in one of the departments, with an umbrella. Almost at the same time two gentlemen in the cabin sprang upon him, and he was pulled back and thrown down.

The moment he was assailed, the President seized his cane, which was lying on the table, and sought to force his way between the gentlemen who surrounded Randolph, insisting that no man should stand between him and the villain who had assaulted him, and that he would chastise him himself. Randolph, by this time, had been borne toward the door of the cabin, and pushed through it to the deck. He made his way from the crowd, and reached the wharf. He stayed for a few moments at a tavern in Alexandria, "to take a drink," and then passed on beyond the District line, and thus escaped.

The affair was of only a few moments' duration.

The grand jury, then in session at Alexandria, found a presentment against him. The court issued a bench-warrant. A magistrate had previously issued a warrant, but Randolph was beyond the reach of an arrest.

The President returned to Washington the next day, meeting at Alexandria and in this city a number of citizens, who paid him the respect due to his station, and testified their disapprobation of the treatment he had experienced while on the boat.

As far as could be ascertained, not a human being besides himself knew of Randolph's intention. He was hurried from the boat by gentlemen present, to prevent him from being killed on the spot, and not with any design of assisting him to escape.

Randolph had been an acting purser in the Navy, and temporarily succeeded Mr. Timberlake, the first husband of Mrs. Eaton. Jackson had dismissed him from the Navy owing to some difficulty or complication in his accounts.

Toward the close of August, 1833, "the earth was feverish and did shake," in this and the adjoining counties of Maryland and Virginia, and even beyond them. At the stone-quarries in Stafford County, the workmen said "the rocks had the fever and ague." Several shocks were felt during the day. At Fredericksburg they were accompanied by a loud rumbling noise, and very much alarmed the inhabitants. Their course was from west to east. The coal-pits at Dover, in Virginia, were somewhat injured from the same cause.

The first time I saw General Jackson, was on the occasion of a balloon ascension, in the summer of 1834. Nicholas J. Ash was the aëronaut. He and I had been children together, in the same neighborhood; but, judging from his profession, his ambition soared higher than my own — to the clouds! The old hero was at a window at the White House, and waved his hand in adieu to the *voyageur*, who, in return, flaunted two miniature flags, and breathed faintly heard huzzas.

General Jackson was very warm and sociable in private life. His habit was, after dinner with friends, to retire with them to the drawing-room. Usually, about nine o'clock, he gave the signal for separation, by ordering wine for the guests, and Jemmy O'Neil, his servant, to bring his pipe for himself.

He was a good friend to Washington, and did much to improve it as the National Metropolis. Before he left here, on the seventh of March, for the Hermitage, the municipal authorities waited on him, and in their address thanked him for the interest he had always manifested in the affairs of the city, and expressed their earnest hopes that in his retirement to private life he might live to enjoy many years of uninterrupted happiness, in the repose so necessary and so desirable after his long service in the various perilous, responsible, and honorable employments, which had been confided to him by the American people.

General Jackson replied, that he deserved their thanks rather for what he intended to do than for what he had done. Nothing could be more gratifying to him than this mark of respect. He reciprocated their kind feeling, and presented to the citizens of Washington, through them, his best regards, and prayers for their happiness both here and hereafter. He then bade them an affectionate farewell.

Before the accession of Andrew Jackson to the

Presidency, the Postmaster-General was looked upon as the head of a bureau, but that President invited Mr. Barry to a seat in his Cabinet meetings. Since that time the head of the Post-Office Department has been considered a regular member of the Cabinet.

John Marshall, Chief-Justice of the Supreme Court of the United States, died in 1835. He had presided in that capacity from 1801, a period of thirty-four years. Roger B. Taney, of Maryland, was appointed as his successor, March 15th, 1836, and Salmon P. Chase in December, 1864, to fill the vacancy occasioned by the death of Mr. Taney.

3

CHAPTER II.

INAUGURATION OF MARTIN VAN BUREN — THE CABINET — EXTRA SESSION OF CONGRESS — ELECTIONS IN THE HOUSE — VIVA VOCE, WHY ESTABLISHED — SECRETARY WOODBURY AND THE AGENT OF THE STATE DEPOSIT BANKS — THE BIG CHEESE — POLITICAL BITTERNESS — AN INSTANCE — INSULT TO SPEAKER POLK — THE CILLEY DUEL — AN "HONORABLE" PROPOSITION TO SHORTEN THE DISTANCE BETWEEN THE COMBATANTS — A FAIR FIGHT — CONDEMNATION OF DUELLING — ANTI-DUELLING LAW — EXCITEMENT OF THE POLITICAL CAMPAIGN — MODES OF WARFARE — WHIG TRIUMPH — MANNERS OF MR. VAN BUREN — HOW HE RECEIVED THE NEWS OF HIS DEFEAT — ANECDOTE OF MR. CLAY.

IN anticipation of the inauguration of Martin Van Buren, a great concourse of strangers from all parts of the Union flocked to Washington. There was difficulty in accommodating them at the hotels and boarding-houses.

On the fourth of March, 1837, a procession was formed and proceeded to the Capitol. The President elect was, as is usual on such occasions, accompanied by the out-going President.

The Vice-President elect, Colonel Richard M. Johnson, of Kentucky, was duly installed in the Senate Chamber.

The delivery of the Inaugural Address, by Mr. Van Buren, on the eastern portico of the Capitol, concluded, the oath of office was administered by the Chief-Justice of the United States. National salutes were fired, and the President and Ex-President returned to the Executive Mansion, attended by the *cortege* which had accompanied them to the Capitol, and whither an immense crowd of citizens repaired, to offer their salutations to the new President, and take leave of his predecessor. The representatives of foreign governments also attended, and through Mr. Calderon, the Spanish Minister, tendered their congratulations to the President in an appropriate and impressive address.

In the evening there was a brilliant ball at Carusi's Saloon, which the President and the Vice-President attended, with a number of senators and representatives, the heads of the departments, many military and naval officers, and all the members of the foreign legations, in the official costumes of their several functions and countries. The presence of the fair sex was a brilliant feature of the assembly.

The party separated soon after the President and his immediate friends retired, without any circumstances of alloy to the pleasant associations.

Mr. Van Buren chose for his Cabinet: Secretary of State, John Forsyth; Secretary of the Treasury, Levi Woodbury; Secretary of War, Joel R. Poinsett; Secretary of the Navy, first, Mahlon Dickerson, and next, James K. Paulding; Postmaster-General, Amos Kendall, and afterward, John M. Niles.

In May, 1837, President Van Buren issued his proclamation convoking an extraordinary session of

Congress, to commence on the first Monday of September following.

James K. Polk was elected Speaker by a majority of three or four votes; but when the President, in his message, recommended to both Houses his Sub-Treasury scheme, trouble at once broke out in the Democratic party. A bill to establish the system was introduced in the Senate and passed; but it was defeated in the House (which had so recently elected Mr. Polk) by thirteen majority.

Mr. Calhoun, who had opposed Mr. Van Buren, declared himself in favor of the bill, which Mr. Clay as earnestly opposed.

The debate in both Houses was not only able, but fiercely spirited.

In the course of time, however—in July, 1840—the bill became a law.

On the twelfth and final balloting, Thomas Allen, editor of "The Madisonian," was elected Printer to the House, over the Van Buren candidates, Blair and Rives.

The elections were, at that day, by ballot; but as this mode afforded a covert to disaffected members, the leading Democrats immediately set about the work of substituting for it the *viva voce* method, by which the true political characters of the representatives were thus made known. The success of their effort continues.

After the removal, by Jackson, of the government deposits from the Bank of the United States, and previous to the Sub-Treasury system, the public funds were placed in the custody of what the Whigs called "Pet Banks," or State institutions.

The Treasury Department was in the row of houses directly opposite to Willard's Hotel, having been temporarily located there after the burning of the Treasury building, which was on the site of the present larger and more substantial structure. Secretary Woodbury was in constant communication with Reuben M. Whitney, who occupied a room adjoining his own. He was the agent of the banks. He furnished all the financial articles to the editorial columns of the "Daily Globe." The establishment of the Sub-Treasury system rendered his services no longer necessary.

President Tyler appointed him Register of the Land Office. His health began to decline. He suffered with an affection of the throat, from the effects of which he died soon after President Polk's inauguration.

It was the custom for some of Mr. Van Buren's New York country friends to annually send him a cheese—a monster cheese. On one occasion the President directed that a cheese should be cut up and distributed to the great crowd at one of the public receptions. This liberality was not productive of an agreeable result, for the crumbs were scattered over the splendid carpet of the East Room, and trodden underfoot; and, besides, the chairs and other articles of furniture were considerably soiled by the greasy substance. From that day to this, no more cheese has been distributed at public receptions.

As an instance of the political bitterness existing in those days, it may be mentioned, that, after an adjournment of the House, as Speaker Polk was on his way to his lodgings, he happened to meet Mr. Henry A. Wise, who was walking in the opposite direction. Wise, after making an ugly face, spat at him; Polk passed on as though he had encountered no such assailant. These facts becoming known, Wise's friends raised the cry of "coward" against Polk — because he was opposed to duelling, and had no desire to kill any one, nor that anybody should kill him!

Duels were of frequent occurrence; and the one which sent a thrill of horror through the country was fought by William J. Graves, of Kentucky, and Jonathan Cilley, a new member from the State of Maine. The particulars are as follows:

Mr. Cilley, in a speech in the House of Representatives, in February, 1838, charged that James Watson Webb, the editor of the "New York Courier and Enquirer," had received a bribe of fifty-two thousand dollars from the Bank of the United States.

On the twentieth of February, Mr. Graves addressed a letter to Mr. Cilley, in which he remarked: "In the interview with you, when you declined to receive from me the note of Mr. Webb, asking whether you were correctly reported in the 'Globe,' did you not say, in substance, that, in declining to receive the note, you hoped I would not consider it in any degree disrespectful to myself, and that the ground on which you declined to receive the note was distinctly this: that you could not consent to get yourself into personal difficulties with conductors of public journals, for what you thought proper to say in debate, and that you did not rest your objection on anything personal to Mr. Webb as a gentleman."

Mr. Cilley, in reply, said, he neither affirmed nor denied anything in regard to Webb's character; and added, "But when you remarked, that this course on my part might place you in an unpleasant situation, I stated to you, and now repeat, that I intended by the refusal no disrespect to you."

Mr. Graves replied: "I have to inquire whether you declined to receive Mr. Webb's communication on the ground of any personal exception to him as a gentleman, or man of honor. A categorical answer is expected."

Mr. Cilley replied, regretting that his note was not satisfactory: and added, "I cannot admit the right on your part to propound the question to which you ask a categorical answer, and therefore decline any further response to it."

Mr. Graves replied: "As you have declined to accept a communication, which I bore to you from Mr. Webb, and as by your note of yesterday you have declined on grounds which would exonerate me from all responsibility, growing out of the affair, I am left no other alternative but to ask the satisfaction which is recognized among gentlemen. My friend, Henry A. Wise, is authorized by me to make the arrangements suited to the occasion."

Mr. Cilley acknowledged the receipt of the note, and stated to Mr. Graves: "My friend, General George W. Jones, will make the arrangements suited to the occasion."

The seconds accordingly made "the arrangements," and the parties proceeded to the duelling-ground, at Bladensburg. Wise won the position, and Jones had the giving of the word. The weapons were rifles.

On the first fire, both the principals missed. The challenge was then suspended, for the purpose of explanation, when Mr. Cilley again repeated he meant no disrespect to Mr. Graves, because he heretofore entertained for him, and did now, the highest respect and most kind feeling; but that he declined to receive Mr. Webb's note because he chose not to be drawn into any controversy with him.

The friends of both parties having retired and consulted, Mr. Wise said to Mr. Jones that this answer left Mr. Graves precisely in the position he occupied before the challenge. Reconciliation having failed, the challenge was renewed, and another shot exchanged. The challenge was again withdrawn, and, in the conference which ensued, Mr. Graves (through Mr. Wise) said he considered himself obliged not only to preserve the respect due to himself, but to defend the honor of Mr. Webb, his friend.

The challenge was again renewed. Immediately previous to the last exchange of shots, Mr. Wise said to Mr. Jones: "If this matter is not terminated by this shot, and is not settled, I will propose to shorten the distance," to which Mr. Jones replied: "After this shot, if without effect, I will entertain the proposition."

The shots were fired, and Cilley fell. Mr. Wise expressed to Mr. Jones the desire of Mr. Graves to see Mr. Cilley. Jones replied, "My friend is dead;" and went over to Mr. Graves and told him there was no objection to his seeing Mr. Cilley. When Mr. Jones approached Mr. Graves, and informed him his request should be granted, Mr. Graves inquired, "How is he?" The reply was, "My friend is dead, sir." Mr. Graves then went to his carriage. Mr. Wise inquired of Mr. Jones, before leaving the ground, whether he could render any service, and tendered him all the aid in his power.

Jones and Wise made a joint statement as to all the facts in the case, in which they said: "We cordially agree in bearing unqualified testimony to the fair and honorable manner in which the duel was conducted. None can regret its termination more than ourselves, and we hope that the last of it will be the signatures of our names to this paper, which we now affix."

The Supreme Court, in order to quietly condemn the practice of duelling, declined to attend Mr. Cilley's funeral.

Sermons were preached in the pulpits against the barbarism of duelling; and outside of the circle or "ring" of the chivalry, there was a general demand that measures should be taken to prevent the repetition of such a mournful catastrophe. Accordingly, Congress passed what is known as "the Anti-Duelling Act," which makes the giving or accepting a challenge to fight a duel in the District of Columbia a misdemeanor, punishable, on conviction, with a fine and imprisonment in the penitentiary.

This did not wholly cure the evil, for since that day challenges have been received and duels fought in the vicinity of Washington.

The administration of Mr. Van Buren was very bitterly opposed, the Whigs making a zealous rally on Harrison and Tyler; and in the contest of 1840, he was put entirely out of reach of further political preferment.

It was a triumph of which the Whigs were justly proud. For twelve long years they had fought the administrations of Jackson and Van Buren, and now they anticipated a realization of all their hopes.

It will be recollected by the "old inhabitants," that "log cabins" were powerful helpers in the Whig cause. They were everywhere erected, and much speaking and cider-drinking were indulged on the "raising" of them. The log cabin was selected to illustrate the simplicity of General Harrison's early days. Although the hard cider was not a political principle, it served to stimulate the zeal of those who were not conspicuous in the temperance cause! The old hero had distinguished himself on Western battle-fields, and especially at Tippecanoe; and hence the songs called him "Tippecanoe," with "Tyler too," in connection with the refrain of "Van, Van, the used-up man." And to show their appreciation of "Tippecanoe," the Whigs hauled from place to place small canoes fixed on wheels, in which were persons seated, waving banners with log cabins and other such devices. Live coons, too, were plentifully displayed. Songs were numerous — sung in the streets by boys, and executed at political meetings by glee-clubs. There never was a more spirited presidential contest

The Democratic party could not endure the "music," and expressed their aversion to the log cabin, coon, and canoe devices. They were attacked so briskly that they had to place themselves altogether on the defensive.

The Whigs raised the cry of "standing army in time of peace," predicated on the scheme of Secretary Poinsett, which proposed that in all the States citizens between specified ages should camp and drill a certain number of weeks every year, in order that the militia might be rendered efficient. The charge was made, too, that Mr. Van Buren, like General Jackson, wanted to hold "the purse in one hand, and the sword in the other."

Mr. Ogle, a member of Congress from Pennsylvania, made a long speech in the House, in which he spoke of the luxurious habits of Mr. Van Buren; and, in effect, described the furniture of the "White House" as being too fine for the President of the Republic, and as being suitable only for potentates who tyrannically wring the means of supporting a splendid establishment, and a glittering retinue, from the labor of oppressed subjects. He was very particular in his description of the style and finish of all the furniture, in contrast with that of men of plain habits, who lived in log cabins. He even gave the number of spittoons, etc., and of spoons, some of which latter he said were of solid gold. Only think! A Democratic President eating with a gold spoon, when men as good as himself ate their mush or soup with a wooden one!

The speech was circulated through the country, both in pamphlet and newspaper form, and in English and Dutch. It was the most popular campaign document of all for the masses.

In vain the Democrats tried to turn aside the effect of this speech. Explanation from them was useless.

They asserted in elaborately written speeches and newspaper articles, that the militia bill was harmless, as its object was merely to drill the people to be their own defenders, that the spoons were not gold, but only washed or plated with that material; and as to the furniture, it did not belong to Mr. Van Buren, but to the people — the Government. Some of it was purchased from Mr. Monroe, who brought it from France, and had caused the ornamentation of the imperial crown on the backs of the chairs to be supplanted by that of the American Eagle.

The Democrats sent out a flood of documents — the best pens were employed to write them; and it is recollected that the speech of Dr. Duncan, a representative from Ohio, was made up of subjects contributed by executive officers of the Government, ornamented with coons and log cabins, — emblems of Whig principles, they said, — and distributed by wholesale.

But log cabins, canoes, and coons, were not the only Whig weapons. The currency was in a very bad condition — "wild-cat" and "red-dog" bank-notes, as well as those of old-established institutions, were at a heavy discount. There had been a suspension of specie payments — trade languished — protection to American industry was demanded; and the people, in the hope of improving their condition, sought a change of administration, which, it is known, was effected.

Mr. Van Buren was quiet in his manners, very courteous, but slightly formal. He did not indulge in jokes. His conversation was pleasant; there was in it no anger or malice; nor was he in the habit of swearing or using tobacco. He was a thorough, well-bred gentleman, remarkably active, and in going up-stairs would spring two steps at a time.

Miner K. Kellogg, Esq., the artist, now a resident of Washington, painted his portrait. The President sat for him every day, and chatted in the most social manner.

Mr. Van Buren received many abusive letters and caricatures during the canvass, but took the matter philosophically. He was cheerful, and hopeful of a re-election. As the returns came in, he would show them to Mr. Kellogg. There were no telegraph arrangements in those days, and the news had to be received by the slow process of the mails, or by pony express. Hence, days passed before the result could positively be ascertained. When he became acquainted with the truth that New York had declared against him, he acknowledged that he was defeated, but attributed the result in that State to the fact that he had sent General Scott to put down the invasion of Canada by the patriots, which rendered him unpopular. He made this further remark to Mr. Kellogg: "It is a singular coincidence that I should be taking my last sitting for my portrait on the reception of the news of my defeat."

During Mr. Van Buren's term of office, a fire broke out in the laundry of the Executive Mansion. The general alarm was given, and engines were hurried to the scene. Mr. Clay, who was in the neighborhood, entered the house to render any assistance which might be required. Mr. Van Buren informed him that the damage was but slight, and that the flames had been suppressed. Mr. Clay and Mr. Van Buren were always good private friends, and the former never neglected an opportunity to indulge in "little jokes" to the confusion of the latter, who was not good at repartee. On this occasion, he remarked, in a low tone to Mr. Van Buren, gently placing his hand on that gentleman's shoulder: "We want you out of the White House, Mr. Van Buren, but we don't want you *burnt* out." Mr. Van Buren could do no more than bow his thanks for this expression of humane feeling toward him.

CHAPTER III.

GENERAL HARRISON'S ADMINISTRATION — PARTICULARS ATTENDING HIS ARRIVAL AT WASHINGTON — HIS APPEARANCE — THE INAUGURATION — INCIDENTS IN THAT CONNECTION — THE "TRUTHFUL REMARK OF A ROMAN CONSUL" — PRESSURE FOR OFFICE — EXCITING OCCURRENCE IN THE UNITED STATES SENATE — A CHALLENGE — CLAY AND KING — THEIR QUARREL — THE RECONCILIATION — MAGNANIMITY APPLAUDED — THE DEATH OF HARRISON — ANECDOTE OF WEBSTER AND COLONEL CHAMBERS — MARTIN RENEHAN AND PRESIDENT HARRISON — WIT AND FRIENDSHIP, ETC.

DIRECTLY after the election of General Harrison to the Presidency, I saw him at the market-house in Cincinnati. He appeared very feeble, as he held his cloak tightly around him. He was, which ever way he moved, congratulated upon his political fortune. He certainly did not appear to be in good physical condition to conduct the affairs of government, and to deal with applicants for place.

He arrived here in the month of February, 1841. The railroad station was at that time on Pennsylvania Avenue, not far from the west gate of the Capitol; and there a committee met and walked with him to the City Hall, about half a mile distant from the depot.

The weather was chilly, with a drizzling of rain, after a slight fall of snow. General Harrison walked all the way, with his hat in his hand, bowing continually to the crowd which lined the pathway and greeted him with cheers. He was different-looking now from what he was, when, during the November before, I had seen him in the Cincinnati market-place. Instead of being bowed with age, and shivering with cold, he walked with an elastic step. His face was slightly tinged with red, caused by the excitement of the hour, or the keen winter's wind, perhaps from these causes combined. Arrived at the City Hall, he was welcomed in a speech by Mayor Seaton, and received the greetings of the crowd.

After a brief sojourn, the President elect paid a visit to Richmond, but was punctual in returning to Washington before the day of inauguration. He was gratified with having met in that city an old negro barber who had shaved him many years before.

The ancient inhabitants did not remember ever before seeing so large a number of strangers in Washington. Hotel-keepers were obliged to turn away applicants for accommodations; and all the private boarding-houses were so crowded, that men were glad to obtain sleeping-places on the floor. And even this crowding together did not afford the required relief. Many of the citizens who had never before kept lodging-houses now consented to do so, large prices having been offered as an inducement to the undertaking. Thousands of persons, with their satchels and carpet-bags, wandered through the streets during the night, or secured good places near the platform at the Capitol, where the President elect was to deliver his inaugural address, and take the oath of office.

A salute of twenty-six guns was fired on the morning of the fourth of March, and soon after ten o'clock the firing of three more guns announced the moving of the procession, which was highly interesting and imposing. Ladies everywhere, in the windows and at the doors, on Pennsylvania Avenue, waved their handkerchiefs and hands in token of their kindly feeling for the President elect, who, as he bowed his thanks, was greeted with repeated cheers by the other sex. The military part of the procession was remarkably fine. Troops were here from distant cities. After the delegation of officers and soldiers who had fought under him, he himself rode on a white charger, accompanied by a suite of personal friends. On his right were seven citizen marshals, and on his left the Marshal of the District of Columbia and his four aides. Next followed Tippecanoe clubs and other organizations. From Prince George's County, Maryland, the delegation was numerous and spirited. Beside their handsome and appropriate banner, was a vehicle drawn by six splendid white horses. All were suitably caparisoned, wearing bells, and drawing a cloth-weaving apparatus, with the operatives at work. Along with this Prince George's delegation, was a large log cabin, drawn by horses. On the sides of the cabin were suitable devices and mottoes, and on its roof numerous white flags, bearing the names of the States which had voted in favor of General Harrison.

Look for a few minutes into the Senate chamber: Among the military, were Generals Scott, Gaines, Macomb, Jones, and Wool; while opposite, sat the nominated members of the Cabinet; and in that company of Senators and Representatives, the Diplomatic Corps, brilliantly decorated, were prominent objects of scrutiny. The Judges of the Supreme Court appeared, as usual, in their gowns of office.

The retiring Vice-President, Colonel Johnson, presented Mr. Tyler, the Vice-President elect, to the presiding officer, who administered the oath of office.

Mr. Tyler then delivered a brief address, and assumed the chair.

General Harrison now entered, and took the seat prepared for him in front of the Secretary's table. He looked cheerful and composed, and appeared to be in good health.

A procession was formed, and proceeded to the eastern portico of the Capitol, where a very large crowd had previously assembled, including those who had escorted the President to that locality.

The Inaugural Address was delivered, and the oath of office administered by the Chief-Justice, when the pealing of cannon announced the proceedings at an end.

General Harrison was fond of the classics, and took much pleasure in reading ancient history; hence there was often to be found in his writings evidence of this fact. His political opponents used to smile at one of the sentences of his Inaugural Address, which set forth a truth, which could not then, and cannot now, be denied, as follows:

"It was the remark of a Roman consul, in the early part of that celebrated republic, that a most striking contrast was observable in the conduct of candidates for offices of power and trust, before and after obtaining them,—they seldom carrying out, in the latter case, the pledges and promises made in the former. However much the world may have improved in many respects in the lapse of upwards of two thousand years, since the remark was made by the virtuous and indignant Roman, I fear that a strict examination of the annals of some of the modern elective governments would develop similar instances of violated confidence."

Nearly the entire throng accompanied the President to the White House from the Capitol, and as many as possible entered it, to pay their respects to him.

In the evening were several inauguration balls, all of them well attended, and which the President visited in turn.

On the 5th of March, an extraordinary session of the Senate was called for the transaction of executive business; among which was the confirmation of the following officers, as members of the Cabinet: Daniel Webster, Secretary of State; Thomas Ewing, Secretary of the Treasury; John Bell, Secretary of War; George E. Badger, Secretary of the Navy; and Francis Granger, Postmaster-General.

On the same day, Mr. Mangum, of North Carolina, offered a resolution, that Blair & Rives be dismissed as printers of the Senate. A debate followed as to whether this could be done at an executive session, some contending that it was a legislative act.

Mr. King, of Alabama, offered a resolution, that Blair & Rives, having been duly elected printers during the late session, it was not competent to annul the election, and defraud them of their contract.

The debate on this subject was continued for some days. In the course of it, Mr. King asked, "Who is this Mr. Blair, who has been so violently assailed on this floor? If my recollection serves me aright, this man Blair resided, years gone by, in Kentucky, where he figured as no inconsiderable personage. He was then the political friend of the Senator from Kentucky, (Mr. Clay,) his intimate associate, and, if I have not been misinformed, his confidential correspondent. Was he infamous *then*, as now pronounced by the Senator from Kentucky? I presume not. I knew nothing of Mr. Blair, or his character, until he made his appearance in Washington, some years ago. Since that time I have been on terms of social intercourse with him, and have observed his conduct in the social and private relations of life, and I feel bound to say that for kindness of heart, humanity, and exemplary deportment as a private citizen, he would proudly compare with the Senator from Kentucky, or with any Senator on this floor by whom he had been assailed."

Mr. Clay repeated: "I have said I believed the 'Globe' to be an infamous paper, and its chief editor an infamous man. I had said nothing of gentlemen on the other side, who had chosen to vote for this editor as printer to the Senate; but, by matter of unlawful inference and illogical deduction, two or three had risen and undertaken to consider that they partook of the infamy of Blair & Rives—if they be infamous. I scarcely ever looked at a paper edited by this man, in which my name appeared, which was not filled with untruths and misrepresentations. Not long ago this same editor called the honorable Senator from South Carolina, *John Catiline Calhoun;* and it was charged by this very editor, that it was impossible for that Senator to speak the truth when a lie would answer his purpose; and in return it had been said of that editor that he looked like a galvanized corpse. Now, if we were to take the character of this editor for what his present friends had said of him, we would find it to be infinitely worse than anything I have said, bad as it might be. But I should be unwilling to take the character of Blair's present friends from what he had said of those friends, for I consider him a common libeller, and the 'Globe' a libel; and for the Senator from Alabama to undertake to put me on an equality with Blair, constrains me to say, it was FALSE, UNTRUE, and COWARDLY."

Mr. King, rising, said: "Mr. President, I have no reply to make—none whatever."

Mr. King withdrew from the chamber. A few minutes afterward, one of the pages came in and whispered to Dr. Linn, of Missouri, who went out with him. Linn soon returned and handed a note to Mr. Clay, who wrote something and handed the paper to Mr. Archer, of Virginia. This was subsequently understood to be a challenge by Mr. King, and its acceptance by Mr. Clay. The friends of the latter, however, perceiving that he was wrong in his assault upon Mr. King, who was a model of senatorial propriety, and that, if pressed to a fight, even if Mr. Clay should not fall in the conflict, it would be death to his political prospects, interfered, and proposed that further proceedings be suspended until an effort could be made for a reconciliation. King would withdraw the challenge only on the condition of an apology by Clay, on the floor of the Senate. Clay, at first, positively refused to make one, and at least four days were spent in arranging the terms of Clay's apology; Colonel Preston, of North Carolina, being a prominent mediator. At last, Colonel Preston rose in the Chamber, and alluded to the "unpleasant collision." He said: "Mr. Clay thought that the language of Mr. King was intended to be injurious to his character and personally offensive; and, acting under that belief, Mr. Clay retorted in language of direct affront; language which, he (Colonel Preston) was convinced he could not have employed but under a deep sense of injury. He believed, however, that Mr. Clay mistook the Senator from Alabama, and from information which had come to him, it was certain that Mr. King did not intend to be personally offensive. At the bottom of this affair, therefore, there was a misapprehension, which he announced with pleasure; and in that confident belief, being thus announced, the honorable and distinguished Senators would have no difficulty in coming to an adjustment, which was earnestly demanded by the Senate."

Mr. Clay said he shared with the Senator from South Carolina in the regret which he had manifested on account of the occurrence which had disturbed the harmony and good feeling which prevailed in the Senate, to which allusion had been made. He, with pleasure, bore testimony to the honorable and high-minded feeling which prompted the Senator to make the explanation he had just presented. While the Senator from Alabama was speaking, he (Mr. Clay) thought there was a studied, premeditated design to make an assault upon him and his character, and when the Senator concluded by instituting a comparison between himself and a man whom he had but the day before declared to be infamous, and of whom he had spoken as a common libeller, and of his paper as a libel, he did not doubt that his object was a personal offence. But it was due to the Senator as well as to himself to state he had since received satisfactory information, on which he placed implicit reliance, that the Senator from Alabama had no purpose or intention to offer a personal insult, or to cast the slightest imputation on his character or honor. Ready at all times promptly to repair an injury, as he ever hoped he should be to repel an indignity, and always taking more pleasure to repair than to repel, and without any regard to the nicety of mere technical forms, to which those acquainted with him knew he never attached great importance, — under the circumstances, as thus explained, and with the understanding which he now had of the real intention of the Senator, it was with infinite pleasure he here declared every epithet in the least derogatory to the Senator's honor or character to be withdrawn.

Mr. King was engaged in writing when Mr. Clay commenced his remarks, and on their conclusion said he concurred with the Senator from Kentucky as to the duty which every Senator owed to himself and to the body of which he was a member, to be studious to avoid all personalities, and confine himself strictly to the Rules of Order, and never depart from decorum in debate. He had long been a member of the Senate, and he could fearlessly appeal to his brother Senators to say whether on any occasion he had violated the prescribed rules, or been guilty of indecorum in debate. The Senator from Kentucky, from whomsoever he received the information concerning his motives in debate, had not been misinformed. The Senator having, with characteristic frankness, explicitly withdrawn the injurious expression used by him, he (Mr. King) now felt himself at liberty to state, as he did in the same spirit of frankness, that nothing which was said by him was intended to be personally offensive to that Senator; nor was it his design in any manner to derogate from his character as a gentleman or man of honor. He made this statement with pleasure; for, while he was always prepared to defend his honor, when assailed, he carefully avoided attacking others.

Mr. Preston expressed his satisfaction at the happy termination of the misunderstanding between the Senators.

Mr. Clay rose from his seat while Mr. Preston was speaking, crossed the chamber, and having arrived in front of Mr. King's seat, exclaimed: "King, give us a pinch of your snuff." King, surprised, sprang to his feet, and held out his hand, which was cordially grasped by Mr. Clay, when there was long-continued applause both by the Senators and spectators in the galleries, in approbation of the return of peace.

The resolution to dismiss Blair & Rives as printers to the Senate was adopted; and on motion by Mr. Clay — yeas 28, nays 18 — it was ordered that their official bond be taken from them.

Mr. Webster was a very strong friend of General James Wilson, of New Hampshire, who was an eloquent and efficient stump-speaker, and had always been in favor of Mr. Webster for the Presidency. Mr. Webster asked President Harrison to appoint General Wilson Governor of the Territory of Iowa; but the President informed him he had offered the place to Colonel Chambers, his private secretary. Shortly after learning of this condition of affairs, Mr. Webster and Colonel Chambers accidentally met near the Department of State, when Mr. Webster thus abruptly addressed him: "Look here, Colonel Chambers, I understand the President has offered to make you Governor of Iowa." "Yes, sir," responded Colonel Chambers. "Well, sir," said Mr. Webster with emphasis, "*you must not take it;* I have promised the place to my friend, General Wilson; you must not accept the office." Colonel Chambers was very indignant at the manner and demand of Mr. Webster, and gave him this answer, namely, "Mr. Webster, I *shall accept the place;* and I admonish you not to practise your insults on me; they will not answer with me, sir."

The parties abruptly separated, and never again came in collision.

Martin Renehan, an American citizen of Irish birth, well known for his wit, intelligence, and warm-heartedness, had served under Jackson and Van Buren's administrations as an usher, or man-of-all-work. He was popular with everybody, and possessed a deservedly good character for integrity. He "still lives," and holds "a little place" in the office of the Sixth Auditor of the Treasury.

In the course of a recent conversation with Martin, he related to me the following incidents: —

The lady of the White House, who did the honors, was a widow, the daughter-in-law of the President. She was an attractive young lady, and popular.

President Harrison was very much of a gentleman, social and kind-hearted. During the first two weeks of his administration, an elderly man, very polite and patronizing, made frequent visits to the White House, in order to see the President *privately.* Martin informed the new-comer that he would gratify him, if he would come some morning at six o'clock. The visitor was punctual to the time. General Harrison was an early riser. Martin went up-stairs gently, and tapped at his door; having received an invitation to enter, he did so. The General was sitting near the grate, in which were a few expiring coals. "Is it possible," Martin said, "the weather being cold, that you have no more fire?" He replied: —

"Martin, when at home I was accustomed to a wood fire; and if I had wood now, I'd replenish this fire myself, as I do not wish to call up my colored man, (the one he had brought with him from Ohio.) Martin responded that he would supply the requisite fuel, and added, "An elderly gentleman, sir, has been repeatedly calling here. He is of respectable appearance and unassuming in his manners, and has elicited my sympathies. I therefore take the liberty of asking whether you will now give him a private audience?" "Where is he?" "In the green room," replied Martin. "Show him up," said the President. Martin accordingly showed him up, and retired in order to give the stranger the full benefit of a strictly private interview. When the visitor had taken his departure, Martin returned to the President's room. "Martin," said the President, "you have been kind to that man." "I have; I took him by the hand." "Are you aware," asked the President, "that he is looking for your place?" Martin replied: "Your Excellency, I expected to go, as I am opposed to you in politics." General Harrison said: "John Quincy Adams told me all about you, and as long as I remain in the White House, the *Cabinet even can't remove you.*" Renehan responded: "I am the last *Martin* in the nest, and I thought you were going to put me to flight." "Oh, no," the President replied, "two *Martins* have already been banished from this house, (meaning Martin Van Buren and his son,) and it would be bad luck to banish *you*, the only remaining *Martin*. So, you remain, and nestle in the battlements."

The President was a good friend to Martin, and made him a companion in all his private dealings.

The President, after taking possession of the White House, was soon annoyed by impatient office-seekers—sometimes a dozen pleaders for the same place. So tiresome had such importunities become to the President, that he caused notice to be given that no office-holder would be removed without cause; but *cause* was soon found to remove those whose places were demanded by Whig applicants! The Democrats, they said, had enjoyed the spoils long enough, and ought, in justice, to give way to the long-suffering Whigs, who were entitled to recognition! The Democrats in office were not prompt to obey the demand; and hence many of them were furnished with small notes, enclosed in yellow covers. The *color* of the envelope itself was significant of its laconic *contents!*

Among the applicants for office were men who many years before had visited Washington, and now again made their appearance for Executive favor. As usual, in such times, all did not get what they persistently claimed; but comparatively few of the "vast multitude" were chosen.

On the 9th of March, President Harrison received the diplomatic corps; and Mr. Fox, the British Minister, delivered to him a formal address in their name, to which the President replied, saying that, "Both from duty and inclination, I shall omit nothing in my power to contribute to your own personal happiness, and that of the friends who on this occasion you represent, as long as you may continue among us."

The ministers were then severally presented to the President.

General Harrison, at first, attended market here, but he did not long continue to do so, for the worry of office and the importunity of place-hunters seriously interfered with his culinary arrangements, and forced him to rely solely upon his steward.

Only think of men who had been for many years deprived of official patronage, now pressing indecently upon the aged President for their coveted supplies; and, at the same time, though, of course, unintentionally, hurrying him to a bed from which he was never more to rise.

In exactly one month from the day of his inauguration, General Harrison died; the reports said of pneumonia, but it is just as true, that his delicate frame was shattered by the assaults of office-seekers! The funeral observances were marked by much "pomp and circumstance."

Many political hopes were blasted by his decease, for John Tyler, though elected Vice-President on the same ticket, was not considered to be the best exponent of Whig principles. His antecedents did not operate in his favor. He had been too "straight" on the State Rights principles, and swore by the expositions of "John Taylor, of Caroline."

CHAPTER IV.

SUCCESSION OF JOHN TYLER — THE CABINET — THE POLITICAL DEFECTION — CLAY'S WAR-BLAST — TYLER'S COMPLAINTS — JOHN M. BOTTS'S IMPEACHMENT ARTICLES — "HEAD HIM, OR DIE" — "THE DAILY MADISONIAN" — JOHN B. JONES, NOT OF "THE WAR OFFICE" — INSULTS TO THE PRESIDENT — THE AUXILIARY GUARD — DANGERS AHEAD — ANNEXATION OF TEXAS PROPOSED BY TREATY AND REJECTED — ANOTHER APPEAL TO THE DUELLO — THE "FLASH IN THE PAN!" — THE EXPLOSION ON BOARD THE PRINCETON — TYLER'S POLITICAL PROSPECTS — DOUGLAS AND WENTWORTH'S PROMISES — AN INFERNAL MACHINE — THE INVALID TELESCOPE — AN ANECDOTE — MR. WEBSTER AND MARTIN RENEHAN, ETC.

MR. JOHN TYLER succeeded General Harrison to the Presidency. The following gentlemen composed his cabinet officers: —

Daniel Webster continued to be Secretary of State till May 8th, 1843. Hugh S. Legaré was appointed his successor, but died in June, 1843. A. P. Upshur, appointed June 24th, 1843, was killed by the explosion of the gun on the steamer *Princeton*, February 28th, 1844. John Nelson, acting, February 29th, 1844. John C. Calhoun served out the term.

Thomas Ewing resigned the office of Secretary of the Treasury in September, 1841, and was succeeded by Walter Forward, who resigned in June, 1844. George M. Bibb served out the term.

John Bell resigned the office of Secretary of War in October, 1841. John C. Spencer was appointed his successor, and was afterward transferred to the Treasury Department. James M. Porter, appointed March 8th, 1843, was rejected by the Senate. William Wilkins, appointed February 15th, 1844, served out the term.

George E. Badger resigned in September, 1841. Abel P. Upshur was appointed his successor, but transferred to the Department of State. David Henshaw, appointed July 24th, 1843, was rejected by the Senate. Thomas W. Gilmer, appointed February 15th, 1844, was killed by the explosion on the *Princeton*. John Y. Mason, appointed March 14th, 1844, served out the term.

Francis Granger resigned as Postmaster-General in September, 1841, and was succeeded by Charles A. Wickliffe.

The Extraordinary Session of Congress convened on the last Monday in May, 1841.

Mr. Clay was made chairman of the Senate's Committee on Finance. The bill reported by him for the establishment of a National Bank, which passed the two Houses of Congress, was vetoed by Mr. Tyler, who, in the place of such an institution, proposed to give the country a Fiscal Agent, a scheme of his own. But this substitute was not acceptable.

Mr. Clay and his friends turned against Mr. Tyler,

while the Democrats took every opportunity to widen the breach between them.

Mr. Clay, at a great barbecue in Kentucky, thus sounded the war-trumpet.

"Whigs, arouse from the supineness which encompasses you! awake from the lethargy to which you lie bound! Cast from you that apathy which seems to make you indifferent to the fate of your country. Arouse! awake! Shake off the dew-drops that glitter on your garments. Once more to the battle, and to victory. You have been disappointed, deceived, betrayed—shamefully deceived and betrayed. Will you also prove false and faithless to your country, or obey the impulses of a just and patriotic indignation? As for Captain Tyler, he is a mere snap, a flash in the pan; pick your Whig flints, and try your rifles again!"

The political war against John Tyler, by the Whigs, grew more and more bitter. His acts were so earnestly assailed that he thought proper to send in a protest against the report of a select committee, the chairman of which was John Quincy Adams. He complained that his motives had been arraigned in his official conduct, without the shadow of a pretext for such charges, and that he had been accused of acts declared to deserve impeachment.

John M. Botts said that the President showed his weakness and vacillation in this protest, and gave notice that at the next session he would prefer articles of impeachment against him.

Botts had been his intimate personal friend. He now, however, intended to "head him, or die." He had slept in the same bed with "Captain Tyler," but was determined to do his patriotic duty in the work of decapitation. Accordingly, he drew up articles of impeachment, and made a loud and long speech in support of them. The House at that day was not so full of impeachment as it was in the year 1868! Botts's effort was unsuccessful. He did not "head" "Captain Tyler," nor did he "die."

Not many months passed before the supporters of the President dwindled down to what was called "a corporal's guard." He was literally a President without a party!

His organ was "The Madisonian," a newspaper originally established by Thomas Allen, under the auspices of William C. Rives, James Garland, and other recusant Democrats in Congress, who declared for "Conservative" doctrines, and succeeded in diverting the Congressional printing to that establishment. Blair, of the "Globe" was, of course, bitter on this "split" from the Democracy, and, in his own figurative language, proceeded to "shoot the deserters." Allen sold out to John B. Jones. In those days it was everywhere said that Jones was of the "War Office." This was a mistake. Others declared that he was a myth. Notwithstanding such annunciations, he was an actual, breathing man. He scarcely did anything but write editorials about the "brewing storm," and "justice to John Tyler." He was the author of "Wild Western Scenes," a work which was far more popular than his newspaper.

This gentleman was of an amiable disposition — kind and liberal to the persons in his employ, and deservedly respected by all who knew him.

While political excitement was at its height, a company of unthinking politicians, mostly located here, proceeded to the White House, and there "groaned" their disapprobation of the President's political conduct. In order to protect the presidential office from the repetition of such an indignity, a bill was introduced in the Senate to establish an "Auxiliary Guard," for the protection of public and private property against incendiaries, *and for the enforcement of the police regulations of the city of Washington.*" It consisted of a captain and fifteen other persons. For the purchase of the proper implements to distinguish them in the discharge of their duties, the sum of seven thousand dollars was appropriated.

During the debate, Senator Crittenden opposed the bill, particularly the last clause of it. He said that these policemen were to be distinguished by a baton and a star. It was nothing (these sixteen men) but a prætorian band. Rome admonished us how such small numbers increase to multitudes. It would not be long before the President would be surrounded by a body-guard of uniformed men. It was the duty of the lovers of liberty to destroy this attempt to introduce a new element of danger at the National capital.

The prediction has been verified to this extent: that out of the Auxiliary Guard has grown the Metropolitan Police — a battalion as to number, and commanded by a major, with all the lower grades of military officers; — a force, uniformed, carrying batons openly, and revolvers concealed in their trousers' pockets.

In 1844, Mr. Tyler communicated to the Senate a treaty for the annexation of the republic of Texas to the United States. This was, after a long debate in secret session, rejected by a vote of ten against thirty-five. He then sent a message to the House of Representatives, saying: "The treaty negotiated by the Executive with the republic of Texas, without a departure from any forms customarily observed in the negotiation of treaties, for the annexation of that republic to the United States, having been rejected by the Senate, and the subject having excited a part of the people in no ordinary degree, I feel it to be my duty to communicate the rejected treaty, with the correspondence and documents. I thought the best way to secure the annexation was by treaty; but if Congress deem proper to adopt any other expedient compatible with the Constitution, and likely to accomplish the object, I stand prepared to yield my prompt co-operation."

The republic of Texas was subsequently annexed by joint resolution, and this led to the war between the United States and Mexico.

During Mr. Tyler's administration—in May, 1842—Mr. Stanley, of North Carolina, through his friends, made a written demand for personal satisfaction from Mr. Wise, of Virginia, reciting the circumstances of the affront, the scene of which was near the race-course in Washington. He repeated, literally, the disclaimer he offered to Mr. Wise on that occasion. After much preliminary correspondence between their respective friends, Wise proposed a suspension of Stanley's demand, with a view to explanation. The proposition was accepted, and Wise proceeded to state that, understanding Stanley unintentionally came in collision with him near the race-course, he deemed it to be his duty, as a gentleman, to say that the blow inflicted by him on Stanley, through a sudden impulse induced by erroneous impressions, demanded his profound regret. The friend of Stanley told him he was bound to acknowledge the explanation as entirely satisfactory, which Stanley did.

In February, 1844, a day was appointed by Captain Stockton, commanding the *Princeton*, to receive visitors to his ship, lying off Alexandria. A large number of guests, with their families, were invited to spend the day on board. The weather was favorable. The company, of both sexes, was not less than four hundred persons. There were among them President Tyler, the heads of departments and their families, and members of Congress. The vessel proceeded down the river below Fort Washington. During the passage one of the large guns on board, carrying a ball of two hundred and twenty-five pounds, was fired more than once, exhibiting the great power and capacity of that formidable weapon of war. It was called "The Peacemaker." The ladies had partaken of a sumptuous repast, and the gentlemen had succeeded them at the table; and some of them had left it. The vessel was on the return up the river, opposite to the fort, when Captain Stockton consented to fire another shot from the same gun, around and near which, to observe its effects, many persons had gathered, though by no means as many as in the morning, the ladies who then thronged the deck being, on this fatal occasion, almost all between-decks, and out of the reach of harm. The gun was fired. Before the smoke cleared away, there were shrieks of woe, which announced a dire calamity. The gun had burst at a point three or four inches from the breach, and scattered death and desolation. Mr. Upshur, Secretary of State; Mr. Gilmer, recently placed at the head of the Navy Department; Commander Kennon, one of the officers of the vessel; Virgil Maxey, lately returned as Minister from the Hague, and Mr. Gardner, of New York, formerly a Senator from that State, were slain; the watch of Mr. Upshur having stopped at the precise time of the catastrophe! Besides these, seventeen seamen were wounded, several of them badly. Among those stunned by the concussion, not all seriously injured, were Captan Stockton himself, Senator Benton, and Lieutenant Hunt, of the *Princeton;* W. D. Robertson, of Georgetown, and also a servant of the President.

The scene was beyond description — wives widowed in an instant by the murderous blast, and daughters agonized by the heart-rending sight of the lifeless bodies of their fathers — to all beholders objects of sympathy and deep commiseration.

The *Princeton,* under the command of Lieutenant McLaughlin, came to an anchor opposite to Alexandria, and the surviving visitors reached Washington by the steamer *Joseph Johnson.*

The ship received but comparatively little injury.

The dead bodies were brought to the Executive Mansion, and lay in their coffins in the East Room.

President Tyler sent a message to Congress relative to the mournful occurrence. Members of both Houses, together with the most distinguished gentlemen in the city, attended the funeral.

A committee was appointed to investigate the cause of the accident, and in its report Captain Stockton and his officers were exonerated from blame.

The gun was loaded with twenty-five pounds of powder, and single-shotted; and, at the previous discharges, with thirty and thirty-five pounds of powder.

While Mr. John B. Jones published "The Madisonian," he printed, by subscription, hundreds of thousands of pamphlets, in advocacy of President Tyler's re-election; and these were distributed through office-holders. In addition to this, a Tyler club was formed in this city, consisting of probably thirty persons, who met regularly at Mr. Jones's house to arrange plans for the campaign. They all appeared to be fearfully in earnest, and some of them spoke of Tyler's re-election as already secured, "counting," of course "without the host," the people! Tyler clubs were also organized in several other cities. They were *not* formidable.

Less than a month after the convention which nominated Mr. Clay for the Presidency, two other conventions met in Baltimore; one of them nominated James K. Polk, whom nobody seemed to know! The other presented the name of John Tyler, unanimously. Both of the other parties laughed at this proceeding. He gravely accepted the honor of being the standard-bearer of his little party; but in a short time, having been convinced there was no chance for him, he formally withdrew from the canvass in favor of Mr. Polk. The Tyler party had almost entirely disappeared in this country!

John Wentworth and Stephen A. Douglas were in "The Madisonian" office when Mr. Tyler's purpose to sustain Mr. Polk was made known. They were here to begin their first Congressional term, and were then scarcely known beyond the limits of their own State of Illinois. They seemed to be very intimate friends personally, and both were Democrats. They expressed their joy at Tyler's declination, Douglas remarking, "That's good — Tyler is yet *young enough* to be elected President the *next* time." Wentworth acquiesced in the remark. But that was the first and the last occasion that these gentlemen advocated John Tyler for a second term.

Mr. Tyler was, during his administration, the recipient of a small wooden box. There was no accompanying note, giving an inventory of its contents, nor was there, at first, any one near by possessed of sufficient courage to open the box, after it had been whispered that it might be an infernal machine. The alarm of a little group, consisting of the President, Captain Waggaman, a relative of the President, and a negro servant, soon rose to a fearful height, when

Martin Renehan was summoned in this great crisis. He came with quick breathing and hurried step, and soon learned the cause of the commotion.

"Your Excellency," he said, with an apparently serious look, and in his own vernacular, "does well to be cautious in these high party-times. The divil himself puts it into the heads of his children to manufacture infernal machines, and who knows but that powder and balls, and percussion dust, have been arranged with a view to blow you up for vetoing the Bank bill!"

"True, true," remarked Mr. Tyler, receding a few steps from the box, and starting back as if it were on the eve of explosion; "b-u-t I should like to see the contents, M-a-r-tin."

"By the powers," said the son of Erin, "I'll chop it up in less than no time." And away he ran down into the kitchen, and picking up a cleaver, hastily returned to execute his purpose.

To this no objection was interposed. Martin placed the box on a table, turned up his cuffs, and prepared for the work.

Captain Waggaman, who was in military costume, retreated to a nook from which he could behold the operation without danger. The negro stood afar off, holding up his hands before him as a shield of defence, and Mr. Tyler took refuge behind a huge pillar. In peeping around it, his nose, which was by no means small, was alone perceptible to the brave Irishman.

"Martin! Martin! a'n't you afraid?" asked the President.

"No, sir," said Martin; "it's better for me to die than that the President should be killed by such a divil of a machine. My death is nothing compared with your Excellency's."

But Martin went to work. Every cut of the cleaver caused a winking of the spectators' eyes, and a cold chill. At last, after much hacking, the inside of the box was exposed, and great was the joy of the alarmed company, when Martin put in *his hand and took out the model of a stove!* Why, or by whom, it was sent to the President has never been ascertained. It is certain, however, that the timid group breathed "freer and deeper" after this exposure.

Mr. Tyler solemnly and emphatically counselled Martin not to talk about the matter, "For," said he, "if you do, they 'll have me caricatured."

Martin, while "fixing things to rights" in the garret, found an old telescope, and laid it by for future use. One evening, the stars shining brightly, the sky unclouded, and while President Tyler was entertaining the Cabinet and foreign representatives at dinner, Martin, having nothing else to do, brought down his instrument and mounted it upon a table on the southern portico. But he could see through it no better than with his naked eyes. In vain he tried to get the focus, and a long time elapsed before he discovered that "the thing," as he called it, with an emphatic adjective, had no glass in it! He talked to the telescope, and, in earnest words, to himself, in the true Irish accent, expressing his disappointment and displeasure.

Mr. Webster, meantime, came from the dining-room to breathe the fresh air. Standing behind Martin, with his hands deep down in his own pockets, he was an attentive and pleased listener to Martin's imprecations on the telescope and his confusion in the effort to "get the focus."

Martin accidentally turning round, descried Mr. Webster, who said: "Why, Martin, can't you see anything?" Martin was much embarrassed on discovering that his complaint and address to the telescope had been heard by Mr. Webster; but soon recovering his self-possession, he with his usual ready wit, said: "Mr. Webster, I have been disappointed — I can't, as I wished, contemplate the heavenly bodies, but I am equally gratified in seeing an earthly luminary now before me." Mr. Webster was so well pleased with what he had witnessed and heard, that he returned to the company and related accurately the whole story, to the delight of the entire dinner-party.

Mr. Henry Clay wrote a letter to a citizen of Alabama, in 1844, in which he said: "From developments now being made in South Carolina, it is perfectly manifest that a party exists in that State seeking a dissolution of the Union; and for that purpose employed the pretext of the rejection of Tyler's abominable treaty. South Carolina being surrounded by Slave States, would, in the event of a dissolution of the Union, suffer only comparative evil; but it is otherwise with Kentucky. She is the boundary of Ohio, extending four hundred miles on through the free States. What would her condition be in the event of the greatest calamity that could befall the nation? The election of Polk, who was in favor of immediate annexation, caused South Carolina to postpone her quarrel with the Union to a more suitable opportunity."

On the 19th of June, 1844, Professor Morse got his magnetic telegraph in order between Washington and Baltimore, which was then established as an experiment. The "National Intelligencer" of that date said: "It continues to work wonders. It was employed on Monday morning in apprising our friends in Baltimore of the action of the two Houses of Congress, during the final sitting. Among the reports of its marvels is, that at twelve o'clock, Chief-Justice Taney being at the electric register in Baltimore, sent his respects to the President, who was then at the Capitol, with the hope he was well. The President returned his compliments immediately, stating that he enjoyed good health, and felt much better, since Congress had finally adjourned."

President Tyler's first wife died in the White House. She had long been an invalid, and suffered from paralysis. After the explosion of the big gun on board the *Princeton*, he was married to the daughter of Mr. Gardner, who was killed by the accident. The latter lady then did the honors of the mansion, and gave balls in the East Room. It was she, it is said, who first introduced the etiquette of Windsor Castle, in announcing at the door, on entering, the names of the guests. She presided with marked grace and dignity.

On the eve of Mr. Tyler's retirement from the Presidency, there was a kind of farewell meeting at the Executive Mansion. A speech was delivered to the President by General Van Ness, to which Mr. Tyler responded.

The President's family removed to Fuller's Hotel (now Willard's), not far from the White House. The Empire Club, of New York, numbering one hundred and fifty men, were present. They brought with them a cannon, which they fired opposite to the President's lodging.

Mr. Tyler possessed many excellent traits of character, and was very hospitable and genial to all who entered his household.

CHAPTER V.

PRESIDENT POLK'S INAUGURATION — SOME THINGS ABOUT IT — THE CABINET — REPUDIATION OF BLAIR & RIVES AS THE OFFICIAL ORGAN — THE SUCCESSION OF THOMAS RITCHIE TO THAT INSTRUMENT — THE OREGON QUESTION — THE BACK-DOWN— SENATORIAL INDIGNATION — THE GREAT SAUSAGE EXCITEMENT — "RICHELIEU" AND THE HON. WILLIAM SAWYER — THE "LAST LINK BROKEN" —SUICIDE OF COMMODORE CRANE — A CURIOUS TRIAL — THE MEXICAN QUESTION—ANNEXATION OF TEXAS—SCOTT'S TROUBLES AND TRIUMPHS —AN EXTRAORDINARY EXPEDIENT — SANTA ANA — THE WAR WITH MEXICO — PEACE — A NEWSPAPER CORRESPONDENT IN "CONTEMPT" —PRIVATE CHARACTER OF POLK — MRS. POLK — THE MYSTERIOUS BOX — MR. CLAY AND THE CRY OF "BUFFALO" —SHOWING THE HORNS — A SLAVERY EXCITEMENT — ATTEMPT TO MOB THE OFFICE OF THE NATIONAL ERA, AN ANTI-SLAVERY JOURNAL — THE SUBJECT IN AND OUT OF CONGRESS — HOW IT ENDED — DEATH OF JOHN QUINCY ADAMS.

JAMES K. POLK was inaugurated President on the 4th of March, 1845.

It was a disagreeable day, with rain and mud.

A procession escorted him to the Capitol, in company with the retiring President. The New York Empire Club and other political organizations, and a tolerably fàir show of military, were in the throng. A white man, painted and dressed like a wild Indian, with a ring in his nose, and in a drunken condition, jumped about and yelled; thus causing much merriment to the spectators.

The usual ceremonies took place at the Capitol — Vice-President Dallas was duly installed, and the President delivered his Inaugural Address, and took the oath of office.

The Cabinet of President Polk consisted of James Buchanan, Secretary of State; Robert J. Walker, Secretary of the Treasury; William L. Marcy, Secretary of War; George Bancroft, Secretary of the Navy; and also John Y. Mason (the last-named appointed in 1846); Postmaster-General, Cave Johnson.

One of the earliest things the President did, was to look out for an editor, to supplant Mr. Blair in the conduct of the official organ. He selected Thomas Ritchie, at that time editor of the "Richmond Enquirer," for the position. That journal had a good reputation, owing to the contributions to its columns by the best political writers of Virginia. Mr. Ritchie was an old man, but vigorous in body and mind. He estimated age, as he frequently said, by *feeling and activity*, and not by *years*, and in these respects he might have passed for a younger man than he was, despite his withered face and gray hairs. The veteran editor brought with him from Richmond his writing-chair, and placed it in his parlor. This piece of furniture had a history, for, he remarked, pointing to it, in my presence, "That 's the chair in which I used to write my editorials against General Jackson." Mr. Ritchie originally opposed General Jackson, but was brought to the support of the nomination by the force of party.

Blair & Rives sold out their establishment to Messrs. Ritchie & Heiss, but retained the name of "The Globe." The latter gentlemen called their paper "The Union." Of course, Blair & Rives were much mortified by Mr. Polk's act of repudiation.

Early in 1846, Congress and the country were intensely agitated with the Oregon question. That territory had been in the joint occupancy of the United States and Great Britain, by convention, to terminate which was the wish of the President and the majority of Congress. Mr. Polk set up the claim for the whole of the territory. This met a warm response from his political friends.

"All or none!" "54.40 or fight!" and similar sentences, were not only paraded in speeches and in newspapers, but written or posted on fences and other places, after the manner of advertising patent-medicines and theatrical performances. The President was believed to be, as he doubtless was, in earnest. Great Britain, however, would not yield to the extravagant pretensions. There were two sides to the question. And the lion on the other side of the Atlantic wanted his share.

The ardent Democrats made the claim on the part of our people heard; and no one among the party seemed to question our right to the whole of the territory of Oregon, until Senator Haywood, of North Carolina, a courteous gentleman, neat in his dress, and particularly fond of tight-fitting gloves and sweet-scented handkerchiefs, made a speech, which took everybody by surprise. He openly declared for a compromise, and was willing to "back down" from "54.40" to the forty-ninth parallel of north latitude, or even to the forty-sixth!

Senator Hannegan, of Indiana, characterized Haywood's speech as extraordinary — the most extraordinary to which he had ever listened. He asked, with great anxiety, whether the Senator had the authority of *the President* for his utterances.

Senator Haywood evaded a direct answer, and replied he had spoken fully, and his speech would be *printed;* a fact of which Senators were aware, for he had taken much pains to prepare it.

Senator Allen, of Ohio, also demanded to know, in his usually loud and distinct voice — whether the Senator meant to be understood as speaking by authority of the President.

Senator Haywood answered, earnestly, and in slow tones: "I am an independent Senator. I recognize no man's right to question me. I will answer no demands."

Senator Hannegan was exercised with indignation, and declared that the man (meaning President Polk) who would make such a surrender of our rights would be buried so deep under public indignation that the hand of resurrection would never reach him!

Senator Allen made fierce speeches, the object of which he declared was to fire up "the popular heart to war."

After much debate in both Houses, we came down from our lofty position of 54.40, to the forty-ninth parallel of north latitude! We got neither "54.40," nor "fight."

Oregon, in 1848, was provided with a territorial government. The bill for that purpose contained a provision, in effect prohibiting the institution of slavery. The House had added a clause extending to this territory the Missouri Compromise line, but the Senate disagreed to the amendment.

President Polk communicated his approval of the bill in a message, in which he justified his action by saying: "The territory of Oregon lies far north of thirty-six degrees, thirty minutes, the Missouri and Texas Compromise line. Its southern boundary is the parallel of forty-two, leaving the intermediate distance to be three hundred and thirty geographical miles. And it is because the provisions of this bill are not inconsistent with the terms of the Missouri Compromise, if extended from the Rio Grande to the Pacific Ocean, that I have not felt at liberty to withhold my sanction."

About the same time, a little fume about sausages was raised in the House of Representatives. On the 27th of February, the "New York Tribune" contained a letter from Washington, signed "Persimmon," in which occurred the following paragraph about the Hon. William Sawyer, of Ohio.

"Though his name would indicate as much, yet he is not a woodsawyer. He is, I believe, a blacksmith — not that I consider the trade would disgrace him — the reputation of this trade is probably the greatest sufferer. All occupations are honorable for hard-working men. It is only disgraceful to live on the toil of another. But I digress from Mr. Sawyer. As Zoölogy is an important part of knowledge, I proceed to give you such account of the *critter's* habits as may assist you in classing him under the proper head in the system of animated nature. Every day at two o'clock he feeds. About that hour he is seen leaving his seat and taking a position in the window back of the Speaker's chair, to the left. He unfolds a greasy paper, in which is contained a chunk of bread and sausage, or some other unctuous substance. Then he disposes of them rapidly — wipes his hands with the greasy paper for a napkin, and throws it out of the window. What little grease is left on his hands he wipes on his almost bald head, which saves an outlay for pomatum. His mouth sometimes seems a finger-glass, his coat-sleeves and pantaloons being called into requisition for a napkin. He uses a jack-knife for a toothpick, and then goes on the floor again to abuse the Whigs as the British party, and claims the whole of Oregon as necessary for the spread of civilization. Some suspect he has a store of vegetables in his drawer. But enough of the habits of an old Loco Foco."

This article caused much commotion; and Mr. Sawyer, finding himself thus caricatured, was naturally indignant. "Richelieu" (now the Hon. William E. Robinson, from the Brooklyn district, in Congress, and the author of the Persimmon letter) wrote in March:

"What was the offence of the 'Tribune,' after all? Nothing in the world but stating a few facts, not against the moral character of anybody, but about the personal habits of a member of the House. Turn to your files, and you will see that 'Persimmon' states that Mr. Sawyer, of Ohio, feeds about two o'clock every day,— that he has his food rolled up in a piece of paper,—that after eating he throws the paper from the window,—that he wipes his hands upon his coat-sleeves, head, etc. While I would not have put these things in my letter, I may be permitted to say—nay, indeed, Mr. Sawyer himself said to-day—that they were mainly correct. He also acknowledged that he had had things said about him before this time, fifty times as bad as this *jeu d'esprit* in the 'Tribune.' I understand that several gentlemen of both parties have expressed the things mentioned upon several occasions, and can attest to the truth of 'Persimmon.'"

When this letter appeared, Mr. Sawyer rose to a question of privilege, and caused the paragraphs in the "Tribune" to be read by the clerk. He acknowledged eating as described; but if any more liberties were taken with his habits of life, he would take the matter in his own hands. He thought the author of the attack had light hair, but of this he was not certain!

Mr. Brinkerhoff, one of Sawyer's colleagues, rose and moved to exclude the reporters and letter-writers of the "Tribune" from the privilege of the seats or desks on the floor.

Several members wished to be excused from voting, because the House had refused to censure the Democratic administration organ for calling a member of the House a liar. This letter of "Persimmon" only described the habits of a member—its contents substantially correct, yet the writers were to be driven from their seats, while the former was retained as an officer of the House. Everything like explanation was voted down; and, under the operation of the previous question, the resolution of Mr. Brinkerhoff was agreed to, by a vote of 119 against 46.

"Richelieu," March 11th, wrote:

"The House have carried their highhanded outrage to an extent further than their own original depravity intended. Not only have they expelled the reporters of the 'Tribune,' but they have actually expelled the ladies from their presence also — not, to be sure, by a formal vote, but by their uncouth manners. As the 'Tribune' cannot be without the smiles of the ladies, your reporter has naturally followed them, and, attracted by the magnetism of their smiles, finds himself in their immediate presence."

The House sent the doorkeeper to expel Mr. Robinson from the ladies' gallery. In this gallery, strangers were admitted on the introduction of a member of the House, particularly if accompanied by ladies. "There are fifty members," he says, "to introduce me to this gallery, and even the ladies have volunteered their services not only to accompany me to the gallery, but to help me to report, if necessary."

Among the members who repeatedly went all the way up-stairs with Mr. Robinson, to pass him into the gallery, was John Quincy Adams.

Mr. Robinson continued to write about members, and criticise them from his perch in the gallery; and when, in his own good time, he retired from his vocation, he took an affectionate farewell; and, in the language of the poet, expressed his regret that the last "link" was "broken" that bound him to the House.

In this year — March, 1846 — Commodore Crane, Chief of the Bureau of Ordnance and Hydrography, committed suicide. He had been in his office, at the Navy Department, and read his papers on business.

About twelve o'clock, one of the clerks went to the door, found it locked, and supposed he had gone to sleep. The clerk looked through the keyhole, and saw him in his rocking-chair. As he had continued in the office till four o'clock, suspicion was aroused, and the door was burst open. He was found with his throat cut, and dead. The cause for taking his own life was not ascertained.

And in that year, a very curious and interesting law-case was tried. The facts are briefly as follows:

Mrs. Mary A. Conner, having been called upon for house-rent, refused to comply with the demand of the property-agent, saying that the premises belonged to herself, by virtue of her being the widow of General John P. Van Ness, to whom the property had belonged. This at once raised a legal issue. Eminent counsel were employed on both sides. The lady claimed that she was married to the deceased in the City of Philadelphia by an alderman. She was very particular in stating the time when, it was alleged, they were married, and all the circumstances of the wedding. The alderman, at the time of the trial, was dead; but his son and a servant-woman in the family were summoned hither as witnesses for the lady. The son said that Mrs. Conner had described his father's features with more accuracy than he could himself; but still, he had no recollection of his father's having performed the marriage ceremony; nor was the entry in his father's book. Neither had the servant-woman any knowledge on that subject. She remembered, that

Mrs. Conner had called at the house to make inquiries of her, and had intimated something about paying her to testify. And this was all she knew about the matter.

Another feature in this extraordinary trial: letters were produced, as if written by General Van Ness to his "dear wife." Doubts arising about the authorship, witnesses were called to prove handwriting; among them, the late John C. Rives, of the "Globe;" and he swore, "to the best of his knowledge and belief," that the handwriting was that of the General.

The dates of post-marks, and their cancellation, occupied much time. Mr. Gardner, the postmaster, and Mr. Tree, chief clerk, were witnesses.

Mrs. Conner's immediate relatives — mother, sister, daughter, and others — testified in her behalf. But, after all the long and interesting trial, the jury failed to be convinced that Mrs. Conner was the widow of General Van Ness.

To return to matters political. The treaty negotiated with Texas for its annexation to the Union having been rejected, joint resolutions to annex that republic to the United States were introduced in the House by Milton Brown, of Tennessee; and these were subsequently passed, and Texas became a State in our Union.

Mexico was incensed. An effort was made to open communication with Mexico, to adjust all questions in dispute between the two countries. John Slidell was sent as envoy to that republic, which refused to receive him. He returned home, and reported the facts to the Government.

Hon. Charles J. Ingersoll, the chairman of the Committee on Foreign Affairs, and other Democrats, at that time, only claimed the Texas boundary up to the Nueces; but Texas herself had more extravagant demands, in which the majority of Congress afterward acquiesced, and insisted that the true boundary was the Rio Grande del Norte.

General Taylor was sent to the banks of that river; and, appearing before Matamoras, the Mexican forces assumed a belligerent attitude. A body of United States troops having been sent up the river to discover whether the Mexican troops had crossed it, became engaged with a body of them, and after a short battle were surrounded and compelled to surrender. These facts were all communicated to Congress by President Polk, in May, 1846, who asked for supplies of men and money wherewith to carry on hostilities with Mexico. He said: "As war exists, and notwithstanding all our efforts to avoid it, by the act of Mexico herself, we are called upon by every consideration of duty and patriotism, to vindicate with decision the honor, the rights, and the interests of our country."

On the same day, a bill was reported to the House of Representatives, responding to the recommendation of the President. A substitute was moved for the first section of it as follows:

"Whereas, by the act of the republic of Mexico, a state of war exists between that Government and the United States, therefore be it enacted," etc.

This caused much excitement. Mr. Holmes, of

South Carolina, denounced the preamble as " base fraudulent, and false."

Mr. Bayly, of Virginia, was unwilling at that time "to vote a declaration of war, but considered withholding the supplies under the circumstances a greater evil."

Mr. Albert Smith, of Maine, declared the preamble to be " false in facts, and operating as a fraud upon the nation."

The bill, as thus amended, passed by a vote of one hundred and twelve yeas, against twelve nays; among the latter were John Quincy Adams and Joshua R. Giddings.

The bill went to the Senate, where the obnoxious preamble met with a stern opposition. It was assailed bitterly by the minority, which included such men as Berrien, Calhoun, John M. Clayton, Corwin, Crittenden, McDuffie, and Mangum.

Among the prominent Democrats who advocated the preamble were Allen, Benton, Cass, Dix, Houston, and Rusk.

Meanwhile preparations were made for war, which was inherited from the preceding administration.

Major-General Gaines, who was at New Orleans, made arrangements for " swooping to Mexico." He wanted to attack the Mexicans before they had time to gather force. But the administration checked his impulse, and ordered him to Washington.

The Thirtieth Congress assembled in December, 1847, with a Whig majority of eight opposed to the administration of Mr. Polk; and there was the remarkable gain of seventy-one "opposition" members over the preceding Congress.

Mr. Calhoun introduced a resolution declaring that to conquer and hold Mexico, either as a province, or incorporating it into the Union, was inconsistent with the avowed object of the war, contrary to the settled policy of the Government, in conflict with its character and genius, and in the end must be subversive of all our free and popular institutions; and that no line of policy in the further prosecution of the war should be adopted which might tend to consequences so disastrous.

Various resolutions were introduced in both branches, by different members, relative to the war; among them, Abraham Lincoln offered one calling upon the President to inform Congress whether the "spot" on which the first blood was shed was American or Mexican soil, and that he particularly point it out.

The country is already acquainted with the brilliant exploits and successes of our armies in Mexico. They will always be remembered.

Mr. Polk became weary of the war, and resorted to an extraordinary expedient for ending it, a plan which called down upon him denunciations both loud and deep.

General Lopez de Santa Ana had been exiled from Mexico, and was in Havana. Great indeed was the surprise when it became known that he had slipped over to Vera Cruz in an American man-of-war, with the permission of President Polk, and this, too, at a time when our military forces occupied a portion of that republic. His friends in Vera Cruz had notice of his coming, and the grandiloquent *pronunciamento* was already prepared by them. The first effect of his presence was the declaration of the garrison of Vera Cruz for their old chief, whose shout, like that of all his countrymen ever had been and was, "God and Liberty!"

Santa Ana had scarcely landed, and restrapped his wooden leg, before he was approached by an agent of this Government, "The man with a white hat," (as he was called by newspaper correspondents) following the army. He was asked to make a treaty, to which he responded: "Sir: I am not ready yet. I have just gained a welcome in Vera Cruz, and I do not know but that my countrymen elsewhere are still against me. I have, as you know, just returned from exile."

The administration of Mr. Polk had received promises from Santa Ana, the old wily Mexican, that if he were permitted to return to his native land, he would take such action as would end the war. And the administration confided in his promises.

So a little longer time was afforded to the General, which he improved, not in the interests of the United States, but in favor of his own country. The people everywhere welcomed him, being glad of his assistance in the war. He set to work, organized armies, and infused great vigor into *los Mexicanos.* Every man capable of bearing arms had to become a soldier. He did wonders, considering the impoverished condition of the country. In camp or on the march there was no commissariat, as with us. A little corn and salt, and jerked beef, sufficed for their support. The food was plain, but wholesome, with such fruits as might be picked up, or picked off, upon the march, washed down with *aqua ardiente.* The "man with the white hat" postponed his business until Santa Ana had a "more convenient season."

I know that a short time before the order was issued to the commander of the fleet off Vera Cruz for Santa Ana's return to Mexico in a United States vessel, his agent was in Washington, and had frequent interviews with President Polk and members of the Cabinet. I had a private friend, who was intimate with this agent, and who had abundant means of keeping himself advised of the progress of the negotiation. Mr. Ritchie, of the "Union," who was always ready to deny the truth of anything said against Mr. Polk, while admitting that this secret agent frequently visited the White House, endeavored to make it appear that he was, (using his own well-remembered term,) "a mere *chevalier d'industrie.*" So he was, as the sequel proved, and stole the confidence of President Polk and his advisers.

Santa Anna, despite the sneers against him, was an able General, and certainly out-generalled Polk and Marcy, and showed himself by the "little arrangement" to be a superior diplomate.

General Scott, however, was more than a match for Santa Ana, and gloriously succeeded in reaching the Capital of Mexico, where our troops "revelled in the halls of the Montezumas."

The campaign was not free from disagreeable events from our own side. The history of that period records the quarrel between Mr. Marcy, the Secretary of War, and Major-General Scott. The correspondence was spicy.

The war ended on the 30th of May, 1848, the date of the treaty of peace and boundaries, and acquisition of territory — California and New Mexico.

The treaty was communicated to the Senate, as a *confidential* document, and was ordered to be printed for the use of that body. Somehow, Mr. John Nugent, the correspondent of the "New York Herald," obtained a copy of it, and caused it to be printed in that newspaper.

The Senate ordered his arrest, and he was brought to its bar, in secret session, on the charge of committing "a breach of privilege." Thus arraigned, he refused to tell where or from whom he obtained the document. He was, for this "contempt," kept in close confinement. The prisoner was brought before the Circuit Court of this District, under a writ of *habeas corpus*, issued on the application of Joseph H. Bradley, Sen., his counsel. The late Richard S. Coxe, Esq., appeared on behalf of the Senate. After elaborate argument, the Court decided that it was not within its jurisdiction to order the release of Mr.

Nugent; and he was accordingly remanded to the custody of the Sergeant-at-arms of the Senate. The Senate never did ascertain from him the name of the person from whom he received the treaty. He remained a prisoner until the close of the session of Congress.

President Polk was a courteous gentleman; very dignified in his manners; his conversation was pleasant, but was free from joke and humor. Mrs. Polk always attended the receptions, and was easy and elegant in her manners.

Mr. Polk was, like his predecessor, the recipient of a box from an unknown source. Instead of exhibiting symptoms of fear, he *carelessly* found occasion to step aside five or six feet to spit, but did not return to inspect the suspicious box. Mr. Secretary Walker was in company, and neither did he expose himself to apprehended danger. Martin, as in the former instance, by permission, opened the box, and announced that there was nothing in it but an "ould rust-eaten gun, and without a lock."

It was probably sent to him by an opponent of the war, which was at that time in progress, and who resorted to this method to express his contempt for the hostile proceedings.

To relieve the President from his embarrassment, Martin remarked: "Perhaps, your Excellency, some friend has sent this to you, as a relic of the Revolutionary war."

"Oh yes!" quickly rejoined the President, "I recollect. I received a letter from North Carolina, several days ago, advising me of the fact."

The scene presented nothing of an exciting character, and was tame in comparison with that on the occasion of the box-opening during the term of his immediate predecessor.

In the early part of the year 1848, Mr. Henry Clay gave a dinner to a number of his friends, the object being, as it was shrewdly suspected, of discovering, in the course of conversation, the sincerity of some of those who professed to be earnest in their political attachments. Botts, Pendleton, and Crittenden were among the guests. It was not long before Botts and Crittenden engaged in an earnest and spirited conversation about the "loyalty" of Reverdy Johnson, at that time a Senator of the United States. Mr. Botts doubted the sincerity of Mr. Johnson, and proceeded to show, by the words and conduct of that gentleman, the truth of his bold assertion. Mr. Crittenden was surprised that the charge should be made, and vindicated his friend Johnson from the aspersion. The dialogue became so noisy, that Mr. Clay interfered to calm the perturbed spirits. He said: "Gentlemen, during the war of 1812, our mess occasioned much unkind feeling by constantly discussing the merits of that conflict; and many acrimonious remarks were made to the disgust of those who supported it; in fact, there was much dissatisfaction, which threatened to separate the members of the mess. So one day we agreed, that when the subject should again be introduced, any one was at liberty to cry out 'Buffalo!' as much as to say that the strife should stop, and that some other topic be introduced. In the course of a few days, the cry of 'Buffalo' had its desired effect." Mr. Clay's dinner-party were pleased with the narrative; but it soon passed from the minds of Messrs. Botts and Crittenden, for they resumed the heated conversation about Reverdy Johnson, when Mr. Clay suddenly called out "Buffalo!" wishing to end the conversation: Mr. Botts, in response to this friendly command of Mr. Clay, said: "It is well enough for you, Mr. Clay, to cry 'Buffalo' to us, but if we were to cry 'Buffalo' to you, you would show your horns very quickly." Whereupon Mr. Clay, in the blandest manner possible, said in his deep and sonorous voice: "That may be true, my friends; but you must make some allowance for 'THE DICTATOR.'"

[The point in the remark is, that Mr. Clay had been called "the Dictator" by his political opponents.]

During the three days preceding the 19th of April, 1848, very great excitement prevailed in Washington and our neighboring city of Georgetown, arising out of the fact that many citizens of the two places had been deprived of their servants, and its being reported that they were taken on board of a suspicious vessel, which had brought wood to Washington, and then left the wharf during Saturday night and sailed down the Potomac River. The citizens of Georgetown determined on Sunday to chase the schooner, and for this purpose they chartered the steamboat *Salem;* the pursuers, about thirty in number, being armed with muskets, pistols, and other weapons. Nothing was known of either the fugitives or the pursuers until Tuesday morning, when the steamer arrived at the steamboat wharf, bringing with her the schooner and all the slave passengers, together with Edward Sayers, a white man, captain of the schooner, and a person named Daniel Drayton, of Philadelphia, who had chartered the schooner.

The *Salem* discovered the *Pearl* lying in Cornfield Harbor, at the mouth of the Potomac River, about two o'clock on Monday morning.

The fugitives, seventy-seven in number, were fast asleep below, as were also Sayers, Charles English, (a white boatman,) and Drayton. The *Salem* having been run alongside the *Pearl*, the Georgetown party boarded her, fastened the hatches, and thus secured the fugitives and their white companions.

A large number of persons were on the wharf when the vessels arrived, some of whom used threatening language toward the white men who were brought up as prisoners, but no assault was attempted. They were hurried before a magistrate, who committed them for further examination on the charge of aiding slaves to escape from their owners.

The fugitives, numbering thirty-eight men, twenty-six women, and thirteen children, were also lodged in prison.

Mr. Gamaliel Bailey, Jr., the Editor of the "National Era," published an address to the citizens of

Washington, saying, "A rumor has been circulated that the office of the 'Era,' was concerned, directly or indirectly, with the recent attempt of a number of slaves to escape on the *Pearl*, it is due to respectable citizens of this place and to myself to give a plain, full, and unequivocal denial to this report." (Which he did; and then added:) "While determined to yield no right to menace or violence—a concession which no true-hearted American would be ungenerous enough to demand,—I feel it my duty to do all I can to remove a serious misapprehension, calculated to provoke unpleasant excitement. Certainly I feel a great repugnance to be assailed for what I have never done, or dreamed of; but if illegal violence be inflicted upon me for writing and printing freely about slavery, or any other subject which it may suit an American citizen to discuss, then will I suffer cheerfully, in the confident hope that when passion and prejudice shall have been dispelled, justice will be done to my character."

Notwithstanding the disclaimer of Mr. Bailey, a large number of persons assembled before the office of the "National Era," which was at that time on Seventh Street, opposite to the Patent Office. Some of them, with frantic yells, and bitter imprecations, demanded that the office be entered, and the printing material destroyed. It was remarked at the time that none of those who had been despoiled of their slaves were present on the occasion. The mob was composed, in part, of half-grown boys, who certainly were ready to take part in the work of destruction. John H. Goddard was the captain of the Auxiliary Guard, and exhibited great firmness and presence of mind in all his movements. He had a comparatively small force to assist him, but he ranged his men in front of the office, and gave due notice that the first person who attempted an entrance should be stricken to the earth. The mob swayed up to the front, but were gallantly pressed back by the policemen. Shouts, and yells, and curses, were frequently uttered by the rioters. If such vocal performances had been of avail, the rickety printing-office building would surely have tumbled to the earth!

Several citizens, with a view of quieting the excitement, resorted to an expedient for that purpose. They pretended to sympathize with the mob, and invited all who desired to take counsel to accompany them to the Patent Office steps, on F Street. Thither the larger part of the crowd repaired, where these citizens made speeches; one of them obtaining the consent of many of the rioters to meet at the same place the next morning, to perform the work of destruction. This postponement afforded time to make preparations to defeat all unlawful purposes.

Mr. Lenox, at that time President of the Board of Aldermen, issued, in handbill form, an address to the citizens of Washington, in which he said:

> "It is well known to you that events have transpired within the last few days, deeply affecting the peace and character of our community. The danger is not past, but demands in-

creased vigilance from the friends of order. The calm, deliberate judgment of the people of this city, unequivocally declared, is that the law will be found sufficient for the redress of any grievance, while fearful acts of lawless violence can only aggravate the evil. The authorities, municipal and police, have thus far restrained acts of violence, and now invoke the citizens of Washington to sustain them in their further efforts to maintain the peace and preserve the honor of the city. The peace and character of the Capital of this Republic *must* be preserved.

"The Mayor of this city, (Colonel Seaton,) confined to bed by sickness, fully concurs in the above.

"WALTER LENOX,
President of the Board of Aldermen.
"J. H. GODDARD,
Captain Auxiliary Guard.

"*April* 20, 1848."

The City Councils elected Colonel Peter Force to act as Mayor during Colonel Seaton's illness, and, by formal resolution, authorized him to take such measures as were necessary to preserve the public peace.

The next night there was another crowd before the "National Era" Office, but considerably tamed in spirit; the municipal authorities having engaged extra policemen, and taken other measures to prevent violence of action. The "National Era" Office was preserved.

Meanwhile the halls of Congress were disturbed with the subject.

Mr. Giddings, of Ohio, sought to introduce the following preamble and resolution:

"Whereas, more than eighty men, women, and children are said to be now confined in the prison of this District, without being charged with crime or any impropriety other than an attempt to enjoy the liberty for which our fathers encountered toil, suffering, and death itself, and for which the people of many European governments are now struggling;

"And whereas, said prison was erected, and is now sustained by funds, contributed by the people of the Free as well as the Slave States, and is under the control of the law-officers of the United States;

"And whereas, such practice is contrary to our national character, incompatible with the duty of a civilized and Christian people, and unworthy of being sustained by an American Congress, therefore,

"*Resolved*, That a select committee of five members of this body be appointed to inquire into and report to this House, by what authority said prison is used for the purpose of confining persons who had attempted to escape from slavery, with leave to report what legislation is proper in regard to such persons."

Mr. Giddings had asked leave to introduce this proposition, but several gentlemen objected.

Mr. Holmes, of South Carolina, said, that if the resolution were considered, he would move to amend by an inquiry whether the scoundrels who caused them to be in jail ought not to be hung.

This sally caused much laughter, for Mr. Holmes was an ill-tempered man. He was small in stature, but always had "large-sounding words."

Mr. Palfrey, of Massachusetts, the next day, rose to a question of privilege, presented in the following form: —

"Whereas, common report has represented to members of this House that a lawless mob has assembled within the District of Columbia on the two nights just passed, and has committed acts of violence, setting at defiance the laws and constituted authorities of the United States, and menacing individuals of this body and other persons residing in said District, therefore,

"*Resolved*, That a select committee of five members be appointed to inquire into the facts above referred to, and to report the facts with their opinion, whether any legislation is necessary or expedient in the premises, and that they have leave to sit during the session of the House."

A debate followed, continuing for two days. It involved the point whether the declarations in the proposition amounted to a question of privilege. The House laid the whole subject on the table by a vote of yeas 130, nays 42.

The slaves were delivered to their respective owners, and a few of them, nearly white, were purchased by voluntary subscriptions and set at liberty.

In the criminal court of the District of Columbia, at the March term, 1849, Daniel Drayton was convicted of transporting slaves in seventy-three cases, and sentenced by the court, in each case, to pay a fine of one hundred and forty dollars and costs; one half of the fine to the owner of the slaves, according to the act of Maryland, 1796. He was ordered to be committed to the jail of Washington County till fines and costs were paid.

The same number of cases against Edward Sayres, who was fined one hundred dollars and costs in each, and committed as above.

Under the law of Maryland, in force in the District of Columbia, the penalty was a fine not exceeding two hundred dollars, with imprisonment in the county jail as the alternative of non-payment. This Act was passed in 1796. The court did not impose the maximum fine in either case, one half of which, under the terms of the law, inured to the owners of the slaves, and the other to the "commissioners of the county." The costs belonged to the United States, by whom all the expenses of the prosecution had been paid.

They remained in jail four years, when President Fillmore pardoned them — 12th of August, 1852 — having been sustained by the opinion of Attorney-General Crittenden.

When the order was sent to the jail for the release of Drayton and Sayres, the Marshal of the United States for the District of Columbia hesitated to comply with it. The Secretary of the Interior wanted to detain them, to wait for a requisition from the Governor of Virginia; the laws of which State, it was said, they had violated. Senator Sumner was very much troubled about the detention, and spoke to Mr. Lewis Clephane, one of the publishers of the "National Era," on the subject. Mr. Clephane suggested that Mr. Sumner insist on their discharge, the President's order requiring this to be done.

The Marshal finally obeyed the order; and Drayton and Sayres, by Mr. Clephane's request, were sent to him. Mr. Clephane hired a hack, and, in the darkness of the night, took them to Baltimore, and placed them on the train for Harrisburg. Nothing more has been heard of them.

On the 21st of February, 1848, John Quincy Adams, while in his seat in the House of Representatives, was seized with paralysis. Mr. Hubbard, of Connecticut, called upon Mr. Fisher, of Ohio, who occupied a seat at Mr. Adams's right, to support the latter, who was apparently in the act of endeavoring to grasp the front of his desk, but sinking back in his seat, he dropped away to the left. He rallied, however, and as Mr. Fisher rose to assist him, he again fell back in the same position as before. Mr. Grinnell, his colleague, and others sitting near, flew to his side, when, the occurrence generally becoming known, many of the members rushed toward the spot, but retired upon the exclamations, "Keep back!" "Give him air!" The business of the House was by this time altogether suspended—everything in confusion. The windows were raised, and Mr. Grinnell bathed his face with ice-water; when he rallied for an instant and gave utterance, in a feeble voice, to the sentence: "This is the last of earth—I am content." Mr. Fries, of Ohio,—a regular physician,—raised him in his arms, and carried him to the Speaker's room, about fifty yards from Mr. Adams's seat in the House; the Speaker and several members of the Massachusetts delegation accompanying him.

Mr. Adams died on Wednesday evening, on the sofa in the Speaker's room, where he lay in an apparently insensible condition, from the Monday previous. The funeral ceremonies were performed on the 26th of February. The remains were embalmed, and lay in state, and were visited by thousands of persons. On the day of the funeral, the House was called to order by the Speaker. The President of the United States, and heads of the Departments, entered the Hall, the former taking his seat on the right of the Speaker. The Judges of the Supreme Court, in their gowns of office; officers of the Army and Navy, in full uniform; foreign Ministers and their suites, in rich costume, followed, and took their seats right and left of the area in front of the Speaker's chair. The Senate then came into the Hall, with the Vice-President, who took his seat on the Speaker's left. After this, the family of the deceased and the Massachusetts delegation, preceding the coffin, appeared as chief mourners. The chaplain, Rev. R. R. Gurley, pronounced an eloquent discourse from *Job* vi. 17 : "And thine age shall be clearer than the noonday; thou shalt be as the morning; and thou shalt be secure, because there is hope."

The remains were subsequently placed in the receiving-vault of the Congressional Cemetery; being carried in a funeral-car drawn by six white horses, and led by grooms in white scarfs; and finally, removed hence and deposited in the family vault at Quincy, Massachusetts.

CHAPTER VI.

THE INAUGURATION OF GENERAL TAYLOR — THE CABINET — RECEPTIONS — A BLUNDER — ANECDOTE OF MRS. MADISON AND MR. CLAY — DEATH OF MRS. MADISON — POLITICAL AND SECTIONAL TROUBLES — ELECTION OF SPEAKER — TOOMBS ON THE RAMPAGE — A DISSOLUTION OF THE UNION! — THE COMPROMISE MEASURES — WASHINGTON'S COFFIN — DEATH OF MR. CALHOUN — LAYING OF THE CORNER-STONE OF THE WASHINGTON NATIONAL MONUMENT — DEATH OF ZACHARY TAYLOR—CHOLERA MEDICINE—ANECDOTE — SUCCESSION OF MR. FILLMORE.

THE inauguration of General Zachary Taylor, as President of the United States, took place on the 4th of March, 1849.

The procession which escorted him to the Capitol was large and imposing, composed, in part, of twelve military companies. The carriage in which the President elect rode was drawn by four handsome gray horses, protected from the pressure of the multitude by one hundred marshals. The gentlemen who rode in the carriage with him, were the Speaker of the House of Representatives and the Mayor of Washington. According to previous arrangements, when the carriage arrived in front of the Irving Hotel, where the retiring President (Polk) was sojourning, the procession halted, and he was placed in the carriage, and took a seat on the right of the President elect, who shook his predecessor cordially by the hand. The friendly delicacy of the movement was duly appreciated by the multitude of persons who witnessed it; thereupon rung out spontaneously nine loud huzzas.

In the Senate chamber, Mr. Fillmore, the Vice-President elect, was escorted to the Chair by Mr. Dallas, the retiring Vice-President. Having taken the oath of office, Mr. Fillmore (as usual on such occasions) delivered an address.

The chamber was filled with members of Congress, foreign Ministers, Judges of the Supreme Court, and other distinguished personages.

The ceremonies in the Senate over, there was a long interval, awaiting the arrival of General Taylor. He at length drew near, sat for a few moments in the chair assigned to him, and was then escorted to the platform on the eastern portico. There, in the presence of many thousands of spectators, he delivered his inaugural address and took the oath of office.

The ceremonies terminated by salvos of artillery; the procession was re-formed, and escorted General Taylor to the Executive mansion. He was met there by a vast multitude. Passing along the area in front of him, he took the ladies, one after another, by the hand: a ceremony which, from their great number, it was not possible for him to perform with the crowd of the other sex.

There were three inauguration balls at night — at Jackson Hall, Carusi's Saloon, and the City Hall. President Taylor and Vice-President Fillmore attended all of them in succession. The display at each ball was noted for its brilliancy.

President Taylor chose for his Cabinet: John M. Clayton, Secretary of State; William M. Meredith, Secretary of the Treasury; George W. Crawford, Secretary of War; William B. Preston, Secretary of the Navy; Thomas Ewing, Secretary of the Interior; Jacob Collamer, Postmaster-General; and Reverdy Johnson, Attorney-General.

On the 13th of March, President Taylor received the diplomatic corps. The address was made to him on their behalf by the Minister representing the Argentine Confederation.

The usual pressure for office commenced, as on the incoming of every President. General Taylor and the Cabinet and Bureau officers were so much annoyed by the importunities of the place-hunters, that, during the month of March, the following notice was published by authority:

"We understand that it has been found necessary by the President of the United States, to require that all applications for office shall be made to the chief of the several departments, by whom they will be submitted at the proper time. No direct application can be entertained by the President for any office whatever."

A great error was made in the President's annual message, in the December following. Some copies had been printed, containing the sentence: "We are at peace with all the nations of the world, *and the rest of mankind*." The blunder caused much diversion to his political opponents. But it was corrected, so that the sentence read: "We are at peace with all the nations of the world, and seek to maintain our cherished relations of amity with them."

Mrs. Madison, relict of President Madison, died in this city, on the 13th of July, 1849. Her funeral was attended by the most prominent civilians at that time in Washington. She was a lady of elegant manners, and for a long period received her friends on New Years' days.

An old citizen has informed me that the levee of Mr. Madison, in February, 1816, was remembered for years as the most brilliant ever held up to that date in the Executive mansion. The Justices of the Supreme Court were present in their gowns, at the head of whom was Chief-Justice Marshall. The Peace Commissioners to Ghent — Gallatin, Bayard, Clay, and Russell — were in the company. Mr. Adams alone was absent. The levee was additionally brilliant — the heroes of the war of 1812 — Major-Generals Brown, Gaines, Scott, and Ripley, with their aides, all in full dress, forming an attractive feature. The return of peace had restored the kindest feeling at home and abroad. The Federalists and Republicans of both Houses of Congress, party politicians, citizens and strangers, were brought together as friends, to be thankful for the present, and to look forward with delight to the great future.

The most notable feature of the evening was the magnificent display of the diplomatic corps, prominent in which was Sir Charles Bagot, special ambassador from our late enemy, Great Britain. It was on that occasion that Mr. Bagot made the remark, that Mrs. Madison "looked every inch a queen." The only incident of a disagreeable character was the coolness toward the French Minister (who was very popular with the Republicans) by the Representatives of the Holy Alliance.

Mrs. Madison, like Mr. Clay, was very fond of snuff. The lady offered him a pinch from her splendid box, which the gentleman accepted with the grace for which he was distinguished. Mrs. Madison put her hand into her pocket, and pulling out a bandanna handkerchief, said, "Mr. Clay, this is for rough work," at the same time applying it at the proper place; "and this," producing a fine lace handkerchief from another pocket, "is my polisher." She suited the actions to the words, removing from her nose the remaining grains of snuff.

Mr. Van Buren inherited from General Jackson the financial troubles; Mr. Polk from Mr. Tyler a war with Mexico; and General Taylor the troubles growing out of the acquisition of territory from Mexico. The difficulty now was to compromise, or settle, political and sectional differences.

The Congress which met on the first Monday of December, 1849, was remarkably excited. The slavery question was prominent in the legislative halls. Northern members were determined not to be driven from their "free soil" position, while the representatives of the South clamorously insisted upon being allowed the right of carrying their slaves into all the territories of the United States. The issue had been fairly joined; neither side was disposed to yield anything; and under this condition of affairs, members sternly met face to face.

The first business was to organize the House. Frequent votes had been taken for the election of a Speaker, but without success. Members desired to open up discussion before this necessary preliminary was effected, and Mr. Toombs, of Georgia, was loudly in favor of latitude of debate. He considered that the House, at the time, was nothing more than a town-meeting, or a mob, and vociferously declared, with extravagant gestures, that the Union was at an end! Practically, however, we had not reached the catastrophe.

The House adopted a resolution that no debate was in order previous to the election of a Speaker and other officers.

Mr. Toombs determined to speak. He denied the right to pass any order prohibiting debate. He *would* exercise his right of discussion! He was saluted with deafening cries of "Order!" "Order!" to which he responded: "You may cry 'order, order, 'till the heavens fall, but you cannot take this place from *me!*" He had a right, he said, to protest against such a gag!

While Toombs was engaged in declamation, some one moved to rescind the anti-speaking rule; when the clerk proceeded to call the roll on that question, amid the combined noise made by "the gentleman from Georgia" and the repeated calls to order.

"I know my right," he repeated for the twentieth time; "you may call the roll, but you cannot *silence me*. I stand on the constitution of my country, and on the liberty of speech. [Cries of "Order!"] You have treacherously violated and opposed the rights of my constituents, and your fiendish yells may well be raised to drown an argument which you tremble to hear! I ask by what authority *that* man (pointing at the clerk) stands there and calls the roll? A member in defending his constitutional rights must not thus be interrupted."

Mr. Toombs was becoming weaker and weaker. No one seemed to have any "constitutional right" but himself; at last, exhausted, hoarse, and panting for breath, from his violent oratorical effort, he sank into his seat, apparently satisfied that he had indulged in "freedom of debate."

Members from the North had no disposition to come in personal collision with Mr. Toombs and his partisans, for they knew that he was earnestly seeking an opportunity to break up the assemblage altogether, if he could, and thus give practical effect to his declaration that the Union was at an end!

The clerk was finally allowed to call the roll, when the announcement was made by him that the House had refused to rescind the rule forbidding debate.

A resolution was then agreed to, in effect: that on the next ballot, the House shall proceed to elect a Speaker from the four candidates receiving the largest number of votes. If neither have a majority, the

House shall then select from the three candidates having the largest number of votes. If no choice, then the two candidates having the largest number of votes shall be the only candidates.

Thus the choice was narrowed down to Howell Cobb, of Georgia, and Robert C. Winthrop, of Massachusetts: the former receiving one hundred and two, and the latter one hundred votes. The House passed a resolution, declaring Mr. Cobb elected Speaker. A slight manifestation of applause followed this result.

Mr. Cobb, on being conducted to the chair, made an appropriate speech.

Thus, three weeks were spent in securing a presiding officer.

Early in February, 1850, Mr. Clay, in the Senate, presented a series of resolutions, having for their object, he said, "the peace, concord, and harmony of the Union, and a settlement of the questions relating to slavery, etc." Toward the close of his remarks on that occasion, he told this incident: "A man came to my room—the same at whose instance, a few days ago, I presented a memorial calling upon Congress for the purchase of Mount Vernon for the use of the public,—and without being at all aware of what purpose I entertained in the discharge of my public duty to-day, he said to me: 'Mr. Clay, I heard you make a remark the other day, which induces me to suppose that a precious relic in my possession would be acceptable to you.' He then drew out of his pocket, and presented to me, the object which I now hold in my hand. And what, Mr. President, do you suppose it is? It is a fragment of the coffin of Washington—a fragment of that coffin in which now repose, in silence, in sleep, and speechless, all the earthly remains of the venerated Father of his Country. Was it portentous that it should have been thus presented to me? Was it a sad presage of what might happen to that fabric which Washington's virtue, patriotism, and valor established? No, sir, no. It was a warning voice, coming from the grave to the Congress now in session, to beware, to pause, to reflect, before they lend themselves to any purposes which shall destroy the Union which was cemented by his exertions and example. Sir, I hope an impression may be made on your mind such as that which was made on mine by the reception of this precious relic."

No one who regularly attended the sessions of Congress, in 1850, can ever forget the ability and spirit of the debates by the great men; the most prominent of whom will never more appear, the grave having closed over their remains. Mr. Calhoun was not able to be present during the discussion, but caused to be read a speech expressive of his views. He had been suffering during the winter with a menacing pleuritic affection which, for eight or ten weeks, with only a few brief intervals, confined him to his room. Thus gradually sinking, he died, aged sixty-eight years, at his boarding-house, the old Capitol building, (which was during the rebellion used as a prison.) His death was announced in both Houses of Congress, and more than the usual number of addresses delivered on the occasion. The Departments were clothed in mourning.

Passing over intermediate events, it may be stated, that on the occasion of the laying of the corner-stone of the Washington National Monument, on the 4th of July, of the same year, a very large crowd of spectators was present. The oration was delivered by General Foote. When the speaker quoted from the letter of Hamilton to Washington, protesting against the first President's retiring from office, as he himself desired, President Taylor, who sat to the left of the orator, aroused himself, as if to catch every word that was uttered.

George Washington Parke Custis, the grandson of General Washington's wife, also spoke on the interesting occasion.

A rather unexpected feature was added to the ceremonies — a bag of sand from the tomb of Kosciusko, which was deposited with the corner-stone. This relic was presented by Francis Leiber, by whose son it had been brought to this country for the purpose.

The weather was intensely warm. While on the ground, President Taylor partook freely of ice-water, and on his return to the White House he said he felt very hungry, and ate heartily of cherries, which he washed down with copious draughts of iced milk and water. At dinner, he applied himself again to the cherries, against which Dr. Witherspoon remonstrated. In the course of an hour, he was seized with cramps, which resulted in violent cholera morbus. The disease, from a remittent character, took the form of typhoid. Then the greatest anxiety, in Washington and throughout the country, was expressed concerning him, and hourly telegrams were sent hence as to his condition. They announced, first, that he was seriously ill; next, that he was in a dying condition, and that, therefore, he was beyond the power of human skill; and, finally, that he died on the 9th of July. His death was calm and peaceful; Vice-President Fillmore, the Cabinet ministers, the Mayor of Washington, the Marshal of the District of Columbia, the attending physicians, and his family, surrounded his bed. His last words were, "I have endeavored to do my duty."

Mr. Fillmore sent a short note to the Senate, saying, that, in consequence of the death of President Taylor, he would be no longer able to fulfil the duties of Vice-President, and suggested that this notification might enable the Senate to proceed more promptly to the election of a presiding officer. Soon after, he communicated a message to both Houses of Congress, recommending the adoption of such measures as in their discretion might seem proper, to perform with due solemnities the funereal obsequies to Zachary Taylor, the late President, and thereby signify the great and affectionate regard of the American people for the memory of one whose whole life was passed in the public service, and whose career in arms had not been surpassed for usefulness or brilliancy.

Eulogies were delivered in both Houses, and committees appointed to make preparations for the funeral.

The remains lay in the east room at the White

House, upon a magnificent catafalco of black velvet, trimmed with white satin lace; the body was in a leaden coffin, enclosed in one of mahogany with silver decorations.

The doors of the President's house were opened in the morning for the admission of Heads of Departments, foreign Ministers, and others of prominent official position. Many persons had gathered on the outside. The funeral ceremonies were performed by Rev. Drs. Butler and Pyne, of the Protestant Episcopal Church.

Nearly all the houses on Pennsylvania Avenue — the line of the procession — were draped with mourning. The military, about fifteen hundred men, were under the command of Lieutenant-General Scott. Besides a large number of civilians, hundreds of hacks and private carriages completed the pageant, which exceeded anything of the kind, in order and magnificence, ever before witnessed in Washington. Conspicuous in the procession was "Old Whitey," with all his trappings on, following his master to the grave. The remains were temporarily deposited in the Congressional Cemetery, and afterward removed to his late home.

An Incident. — A few days before the laying of the corner-stone of the monument, a young gentleman from Baltimore brought a letter of introduction to me. His business was to sell cholera medicine. It was thought, by the friend who furnished him with the letter, that I might, perhaps, help him to commend the medicinal preparation to public favor. As I had never been engaged in the physic business, I was quite ignorant of the means to serve his purpose. None of my friends were suffering with cramps, or any other painful internal affliction. The medicine was a genuine painkiller! Fortunately, *I* had no necessity to try it. He asked me whether it was not a good idea to call upon President Taylor, and make him a present of a bottle. I replied that perhaps it *was* a good idea. As I had not yet become intimately acquainted with General Taylor, I could not present him, but I consented to accompany him to the White House, to see how he would act. The young gentleman, as we walked thither, rehearsed his speech. We had no difficulty in getting into the reception-room, which was tolerably well filled. There was the President, in the centre of the parlor, with his hand continually stretched forth, earnestly shaking that of everybody who was ambitious of enjoying the pleasure. Now came the trial. My new acquaintance timidly approached the President, and underwent the stiff and formal ceremony. I saw his lips tremblingly move, and drew nearer to hear what he was saying, but I clearly remember only a few words of that, his first speech, to a President, as he put his hand into his pocket to pull out "the dead shot." President Taylor started back a step or two, and exclaimed in a loud tone, "I thank you — am much obliged to you — but I never take medicine, cholera or no cholera." The young man almost fainted, and hastily took my arm and disappeared from the gaze of the spectators. Less than ten days from that time General Taylor died of cholera.

CHAPTER VII.

MR. FILLMORE TAKES THE OATH OF OFFICE — CONTINUATION OF THE POLITICAL TROUBLES — THE NASHVILLE CONVENTION — ESTABLISHMENT OF A "SOUTHERN PRESS" — THE COMPROMISE — PEACE — THE GREAT PISTOL SCENE IN THE SENATE — THE PARTICULARS OF THE QUARREL BETWEEN FOOTE AND BENTON — THE LAYING OF THE CORNER-STONE OF THE ADDITION TO THE CAPITOL — MR. WEBSTER'S GREAT ORATION — MR. FILLMORE'S ORGAN — RECEPTION OF KOSSUTH — GRAND DINNER — DEATH OF HENRY CLAY — DEATH OF MR. WEBSTER — CONVICTION AND SUICIDE OF DR. CHAS. JOHN GARDNER — CABINET CHANGES, ETC.

ON the 10th of July, by pre-arrangement, Mr. Fillmore came to the House of Representatives, and, in the presence of the Senators and Representatives, and the Cabinet, took the President's oath of office, as prescribed by the Constitution, and then returned to the Executive Mansion.

During June, of 1850, the Nashville Convention passed strongly-worded resolutions, the twelfth declaring "that in the opinion of this Convention the prevailing controversy should be ended, either by a recognition of the constitutional rights of the Southern people, or by an equitable partition of the territories; that the spectacle of a confederacy of States, involved in quarrels over the fruits of the Mexican War, in which the American arms were crowned with glory, is humiliating; that the incorporation of the Wilmot Proviso, in the offer of settlement — a proposition which fourteen States regard as disparaging and dishonorable — is degrading to the country. A termination to this controversy by the disruption of the confederacy, or by the abandonment of the territories to prevent such a result, would be a climax to the shame which attaches to the controversy, which it is the paramount duty of Congress to avoid."

The slavery question had been intensely agitated. From its presentation by a few, it had extended to many politicians, both North and South; and threats had been made on both sides, the one against the machinations of the other.

The Southern members of Congress became alarmed, and held meetings at the Capitol, responsive to the utterances of their constituents; and in May, 1850, resolved to establish in this city a newspaper, devoted exclusively to Southern interests. In order to permanently locate it, they issued an address, in which they said: "We do not propose to meddle with political parties as they exist: we wish to enlist every Southern man in a Southern cause, and in defence of Southern rights, be he Whig or be he Democrat. All that we ask is, that he shall consider the constitutional rights of the South, which are involved in the great abolition movement, as paramount to all party and other political considerations. And surely the time has come when all Southern men should unite for purposes of self-defence." They said, in addition, that they wanted this paper to be sent to every Southern home, and complained that the Northern press had a controlling influence in the South.

So the "Southern Press" was started. It had only a brief existence. Its presses and types entered into more profitable channels.

The session continued to be stormy, and was of ten months' duration. The result of the compromise was:

1. An Act proposing to the State of Texas the establishment of her northern and western boundaries; the relinquishment, by the said State, of all territory claimed by her to the said boundaries, and of all her claim upon the United States, and to establish a territorial government for New Mexico.

2. An Act to establish a territorial government for Utah.

3. An Act for the admission of the State of California.

4. An Act to amend, and supplementary to the Act to more effectually secure fugitives from justice and persons (slaves) escaping from the service of their masters; and

5. An Act to suppress the slave-trade in the District of Columbia, which abolished the importation of slaves into the District of Columbia for the purpose of traffic.

The Nashville Convention reassembled in November, 1850, and among its resolutions was the declaration that all the evils anticipated by the South, and which occasioned the Convention to assemble, had been realized by the failure to extend the Missouri line of compromise to the Pacific Ocean; by the admission of California as a State; by the organization of territorial governments for Utah and New Mexico, without giving adequate protection to the property of the South; by the dismemberment of Texas; by the abolition of the slave-trade and the emancipation of slaves, carried into the District of Columbia for sale.

While the compromise measures were under discussion, on the 17th of April, 1850, much excitement was occasioned in the Senate by the conduct of Messrs. Foote and Benton.

On several occasions prior to that time, Foote had indulged in remarks personal to Benton. On the occasion last preceding the one in question, Benton complained of these personalities in severe and violent language addressed to the Senate, reiterated the personalities on Foote, spoke of the failure of the Senate to protect its members from such insults, and declared his determination, if the Senate did not protect him, to redress the wrong himself, cost what it might. He also said, in substance, that a member offering the insults should be cudgelled. On the following day Benton brought into the Senate the newspaper report of the altercation, which he said had been revised by Foote. He pronounced it a wrong report, and denounced it as cowardly. On the 17th of April he said he intended, by an amendment which he had offered, to cut at the root of all the political agitation, to cut up the whole address of the Southern members, by which the country was thrown into a flame. He proposed to show the Senate that this alarm had been without foundation — that they had been disturbed about nothing, etc.

To this Foote replied, saying they all knew the history of the Southern address. It was the history of a band of patriots. Calhoun was the author of the Southern address. But by whom was this extraordinary denunciation hurled against all the individuals who subscribed this address? By a gentleman long denominated the oldest member of the Senate — the father of the Senate; by a member who, on a late occasion —

At this point of the speech of Foote, Benton rose from his seat, threw or pushed his chair violently from him, passed through the opening in the railing to the passage behind the bar of the Senate, and without remark or gesture, but with angry countenance, quickly strode down the passage without the bar of the Senate, toward the seat of Foote, which was distant about twenty feet from his own, both seats being in the back row, next the bar. Benton had no weapon of any kind in his hand, or about his person. Foote quickly perceiving the movement of Benton, and almost simultaneous with it, left his place on the floor, and proceeded down the Senate aisle which led from his seat to the space in front of the Secretary's table, and which was the next one to the principal aisle. As he did so, he looked over his shoulder, and drew a pistol from his pocket, the pistol being a five-chambered revolver, fully loaded. Foote cocked his pistol, either while going down the aisle or after he had taken his place in front of the Secretary's table. Mr. Dodge, of Wisconsin, quickly followed Benton and overtook him within seven or eight feet of Foote's seat, and seized him by the arms, when Benton said, "Don't stop me, Dodge." Dodge then said, "Don't compromit yourself or the Senate," or words to that effect. Benton then turned with Dodge, and was going back to his seat, when he perceived the pistol in Foote's hands, which seemed to excite him greatly. He got within the bar, near his seat, and struggled with the Senators around him as if desirous of approaching Mr. Foote, exclaiming, "I disdain to carry arms; let him fire! Stand out of the way, and let the assassin fire." While making these exclamations, Benton was brought back to his seat by the Senators around him. In the meantime, amid great noise and confusion, Foote had remained standing in or near the position he had taken, with his pistol in his hand cocked, but with the muzzle down. Mr. Dickinson, of New York, desired him to give up the pistol, which he readily did, when Dickinson locked it up in his desk. Soon after both Senators resumed their seats and order was restored.

Mr. Benton said: A pistol was brought here with which to assassinate me. The gentleman had no reason to think that I was armed, for I carry nothing of the kind, sir.

Mr. Foote. I brought it here to defend myself.

Mr. Benton. Nothing of the kind, sir; it is a false imputation. I carry nothing of the kind, and no assassin has a right to draw a pistol on me. (Several Senators cried "Order.")

Mr. Benton. It is a mere pretext of the assassin. Will the Senate take notice of it, or shall I be forced to take notice of it by going and getting a weapon myself. A pistol has been brought here, and drawn upon me by an assassin.

The Vice-President. The Senator will be seated.

Mr. Foote. Mr. President —

The Vice-President. Senators will be pleased to suspend their remarks until order is restored. The Senator is requested to be seated.

Mr. Clay. Mr. President —

The Vice-President. Business cannot proceed until order is restored.

Mr. Hale. I hope order will be kept in the galleries.

The Vice-President. There is too much noise in the galleries. Quiet and order must be restored.

Mr. Foote. May I proceed in order?

Mr. Benton. I demand the Senate shall take immediate cognizance of the fact of this pistol having been brought here to assassinate me under the felonious pretext that I was armed — the pretext of every assassin who undertakes to constitute a case of self-defence, when laying out the death of his victim. Will the Senate notice it, or shall I myself; for it shall not pass. I will not be satisfied here.

Mr. Foote. If my presenting a pistol has been understood as anything except the necessary means of self-defence, after threats of personal chastisement, it is doing me a wrong. I saw him advance toward me, and I took it for granted he was armed; for had I thought otherwise, I should not have stopped to meet him in the narrow alley. So help me God, to shoot him, without an attack, was not my intention. I also court investigation.

Mr. Mangum's resolution for an investigation was adopted.

The Committee, on the 30th of July, reported all the facts, saying the whole scene was most discreditable to the Senate. Its origin was traced directly to a violation of the Rules of Order, which forbid all personalities. They unanimously gave their opinion that Foote was innocent of any design or desire to assassinate Benton; but they were bound to say that at various times during the session, Foote, without any just provocation, indulged in personalities against Benton, of the most offensive and insulting character, such as were calculated to arouse the fiercest resentment of the human bosom.

They were suffered by Benton for a long time with great forbearance. On the 26th of March they were renewed, and on this occasion Benton manifested his resentment with much violence. On the succeeding day he recriminated in language equally personal, disorderly, and abusive. He complained that the Senate permitted such outrages, and announced his purpose, if the Senate did not protect him in the future, to redress the wrong, cost what it might. On the 17th of April, Foote spoke again, and used language the Committee considered personal and offensive. It is believed that Foote did not know that Benton was not armed. The Committee severely condemned the wearing of arms in the Senate. They forbore to recommend any action to the Senate, and expressed the hope that what had transpired would serve as a sufficient rebuke and warning in the future.

Should such scenes be re-enacted, they could not doubt that the Senate would resort to the proper means of punishment.

During the year 1851, Lopez and a number of daring followers from this country, sought to revolutionize the island of Cuba. The authorities there executed a number of them, including their chief. There was a widespread complaint that our consul at Havana, Hon. A. F. Owen, was recklessly indifferent to their fate, and made no effort to save his countrymen from death, and even President Fillmore was accused of having counselled the "do-nothing" policy. Mr. Owen endeavored to excuse his non-intervention in the affair by explaining, through the public press, that when he heard that the prisoners had been tried and sentenced to be shot, he was at his residence, four miles from Havana, and he said to his informant he should not have time or permission to see the prisoners. He learned soon thereafter that they had been shot. He characterized the charge of indifference as a base falsehood, and repeated it was not in his power either to have had an interview with the prisoners, or to do anything on their behalf.

A number of the filibusters were sent to Spain by the Cuban authorities, to be dealt with by the Government of that country. Through the efforts of our Minister, Mr. Barringer, her Most Catholic Majesty pardoned them.

On the 4th of July, 1851, the extensive grounds of the Capitol were filled to their utmost capacity. The ladies were there in great force, enlivening and adding gayety to the occasion, together with military companies and civil associations. The President of the United States, Heads of Departments, foreign Ministers, Governors of States, and other distinguished personages, were seated upon a platform on the left portico, at the east front. Several bands of music played during the intervals of the proceedings. The scene was brilliant and interesting.

It was the seventy-sixth Anniversary of the nation's independence, and the assembling was to lay the corner-stone of the Capitol extension.

The Grand Master of the Order of Masons, Major B. B. French, attended to his part of the programme, and President Fillmore laid the stone, after the manner of that fraternity.

Mr. Webster was the orator. He said the principles of our government might be thus briefly stated: — First, the recognition of popular representation; second, the popular voice, as expressed by the majority, becomes law; and third, the law governs all the people, and is recognized as the rule of government. He had caused to be deposited in the corner-stone a statement written in his own hand, as follows: —

"On the morning of the first day of the seventy-sixth anniversary of American independence in the City of Washington, being the fourth day of July, 1851, this stone, designed as the corner-stone of the extension of the Capitol, according to a plan approved by the President, in pursuance of an Act of Congress, was laid by MILLARD FILLMORE, President of the United States, assisted by the Grand Master of the Masonic lodges, in the presence of many members of Congress, of officers of the Executive and Judicial departments — National, State, and District,— of officers of the Army and Navy, the corporate authorities of this and neighboring cities; many associations, civil and military; the officers of the Smithsonian Institution and National Institute; professors of colleges and teachers of schools of the District, with their students and pupils, and a vast concourse of people from places near and remote, including a few venerable gentlemen who witnessed the laying of the corner-stone of the Capitol by President Washington on the eighteenth day of September, 1793.

"Therefore, if it shall be hereafter the will of God that this structure shall fall from its base, that its foundation be upturned, and this deposit brought to the eyes of men, be it known that on this day the Union of the United States of America stands firm, and that their Constitution still exists unimpaired, and with all its original usefulness and glory, growing every day stronger and stronger in the affections of the great body of the American people, and attracting more and more the admiration of the world. And all here assembled, whether belonging to public life or to private life, with hearts devoutly thankful to Almighty God for the preservation of the liberty and happiness of the country, unite in sincere and fervent prayers that this deposit, and the walls and cornices, the dome and towers, the columns and entablatures now to be erected over it, may endure forever. God save the United States of America.

"DANIEL WEBSTER,
"*Secretary of State of the U. S.*"

He referred to the fact of Washington's laying the corner-stone of the Capitol, as forming a chain in the bond of union, and invoked the spirit of the illustrious dead in behalf of the present and the future. The new wings about to be added to the Capitol, stretching, as they did, North and South, he regarded as an additional cord in binding the States in union. He would say now, relative to the Capitol, as he had said on another occasion — referring to his speech on the laying of the corner-stone of the Bunker Hill Monument — "Let it rise — let it rise — let it rise until it shall meet the sun in its coming." He thought if the immortal Washington could rise and stand forth there that day, he would rejoice in the feelings which existed, and ask the blessing of Heaven upon our future union and prosperity. "Father immortal!" he exclaimed, "though dead, we shall feel thy influence now and here."

The oration was one of Mr. Webster's best efforts, although it was not delivered under favorable circumstances of health. He exhibited considerable physical weakness, and had to resort to stimulants to sustain himself.

There were present three persons who attended the laying of the corner-stone of the Capitol by Washington, fifty-eight years before the present ceremonies, namely: George Washington Parke Custis, Z. Walker, of Maryland, and Lewis Machen, a clerk in the office of the Senate of the United States.

Louis Kossuth and suite arrived at Washington toward the close of December, 1851. Reaching Brown's Hotel, where arrangements had previously been made for their accommodation, three or four hundred persons gathered at the doors to see the distinguished stranger. He appeared on the balcony to gratify their desire, and made a short speech of thanks for their cordial greeting.

A number of prominent gentlemen, including Secretary of State Webster, Senators Cass and Douglas, and Major-General Scott, formally called on him the next day, to pay their respects.

Kossuth visited President Fillmore, and read to him a short address, to which Mr. Fillmore replied he was happy to welcome him to this land of freedom, and added: "Should your country be restored to independence, I shall then wish, as the greatest blessing for your country's interests, a restoration to your native land."

Kossuth was honored by the Senate, in being invited to a seat in their chamber, which he took in silence.

The House had a long debate before they passed a resolution extending to him a similar courtesy. Early in January, he was formally received in that body. Mr. Cartter, of Ohio, a member of the House, and now Chief-Justice of the Supreme Court of the District of Columbia, was the chairman of the select committee, and introduced him as follows:

"Mr. Speaker, I have the honor, on the part of the Committee, to present Governor Louis Kossuth to the House of Representatives."

Speaker Boyd responded: "As the organ of this body, I have the honor to extend to Louis Kossuth a cordial welcome to the House of Representatives."

Mr. Kossuth (standing meantime in the area in

front of the Clerk's desk) said: "Sir, it is a remarkable fact in the history of mankind, that while, through the past, honors were bestowed upon glory and valor attached only to success, the legislative authorities of this great republic have bestowed honor upon a persecuted exile not conspicuous by glory, not favored by success, but engaged in a just cause. There is a triumph of republican principles in this fact. Sir, I thank, in my own and country's name, the House of Representatives, for the honor of this cordial welcome."

Kossuth was then conducted to the seat assigned to him, and was subsequently greeted by individual members of the House.

A grand public dinner was given in his honor by a large number of Congressmen, at the National Hotel. Among them were Senators Cass, Seward, Shields, King, of Alabama, and Speaker Boyd.

Speeches were made by Judge Wayne, of the Supreme Court, General Cass, General Shields, Mr. Webster, Senator Seward (a very brief one) and others. Kossuth eloquently responded to the toast in his honor.

At least several of the suite of Kossuth were ill-bred. One of them was so drunk when he returned from the banquet, that he tumbled into what is called the "bridal bed"—in the room reserved for couples just married—at Brown's Hotel, where he was lodged, with his heavy clothing on, boots and all! Although Brown's Hotel was not more than two minutes' walk from the National Hotel, where the banquet was held, hired carriages conveyed Kossuth's party to and fro. One of the suite, being too drunk to mount the carriage steps, staggered *Brownward.* The night was very cold. Passing near this Kossuthian, he put his arms around me, gave a hearty hug, and called me by the endearing name of "Mine Bruder!" I never before knew that I had a Hungarian brother.

An interesting meeting between Kossuth and Henry Clay took place the day after the dinner. Accompanied by General Cass, this gentleman introduced him to Mr. Clay. Kossuth commenced a conversation by saying, "I thank you, sir, for the honor of this interview." "No, no," responded Mr. Clay, interrupting him, "it is I who am honored. Will you please be seated?"

Mr. Clay then said that his health was feeble, and proceeded at some length to give his views adverse to Kossuth's errand for material aid in behalf of Hungary, concluding with the remark: "We should adhere to our wise pacific system. We should keep our lamp brighly burning on these shores as a light to all nations, rather than hazard its utter extinction amid the ruins of fallen republics in Europe."

Kossuth was overwhelmed by the warm and earnest sympathy expressed by Mr. Clay for himself and family. Profoundly bowing, he pressed Mr. Clay's hand to his heart, and replied in tones of deep emotion, "I thank you, honored sir. I shall pray for you every day that your health may be restored, and that God may prolong your life."

Clay's eyes filled with tears. He again pressed the hand which clasped his own, for the last time; but he could say no more.

Henry Clay died in Washington on the 29th of June, 1852.

The members of Congress were generally on their way to the Capitol when overtaken by the tidings. In the Senate, before the reading of the Journal, Mr. Hunter, of Virginia, said:

"Mr. President, a rumor has been circulated that Henry Clay is dead. His colleague is absent rendering the last sad offices. I, therefore, move that the Senate adjourn." The motion was agreed to without a division.

The next day, the scene at the Capitol was in the highest degree solemn and impressive. The galleries and lobbies of the Senate Chamber were filled at an early hour, in anticipation of the funeral solemnities. No similar occasion ever before drew so large a crowd of spectators, including the President of the United States, members of both Houses, the diplomatic corps, Cabinet Ministers and Chiefs of Bureaus, and Judges of the Supreme Court, Daniel Webster; the General-in-Chief of the army, Major-General Scott, and Attorney-General Crittenden. The Rev. C. M. Butler officiated. Eloquent addresses were delivered in the Senate, and afterward in the House of Representatives.

The coffin containing the body was borne upon a car appropriately draped, and drawn by gray horses;

festoons of mourning lined the buildings on Pennsylvania Avenue, on each side, to an extent never before witnessed. A large number of distinguished persons were in the procession. The remains were conveyed to Kentucky, accompanied by a Congressional committee.

On the day of the death of Mr. Clay, President Fillmore sent the following letter to the several Heads of Departments : —

"EXECUTIVE MANSION, Tuesday, 12½ P. M."

"SIR : — The tolling of bells announces the death of Henry Clay. Though this event has been long anticipated, yet the painful bereavement could not be fully realized. I am sure that all hearts are at this moment too sad to attend to business. I therefore respectfully suggest that your Department be closed for the remainder of the day.

"MILLARD FILLMORE."

Daniel Webster died at Marshfield, Massachusetts, on the 24th of October, 1852. He filled, at the time of his decease, the office of Secretary of State. His death was announced in both Houses of Congress on the 14th of December. Among those who pronounced eulogies were, Messrs. Butler, of South Carolina; Cass, Seward, Stockton, Preston, of Kentucky; and Mr. Bayly, of Virginia. The last-named said: "Sir, it is but a short time since the American Congress buried the first one that went to the grave of that great Triumvirate, (Calhoun.) We were then called on to bury another, (Clay,) and now the third, (Webster.) In the lives and characters of these great men there is much resembling those of the great triumvirate of the British Parliament. It differs principally in this: Burke preceded Fox and Pitt to the tomb; Webster survived Clay and Calhoun. When Fox and Pitt died, they left no peer behind them. Webster still lived after Calhoun and Clay were dead. Like Fox and Pitt, Clay and Calhoun lived in troubled times. Like Fox and Pitt, they were, each of them, the leader of rival parties. Like Fox and Pitt, they were idolized by their respective friends." The speaker then drew a parallel between Burke and Webster.

The Departments were draped in mourning as a mark of respect for the departed statesman.

As appropriate to the character of the deceased, it may here be stated, that in the Senate of the United States, in 1846, there was a personal quarrel between Mr. Dickinson and Mr. Webster, resulting from a charge by the latter against the former, respecting the Ashburton treaty. Four years after, the feeling left in Mr. Webster's bosom by the quarrel had been so far subdued by Mr. Dickinson's manly and patriotic course in regard to the sectional agitation, that in the year 1850, being on the point of leaving the Department of State, Mr. Webster wrote a letter, dated September 27th, in which he said:

"In the early part of our acquaintance, an occurrence took place which I remember with constantly increasing regret and pain, because the more I have known of you the greater has been my esteem for your character, and my respect for your talents; but it is your noble, able, manly, and patriotic conduct in support of the great measures of the session which has entirely won my heart, and secured my highest regard. I hope you may live long to serve your country, but I do not think you are very likely to see a crisis in which you may be able to do so much, either for your own distinction or the public good. You have stood while others have fallen; you have advanced with firm and manly step where others have wavered, faltered, and fallen back, and for one I desire to thank you, and to commend your conduct out of the fulness of an honest heart. This letter needs no reply. It is, I am aware, of poor value, but I have thought you might be willing to receive it, and propose to leave it where it will be seen by those who shall come after you. I pray you, when you reach your own threshold, to remember me most kindly to your wife and daughter. I remain, dear Sir, with the truest esteem, your friend and obedient servant, DANIEL WEBSTER.

"Hon. D. S. DICKINSON, United States Senate."

During the time that Mr. Webster was Secretary of State, one of the newspaper correspondents managed to obtain the freshest news of Cabinet consultations, etc., to the exclusion of all rivals. Things desired to be kept secret were promptly exposed. The President and his Cabinet, annoyed by such occurrences, had a grave talk; and the conclusion reached by Mr. Webster was, that the "news" must have escaped into the ears of an eavesdropper. His fellow-members did not think this possible. "Oh, yes," remarked Mr. Webster; "I think it is. I'll go into the reception-room — you must talk meantime, and I will report progress." When he returned, he repeated all they had said. This convinced them that he was right in his guessing. An order was the same day given to add another door to the listening place. This effectually stopped the leak.

In the year 1853, a trial of much interest took place in this city—that of Dr. Charles John Gardiner—for forgery, the suit being instituted by the United States. He was a dentist, and had sought to better his fortune in the republic of Mexico. While there, he procured fraudulent titles to silver mines, and was so successful in this branch of his business, that his claim for a large amount of money was allowed and paid by the Commission, which sat in Washington to adjust claims growing out of the war between the United States and Mexico. There were a large number of witnesses and much documentary matter produced on both sides. The first jury failed to agree, and were accordingly discharged, after several days' effort to make up a verdict. Therefore, there was a second trial.

Dr. Gardiner was a man of elegant manners, and bore himself throughout the proceedings as though he were confident of acquittal.

When the jury, on the last day, went out to deliberate, the court-room was crowded, and the greatest anxiety was manifested in regard to the issue.

The jurors having returned to the court-room, their countenances were intently watched by every one, in order to ascertain, if possible, in advance of the formal announcement, the result of their conference.

The jurors, having taken their seats, were asked, in the usual manner, whether they had agreed upon their verdict. An affirmative answer was given in such a tone of solemnity, that its character was known to all in that dense assembly. The counsel for Gardiner asked that the jury be polled, when, in response to the question: "Guilty, or not guilty?" every one of them answered, "Guilty."

Dr. Gardiner stood during these interesting proceedings; his countenance became paler and paler, as the answers were severally given. He cherished hopes of an acquittal, or that the jury would not be unanimous, until the twelfth juror had responded.

That last answer seemed to shatter him completely. His face became deadly pale, with a blue tinge about his mouth, and this appearance strongly contrasted with that of his large, dark, and glaring eyes. He staggered to his seat, a pitiable object to all spectators. Some minutes having elapsed, and after putting into his mouth what was supposed to be a small piece of tobacco, he asked for a glass of water, which evidently afforded partial relief to his intense agony. Soon the order was given by the court to conduct him back to the jail. He had not been there more than half an hour, before he was seized with spasms, which soon resulted in his death. He had taken strychnine in the court-room, the effect having been deferred, owing to its being enclosed in a piece of paper, which he had swallowed with the drug.

This suicide startled the community, and for a long time afforded a theme for comment.

After the death of Mr. Webster, Mr. Everett, of Massachusetts, was appointed Secretary of State. Thomas Corwin succeeded Mr. Meredith (resigned

July 10th 1850) as Secretary of the Treasury; and after the resignation, in the same month and year, of Mr. Crawford, Mr. Conrad was appointed Secretary of War. Messrs. Preston, Ewing, Collamer, and Reverdy Johnson severally resigned their official positions, when John P. Kennedy was appointed Secretary of the Navy; Alexander H. H. Stewart, Secretary of the Interior; Nathan K. Hall, and afterward Samuel D. Hubbard, Postmaster-General, and John J. Crittenden, Attorney-General.

On the 28th of February, a few days before the retirement of President Fillmore from the Executive Mansion, he gave a public reception, which was numerously attended. Ladies of all ranks, and gentlemen of all parties, were there, to express to him their regret at parting, and their wishes for his future welfare.

The City Councils subsequently took their formal leave of him, and in reply to their address he said he could not take his departure from their delightful city, where he had always been treated with so much kindness and consideration, without feeling a pang of regret at the severance of so many social ties, which had been to him a source of unalloyed happiness.

CHAPTER VIII.

ACCESSION OF FRANKLIN PIERCE — THE DEATH OF HIS ONLY CHILD — ILLNESS AND DECEASE OF VICE-PRESIDENT KING — THE INAUGURATION OF THE PRESIDENT — KANSAS AND NEBRASKA — REPEAL OF THE MISSOURI COMPROMISE — FRESH POLITICAL TROUBLES IN CONSEQUENCE — A GLANCE AT THE LEGISLATIVE PROCEEDINGS — EXCITING TIMES — PERSONALITIES — BRECKINRIDGE AND CUTTING — A CHALLENGE — THE TOBACCO SEDATIVE — PIERCE'S PROCLAMATION — PASSAGE OF THE ARMY BILL — AN INTERESTING SCENE IN THE HOUSE — INCENDIARIES — CHURCHWELL AND CULLUM — A PISTOL EXHIBITION — PROPOSITION FOR AN ARMORY IN THE ROTUNDA, ETC.

THE President elect, with his private secretary, Sidney Webster, Esq., dined at the White House on the evening of the 28th of February, 1853, with President Fillmore. No members of the Cabinet were present.

William R. King, of Alabama, had been elected Vice-President on the ticket with Franklin Pierce, but was now in Cuba seeking to repair his shattered health. The American Consul at Havana administered to him the oath of Vice-President on the 4th of March, but he never again visited Washington. Returning to his plantation in Alabama, he died the day after — on the 18th of April.

On the 3d of March, the number of visitors exceeded

that at all former inaugurations. The hotels were unable to accommodate so large an influx of strangers. Many hundreds slept in chairs. The reading-rooms and parlors at the hotels were filled with cots. The capital was thronged with people, and the principal avenue crowded with pedestrians. Seven or eight military companies paraded at night. The flying artillery from Fort McHenry arrived on the morning of the 4th, and reported to the War Department.

The inauguration procession was a mile long; besides the military, there were numerous political and other associations in line.

The President elect rode in a carriage with the retiring President by his side. They were repeatedly cheered by the spectators on the sidewalks, balconies and at windows, the ladies waving their handkerchiefs.

A company of fantasticals, dressed in rags and tatters, marched along the avenue while the procession was passing, and received some rough usage.

President Pierce delivered his inaugural without the aid of his manuscript.

The ceremonies over, bells were rung, cannon fired, and martial music played.

The family of Mr. Fillmore vacated the White House during these proceedings.

A large number of persons followed President Pierce to the Executive Mansion, and were received by him in the reception-room.

President Pierce chose for his Cabinet: William L.

Marcy, Secretary of State; James Guthrie, Secretary of the Treasury; Jefferson Davis, Secretary of War; James C. Dobbin, Secretary of the Navy; Robert McClelland, Secretary of the Interior; James Campbell, Postmaster-General; Caleb Cushing, Attorney-General.

These gentlemen served throughout the administration in their respective offices.

On the 5th of January, previous to General Pierce's arrival in Washington, a dreadful accident occurred on the Boston & Maine Railroad, by which the President elect was placed in imminent jeopardy of life. The train on the road was proceeding northward, when the axle of one of the passenger-cars broke, and the car was thrown down a steep embankment, between Andover and Lawrence. Among the passengers were General Pierce, his wife, and only child, a lad of thirteen years. The boy was instantly killed, and Mrs. Pierce so severely injured, that doubts were entertained of her entire recovery. General Pierce was considerably bruised, but escaped without broken bones, though a report was for a time spread that he was killed, which created intense excitement. The corpse of his son was taken to the workhouse in Andover, until arrangements could be made for its removal. The family were on their return to Concord, when the accident took place. Several other passengers were also injured. The New Hampshire Legislature, on hearing of the accident, and the report that the President elect had been killed by it, immediately adjourned, in the midst of great alarm.

Thus Mrs. Pierce came to Washington, not only in poor health, but in a distressed condition of mind. It was not until near the close of her husband's administration that she appeared at the public receptions.

We in this section of the country had been in the habit of pronouncing the President's name as if spelled *Peerce*, but persons from his own and other New England States persisted in calling it *Purse.*

The President soon found himself involved in trouble. The Kansas-Nebraska bill was introduced, and after long discussions was passed, repealing the Missouri Compromise, and declaring "it being the true intent and meaning of this Act, not to legislate slavery into any Territory or State, nor to exclude it therefrom, but to leave the people thereof perfectly free to form and regulate their domestic institutions in their own way, subject only to the Constitution of the United States."

During the House proceedings on that subject, the following colloquy took place: —

Mr. Cutting asked: How comes it that the "Union" newspaper selected me (a paper conducted, it is said, by the Clerk of this House, Col. Forney, who is united with the printer of this body) in carrying out its order? How is it that a friend of this measure is selected as the victim? Was it to drive off its friends, who have given him their support? Is it to assassinate the friends who stand with me?

Mr. Breckinridge [who had taken a seat in front of Mr. Cutting] asked: Do you apply that remark to me?

Mr. Cutting. Not unless you consider yourself a portion of the "Union." It applies to that newspaper.

Mr. Breckinridge. I want a categorical answer.

Mr. Cutting. I have been charged with being an assassin — with the arm of friendship around the measure, and with the other stabbing it to death. If I did simply retort, the gentleman forced it on me.

Mr. Breckinridge. So far from driving the gentleman from the support of the bill, it was with profound regret and mortification that I saw his course. The gentleman said, I was the last person whom he expected to make an assault on him, because, in the day of my greatest need, the "Hards" came to my aid. The innuendo is so deep that I do not understand it. I ask an explanation.

Mr. Cutting. The explanation will be given. I am informed that during the canvass in Kentucky, when it was intimated that funds were needed in order to accomplish the success of the gentleman, my friends in New York made up the sum of fifteen hundred dollars, and transmitted the fund to Kentucky, to be employed for the benefit of the gentleman, who is now the peer of Presidents and of Cabinets. [Laughter.]

Mr. Breckinridge [proudly and defiantly]. And not only the peer of Presidents and Cabinets, but the peer of the gentleman from New York in every respect. [Applause on the Democratic side of the House.]

Mr. Mike Walsh. I believe I have as good a right to speak for the "Hards" of New York as any gentleman in or out of this House. I have stood and stemmed the torrent of treason in the North, when those who have attempted to speak for them have skulked from the thresholds of the places where the meetings were held; and I do not want any imputation of this character to go out unexplained to the world. When we came here, we protested against the Administration for interfering with our local affairs in New York; and now my colleague states that a portion of those who sent him here interfered in the same way in Kentucky.

Mr. Cutting. Is that all the gentleman rose for?

Mr. Walsh. That 's all. I 'll be on hand by-and-by, though. [Laughter.]

After further colloquy between Messrs. Breckinridge and Cutting—

Mr. Cutting asked: How dare the member undertake to assert that I professed friendship for a measure with a view of killing it, by sending it to the foot of the Calendar? And when I said the Committee of the Whole on the State of the Union had under their control the House bill, which they intended to take up, he retreats and escapes and skulks behind the Senate bill at the foot of the Calendar.

Mr. Breckinridge, rising, said in an earnest tone: I ask the gentleman to withdraw the last words. [Sensation.]

Mr. Cutting [with emphasis]. I will withdraw nothing. What I have said, I have said in answer to the most violent and personal attack ever made upon a gentleman on this floor.

Mr. Breckinridge. When the gentleman says I skulk, he says what is false, and he knows it. [Great excitement—members uneasy in their seats, and cries of "Order."]

Mr. Cutting. I did not answer the remarks such as the gentleman has thought proper to imply. They belong to a different region. I am not here to disregard propriety by answering in such a tone and manner.

The result of this "unpleasantness" was a correspondence, of which the following is the substance:

MR. CUTTING TO MR. BRECKINRIDGE.

WASHINGTON, March 27, 1854.

SIR:—In the course of debate in the House, to-day, in replying to what I considered to be a legitimate criticism upon your argument, you asserted that what I said was false. I now call on you to retract the assertion, or to make the explanation due from one gentleman to another. This will be handed to you by my friend Mr. Maurice, who is authorized to receive your answer, and to act for me.

F. B. CUTTING.

Mr. Breckinridge replied next day: — "My friend, Colonel Hawkins, will present this note, and will act for me in the matter."

Affairs went on, and Colonel Hawkins submitted the terms; among them, it was proposed that the meeting should be between three and four o'clock; the place of meeting at or near the residence of Francis P. Blair, in the State of Maryland, six or seven miles from Washington; weapons, the ordinary rifle, known as the Western rifle. But a reconciliation having been effected, the honorable gentlemen returned to the House with their wounded honor healed. After they had passed between the tellers, on the division of a question, they accidentally met face to face. Mr. Breckinridge looked at Mr. Cutting a moment, and then asked him a favor in the following laconic form: "Cutting, give me a chew of tobacco!" Cutting put his hand into his pocket, and gracefully, but without saying a word, presented the plug, from which Mr. Breckinridge broke off at least one-third, and returned to Mr. Cutting the remainder. The latter also took a fresh chew, and both went to their seats apparently happier men. The chewing of tobacco from the same plug was considered by the few observers of the scene a good substitute for the much-praised "calumet of peace," which is smoked as an indication of friendship by some of our amiable red brethren of the plains.

During the recess, between the 4th of March and the 1st of December, 1855, the events in Kansas were of a startling nature. Both parties in the territory armed themselves to carry out their respective principles of "free soil" and "slavery."

The President, in his annual message, referred to the condition of affairs. They assumed so frightful a character, that he also made them the subject of a special message; and on the 11th of February he issued a proclamation against all disturbers of the peace therein, warning them of the consequences.

Agitation continued both in the territory of Kansas and in the halls of Congress, intensely exciting the entire country.

The Congress which met on the first Monday of December, 1855, was composed of incongruous materials, and hence there was much difficulty in electing a Speaker. It was not until the 2d of February, 1856, that Mr. N. P. Banks was chosen by the plurality rule. The slavery question was on this, as on previous similar occasions, the principal cause of the delay.

The administration of this gentleman did not produce the awful effects prophesied by Southern members. There never was a more popular officer; and as a proof of this fact it may be stated that, at the close of the Congress, Mr. Aiken, of South Carolina, offered a resolution, tendering the thanks of the House to Mr. Banks for the able, impartial, and dignified manner in which he had discharged the duties of the chair. Mr. Aiken had been the competitor of Mr. Banks for the Speakership. Mr. McMullen, of Virginia, delivered himself of a diatribe against Mr.

Banks, and Mr. Seward, of Georgia, replied to his strictures. The resolution was adopted; yeas 119, nays 25.

It was, I think, at the commencement of that Congress that President Pierce sent his annual message to the Senate only, (the House not having organized,) as the document was becoming stale. He was always particular to prevent his messages from getting prematurely into print, and on one occasion had printers engaged in the White House putting a message in type; the "letter" having been conveyed thither for that especial purpose.

President Pierce called an extra session of Congress on the 29th of August, 1856, owing to the failure of Congress during the session just closed to make provision for the support of the Army. A bill was passed in the House precisely the same as that on the previous Monday of the same month — the regular session — including the Kansas restrictive proviso. The Senate received the bill, when, at the instance of Mr. Hunter, the proviso was stricken out, and the bill passed. The House adhered to the proviso, and so informed the Senate. Mr. Hunter thought that the bill should be allowed to fail. Mr. Bell said the proviso was but an abstract idea, Congress could never control the President in the discharge of his duties. General Cass regarded this as the most solemn crisis that had ever occurred in the history of the country. Mr. Wade argued that, instead of the House trying to dictate to the Senate, the Senate were, in fact, trying to dictate to the House; and he argued the propriety of the Senate's receding, so as to pass the bill.

In the House, Mr. Campbell, of Ohio, the chairman of the Committee of Ways and Means, on the 30th of August, reported a bill for the support of the Army, with only the first clause of the proviso, namely: prohibiting the use of the army in enforcing the territorial laws of Kansas.

This bill was strongly opposed in the House. It went to the Senate, where the proviso was struck out by a vote of twenty-five against seven. As thus amended, the bill was returned to the House, and the question was stated on agreeing to the Senate's amendment. This was concurred in; when the result was announced, general satisfaction was manifested, the Republicans, if possible, showing the greater joy; and many members rushed from the Capitol to prepare for leaving in the evening railroad-train. Thus ended the short extra session.

An interesting scene took place in the House of Representatives in June, 1854.

Mr. Joshua R. Giddings solemnly rose and called attention to the Washington "Union," in which, he said, an article appeared, assailing him by name, and, by implication, members of the House.

The criticism alluded to was on the speeches of Messrs. Giddings, Wendell Phillips, Theodore Parker, and others in Boston. A passage in the obnoxious article is as follows:—

"Is there no law which can reach these cowardly incendiaries, who, after throwing the firebrand, skulk away in the darkness to enjoy the blaze? Are those who, on the floor of both houses of Congress, openly declare their disaffection to the Constitution, to that Constitution they have sworn to support, worthy of a seat in the sacred halls of legislation? When any act shall emanate from that source, these are questions that must be answered sooner or later, and the sooner the better."

Mr. Giddings's point was, that the declaration came from an officer in the House that the members are beyond the pale of protection. This was an implication that persons may assassinate them as felons. He offered the following: —

"Whereas, A. O. P. Nicholson, public printer to this body, and a proprietor of the Washington 'Union,' has, in his paper of this morning, published an article most evidently designed to excite unlawful violence on members of this body, therefore,

"*Resolved*, That said Nicholson, and all others connected with the Washington 'Union,' be expelled from this hall."

Mr. Olds, of Ohio, one of Mr. Giddings's colleagues, said, if he recollected right, in Giddings's Boston speech he charged his colleagues with having voted for the Nebraska bill under a bribe.

Mr. Stanton, of Kentucky, said the article was a communication to that paper, and not written by the editor.

Mr. Giddings replied it was unquestionably from the pen of the editor.

NOTE.—The article was headed, "Obsolete Ideas. By an Old Fogy."

Mr. Millson and others opposed the resolution,—they did not think the reporters, who were free from the offence, should be expelled.

Mr. Lane, of Oregon, asked his friend whether he was apprehensive of personal danger. Mr. Giddings replied: "My friend will excuse me. It is the dignity of this body I wish to preserve."

Mr. Lane. I assure him he is in no danger. [Laughter.]

Mr. Giddings. I don't thank the gentleman for assurances of that kind.

Mr. Lane. I can only say, "Conscience makes cowards of us all." I'll go security for the gentleman's safety.

Mr. Giddings. I have not asked for his security. If I recollect right, my colleague (Mr. Olds) voted to expel the reporter for the "Tribune," for holding up a colleague to ridicule. [A voice: "About Sawyer and Sausages, ha! ha!"] The editor has read me out of the pale of human society, but the day will come when no individual will have that power or authority.

Mr. Olds replied, the appeal for protection did not come with a good grace from one who could leave his colleagues, go to a distant city, and there, assassin-like, stab their private reputation in the dark, when his colleagues were not there to reply to him. When he made the accusation, he must have known in his heart it was false in conception and utterance.

A vote was taken on laying the resolution on the table, and resulted — yeas 77; nays, 29.

Another scene may here appropriately be described.

In June, 1854, Mr. Churchwell, of Tennessee, felt compelled to throw himself on the charity of the House for one moment.

The Speaker reminded him that half a dozen members objected.

Mr. Washburne, of Illinois, hoped the gentleman

would be allowed the privilege he asked. He wished to propound a question.

Consent having been given —

Mr. Churchwell said it would be recollected that through the whole of the peculiar debate yesterday good humor prevailed. The point made by the gentleman (Cullum) was, a few words, not of an offensive character, had been inserted in his previous speech. He regretted to find a liberty had been taken by the gentleman to insert language, after the close of the debate, which was not uttered on this floor.

The language referred to by Churchwell, as attributed in the "Daily-Globe," to Cullum, was as follows: —

"I positively deny that I was congratulated by a single Abolitionist on this occasion, and the gentleman should learn to be a little more particular in making this sweeping and random charge, intended to affect others, without the semblance of truth or fact to sustain them. Being untrue, those charges all fall to the ground."

There was much confusion during these proceedings.

Churchwell pronounced the language infamously false.

Cullum, who sat about fifteen feet from Churchwell, before the last word was pronounced, sprung from his seat, with fists upraised, and exclaiming, "G—d d—n you," and "d—n rascal," made a desperate effort to reach Churchwell. He was instantly seized by the coat-collar, legs, and body. Several voices called out, "No words, Cullum" — "Separate them," "Sergeant-at-arms," etc.

Churchwell, too, was restrained from advancing toward his colleague. The persons in the main aisle formed an impassable barrier, apart from those who held the belligerents. A crowd quickly gathered round them. The greatest possible excitement prevailed, both on the floor and in the galleries. The Speaker banged and rapped to order, loudly calling on gentlemen to take their seats. The Sergeant-at-arms rushed first to Cullum and next to Churchwell, and held up his emblem of office — the mace.

Cries of "Order! Order!" were resumed, the Speaker still endeavoring to restore quiet.

Mr. Seward, of Georgia, moved that the House adjourn.

The Speaker said he would entertain no question until quiet was restored, and again and again requested gentlemen to be seated.

Quiet was finally restored. Cullum returned to his seat, and Churchwell to the lobby.

A Minnesota land-bill was then passed, after serious efforts to defeat it.

Mr. Millson, of Virginia, gave notice that on the next day he would introduce a question of privilege, relative to the recent violation of the rules and decorum of the House. [Cries of "Good! that 's right!"]

The House adjourned at three o'clock, after giving the usual quantity of books to members.

The next day, Mr. Churchwell made an apology to the House for a breach of its decorum.

Cullum regretted that an unexpected and unprovoked

attack on him precipitated him into a violation of the rules of the House. The ebullition which he displayed was raised by the exhibition of a deadly weapon.

Mr. Millson, notwithstanding these explanations, or apologies, moved the appointment of a select committee to investigate the disorder which occurred, and the use of warm words and threatening gestures.

Mr. Wheeler. I understand, from Mr. Cullum that a deadly weapon was drawn upon him. Is there such another case of the kind on record?

Mr. Millson. I know nothing of the kind, as on this occasion. I will state that, in the parliamentary records of Great Britain, it is mentioned that several of the parties drew their swords. I will withdraw the resolution.

Mr. McMullen, of Virginia, objected to the withdrawal of the resolution.

The Speaker said the gentleman had a right to withdraw it.

Mr. Orr gave notice that he intended to move an amendment of the rules, as follows: "Any member in violation of the rules of the House refusing to obey the order of the Speaker made in conformity therewith, the Speaker shall be authorized to order a member so offending to the custody of the Sergeant-at-arms, to be dealt with as the House may direct."

Mr. Preston S. Brooks, of South Carolina, gave notice of his intention to offer an amendment, as follows:

Resolved, That any member, who shall bring into the House a concealed weapon, shall be expelled by a vote of two thirds.

Resolved, That the Sergeant-at-arms shall cause to be erected a suitable rack in the rotunda, where members who are addicted to carrying concealed weapons shall be required to place them for the inspection of the curious, so long as the owners are employed in legislation.

Cries of "good," resounded throughout the hall, accompanied with laughter and applause. And thus ended the excitement of that day.

The Kansas troubles continued throughout President Pierce's administration. Comparatively little was said about Nebraska, so far as slavery was concerned, — the great fight was in and about Kansas.

President Pierce was sociable with all parties. Those who were opposed to him in politics liked "Frank Pierce" personally. He was free and liberal in his intercourse with all who visited the White House.

CHAPTER IX.

THE ASSAULT OF BROOKS ON SUMNER — THE PARTICULARS — WHAT SENATOR BUTLER (BROOKS'S UNCLE) SAID — BURLINGAME AND BROOKS — THE CHALLENGE — BROOKS IN COURT, AND WHAT WAS DONE BY WAY OF PUNISHMENT FOR THE OFFENCE — PROCEEDINGS IN CONGRESS ON THE SUBJECT OF THE ASSAULT — RETURN OF SENATOR SUMNER FROM ABROAD — MR. HERBERT, CONGRESSMAN, KILLS AN IRISH WAITER — PRIVILEGES OF FOREIGN MINISTERS — A WAFER SCENE BETWEEN MR. JOHN SHERMAN AND MR. WRIGHT, ETC.

ON the 22d of May, 1856, an assault and battery was committed upon Senator Sumner by Preston S. Brooks, of South Carolina, in the Senate Chamber. The latter had taken exception to the following passage uttered by Mr. Sumner a day or two before that time:

"With regret I come again upon the Senator from South Carolina, (Mr. Butler,) who, misrepresenting the Kansas debate, overflowed with rage at some suggestion that Kansas had applied for admission as a State, and with incoherent phrases discharged the loose expectoration of his speech now upon her representatives, then upon her people. There was nothing extrinsic of the innocent parliamentary debate which he did not repeat, nor was there any possible deviation from truth which he did not make. But the Senator touches nothing which he does not disfigure with error, sometimes of principle, sometimes of fact. He shows an incapacity for accuracy, whether in stating the Constitution, or in stating the law, whether in the details of statistics or the diversions of scholarship.

"He cannot ope his mouth but out there flies a blunder. But it is against the people of Kansas that the sensibilities of the Senator are particularly aroused. Coming, as he announces, from a State — ay, sir, from South Carolina — he turns his load of disgust from this newly formed community, which he will not recognize even as a body politic. Pray, sir, by what title does he indulge in this egotism? Has he read the history of the State which he represents? He cannot surely have forgotten its shameful imbecility from slavery, continued throughout the Revolution, followed by its more shameful assumption for slavery since."

Senator Butler, at this time, was absent on a visit to his family in South Carolina.

Brooks, the day after the speech was delivered, lurked an hour about the lobby, hoping to meet Sumner, with a view to attack him. Failing in this, he entered the Senate Chamber just as that body adjourned. Seeing several ladies present, he seated himself on the opposite side of Sumner. Soon they all but one withdrew. He requested a friend to get her out, and then approached Sumner, and said in a quiet tone of voice: "Mr. Sumner, I have read your speech with great care, and with as much impartiality as I am capable of doing, and I feel it my duty to say to you that you have published a libel on my State, and uttered a slander on a relative, who is aged and absent, and I have come to punish you."

At the conclusion of these words, Sumner attempted to spring to his feet, but was struck by Brooks a back-handed blow across the head with a gutta-percha cane nearly an inch thick, but hollow, and he continued striking him, right and left, until the stick was broken into fragments, and Sumner lay prostrate and bleeding on the floor. No one took hold of Brooks during that time, so quick were his movements. But immediately afterward Senator Crittenden caught him round the body and arms, when Brooks said, "I did not wish to hurt him much, but only to whip him."

When the attack was made on Sumner, there were probably fifteen or twenty persons present, including Crittenden, Foster, Toombs, Fitzpatrick, Murray, and other members of Congress, together with Governor Gorman, several officers of the Senate, and a few strangers.

The anticipated assault was known to Mr. Edmundson, of Virginia, and Mr. Keitt, of South Carolina, who were present when the attack commenced. It had been reported on the streets for several days previous that Sumner would be armed when he delivered his speech, and that if the occasion required, he would use weapons. But he was not armed when he was attacked by Brooks.

Brooks, after his arrest, went to the office of Justice Hollingshead, and tendered his bond for security to appear and answer any charge presented by the grand jury; but the justice, deeming the bond premature, discharged him on his parole of honor to appear before him whenever required.

Subsequently Brooks was complained of by William Y. Leader, on whose oath Justice Hollingshead required Brooks to give a bond of five hundred dollars as security for his presence the next day.

Much excitement prevailed in Congress and throughout the city.

The Senate took action on the subject, and presented the facts to the House for its consideration.

Brooks sent to the Senate a letter, which was read, in which he said he had seen the report, and it was with infinite regret he found in it that what he intended only as a redress for personal wrong should have been considered a breach of the privileges of that body. He regarded himself only as a gentleman in society, and under no political restraint as a member of the House. He did not advert to or consider there was any obligation or restraint imposed upon him by reason that the offence came from a member of the Senate. He had read the speech carefully, and had found the language unjustly reflected, not only upon the history and character of South Carolina, but also upon a friend and relative. The Senator from South Carolina being absent, he had reason to believe that Sumner did not acknowledge his responsibility for wrong in his deportment. If he had, it would have saved him the painful necessity of the collision which he sought; and, therefore, in his judgment, he had no alternative but to act as he did. He offered this as a full explanation, and disavowed any purpose or design to infract the privileges of the Senate, or offend its dignity.

Mr. Brooks sought satisfaction from Senator Henry Wilson, for saying, in his place in the Senate, that the attack upon Mr. Sumner was barbarous and ruffianly, or words to this effect, and sent an invitation to meet him on duelling-ground. Mr. Wilson, being opposed to "the code," declined the challenge, but nevertheless declared, that he would be ready to defend himself whenever assailed.

In the House, on the 2d of June, 1856, Mr. Campbell, of Ohio, from the Select Committee, made a report, setting forth that the Senate had transmitted to the House a message complaining that Preston S. Brooks committed an assault on the person of Charles Sumner, while seated at his desk in the Senate chamber, after the adjournment of that body, on the 22d of May, followed by blows which disabled him from attending to his duties in the Senate. The said assault was a breach of the privileges of that body. The Senate had also stated, that, inasmuch as Brooks was a member of the House, they could not arrest, and *a fortiori*, could not try or punish him for a breach of privilege; it could only complain to the House. Brooks, the Committee said, was guilty of the assault, with the most aggravated circumstances of violence, and, in their opinion, he had thus committed a breach of privilege. The House had the power to punish Brooks, not only for a breach of privilege, but for improper behavior. It further appeared from the investigation, that Henry A. Edmundson, of Virginia, and Lawrence M. Keitt, of South Carolina, some time previous to the assault, were informed that it was the purpose of Brooks to commit violence upon Sumner for words used by him in debate, and took no means to discourage or prevent the same; but on the contrary, anticipating the commission of the violence, were present on the occasion, to witness the same, as friends of the assailant. The Committee concluded their report with a resolution, namely: "That Preston S. Brooks be and he is hereby forthwith expelled from this House, as a Representative from South Carolina; and that this House hereby declare its disapprobation of the said act of Henry A. Edmundson and Lawrence M. Keitt in regard to the said assault."

This report was signed by Messrs. Campbell, Spinner, and Pennington.

Mr. Cobb made a minority report: "That no breach of the privileges of Congress had been committed, and therefore the House had no power to go beyond the Constitution in deciding that a breach of privilege had been committed."

These reports were postponed for future consideration.

When Senator Butler returned to Washington, from South Carolina, he replied to the obnoxious speech of Mr. Sumner. If, he said, he had been here at the time, he should have asked the Senator, before finishing some of the paragraphs personally applicable to himself, to pause; and if the Senator had gone on, he should have demanded of him to retract or to modify his remarks, so as to bring them within the sphere of parliamentary propriety. If Sumner had then refused this, he (Butler) would have done — he would not exactly say; but one thing he knew, and that was, he would not have submitted to it. To what mode of redress he would have resorted, he could not tell; he would, at least, with all the responsibility of a Senator from South Carolina, have silenced him, and taken the consequences, fall where they might. But, instead of that, the speech involved a friend and kinsman to the extent that he was obliged to put his fortune and life at stake. The Senator from Massachusetts made war on the State of South Carolina, and on himself. It was the purpose of the Senator to pander to the prejudices of a portion of the people of Massachusetts. If the Senator were here, he (Butler) would make him hang his head in shame, and prove him to be a calumniator. He accused Sumner of having pretended to quote from the Constitution of South Carolina, that which is not to be found in it. One thing was certain, either the Senator had not read the Constitution, or that he did not understand it. The Senate had before been profaned by the Senator from Massachusetts. For himself, he would rather take ten blows than endure the act of the rhetorician in bringing a calumny upon his State. In conclusion, Mr. Butler, having spoken with much warmth, said that something must be pardoned to the sensibilities of a man acting under the dictates of manhood and honor.

Mr. Anson Burlingame had made a speech in the House of Representatives, in which he said that Brooks entered the Senate Chamber, and smote Sumner as Cain smote his brother Abel. Having afterward been called upon by friends of Mr. Brooks, he directed attention to the fact that his expression related to the assault, and not to the personal character of the assailant. It was, of course, the right of Brooks to take advantage of this distinction. He availed himself of that right, but somewhat studiously paraded the memorandum in which it was recorded as an explanation, by Burlingame, of the obnoxious remark contained in his speech. Finding that this was used to his injury, and hearing, moreover, that Brooks had loudly boasted of having "again conquered Massachusetts," Burlingame promptly withdrew it, and left his speech to interpret itself. Brooks then sent Burlingame a note, as follows:

"SIR: You will do me the kindness to indicate some place outside of this District where it will be convenient to you to negotiate in reference to the differences between us."

Mr. Burlingame, on the same day, answered as follows:

"SIR: Your note of this date was placed in my hands by General Lane this afternoon. In reply, I have to say I will be at the Clifton House, Canada side of Niagara Falls, Saturday next, at twelve M., to 'negotiate' in reference to any 'difference between us,' which in your judgment may require settlement outside of this District."

Burlingame immediately left Washington, accompanied by Mr. James, of Wisconsin, and proceeded to Niagara Falls, to await the coming of Mr. Brooks, who, however, was indisposed to take the journey, and charged that Burlingame had named that place of meeting for the express purpose of making it impossible for him to be present. He added that he had no further demands upon Burlingame, but should he be screwed up to the point of making demands upon him — Brooks — he would yet treat him as a gentleman, and meet him at any convenient accessible place, on equal terms.

Burlingame having been informed by telegraph that Brooks had declined a meeting at Niagara Falls, returned to Washington.

Brooks had been placed under bonds, and now Burlingame gave the required security not to fight a duel. It was said at the time that the latter was under double bonds of peace, for he was also taken in custody by his wife, who started with him for Boston.

A few days after Brooks's assault on Sumner, he was brought into the Criminal Court, accompanied by Representatives Orr and Keitt, but the witnesses had been discharged until further notice. The District Attorney (Philip Barton Key) had received a note from Mr. Sumner, saying his physicians did not think it prudent for him to attend at present, owing to the condition of his health.

Subsequently the case again came up before Judge Crawford. There was a large attendance of auditors, including many members of Congress. The District Attorney read the correspondence between himself and Mr. Sumner, to show he had used due diligence, though unsuccessfully, to obtain the presence of Mr. Sumner, who had expressed himself as having no desire to take part in the proceedings, and had left the city.

Testimony was given by Mr. Leader, who had caused the arrest of Brooks after the assault, and by J. W. Simonton, (the correspondent of the "New York Times,") Mr. Keitt, and Senators Foster, Pearce, and Toombs.

The last-named wished to have read, in mitigation of the assault, an extract from Sumner's speech.

Brooks himself addressed the Court, repeating that while he had a heart to feel and a hand to strike, he would redress the wrong inflicted in the effort of Northern politicians to cover with obloquy his State and honored relative, but would at all times bow to the majesty of the law.

Judge Crawford said he would forbear comment on the testimony as to the conduct of Mr. Brooks, and would therefore render judgment, which was that he be fined three hundred dollars, which sum Brooks paid, and retired with his friends.

About the 18th of July, the report of the Select Committee of the House was taken up for final action in that body.

The debate was very earnest; among the speakers was Mr. Clingman, of North Carolina, who said that no man ought to indulge in vituperation, without, as Franklin said, subjecting himself to be called to account. There was nothing in the assault to justify the indignation of the country. It ought to be left to the judicial tribunals.

Mr. Bingham, of Ohio, in his usually spirited manner, asked who made Clingman a censor of the distinguished Senator from Massachusetts. The gentleman from North Carolina had undertaken to lecture members of the House as to morals and propriety of conduct, when he himself had indulged in the most gross and outrageous personal abuse which could fall from the lips of any man. The Senator was beaten for having denounced slavery, the sum of all villanies, which made merchandise of mortality. He, for this, was made to bleed; a bludgeon was used; the weapon of a barbarous age was the instrument, in perfect keeping with the act.

Mr. Orr said that Sumner was punished for a libel on the State of South Carolina, and a slander on Butler, the near relative of Mr. Brooks. Franklin was right when he declared that the freedom of speech was the freedom of the bludgeon.

Mr. Comins, of Massachusetts, advocated the adoption of the report.

Mr. Aiken, of South Carolina, in reply, pronounced, on his own responsibility, one of the gentleman's statements false.

Other gentlemen indulged in the fiery debate.

Mr. Giddings, of Ohio, tendered to Brooks the whole sympathies of his heart, for he recollected that, fifteen years before that time, he himself stood there, accused, but on a different charge, without being permitted to open his lips, or to have a friend utter a sentence in his behalf. The member had satisfied the law relative to the assault and battery on Sumner, but had not atoned for the great crime committed against the Constitution; for the blow was aimed against the sovereign rights of the people.

The House finally voted on the resolution to expel Brooks, and to censure Edmondson and Keitt. The vote was, yeas 121; nays 94. But as a two-third vote was required, the resolution was not passed.

There were hisses mingled with applause in the galleries.

Mr. Brooks was privileged to speak. He said the rights of his constituents had been violated by the action of the House. Sumner, he added, had slandered his State and his honored relative, who was absent. It was a personal affair altogether, for which he had answered at the law. He made other remarks in justification of his course, and concluded by saying, that, foreseeing what would be the course of this body, he had anticipated the result by placing in the hands of the Governor of South Carolina his resignation. He was therefore no longer a member of the House.

Applause followed, during which Brooks retired from the Hall.

He was re-elected, and took his seat at the extra session of the same year.

Mr. Sumner suffered for a long time from his wounds, and went abroad, and there subjected himself to the "moxa," as a remedy. On his return he resumed his seat in the Senate, where he has continued ever since.

When Mr. Brooks went home to South Carolina, he made a speech at Columbia, in which he said: An ordinary castigation was nothing to excite a people as had this act of his excited the North. Abolitionists, seeking excuses for their vile slanders, had made it a pretext for more fanaticism. It was curious that the castigation of a Black Republican should beget so extraordinary an excitement. But they had used this act of his — executed under the highest sense of duty — as an instrument to kindle more fires of fanaticism. Their motive was political power; they wished to enjoy the patronage and emoluments of the Government. Every foot of the way from Washington to this city he had met with kindness from the people of the South; and it gratified him to believe that, were he to travel to the extremest verge of the South, he should meet with the same hearty welcome that he had experienced here and elsewhere. . . . . . When he said in the House of Representatives that he had it in his power to raise a revolution, it was no egotistic boast. He felt that he had done as much as any one man to concentrate the feeling of the South; and when he spoke of revolution, he knew that, had he stepped forward and smote one of their abolition crew in the House, their enmity to him would have precipitated them against him, and caused a revolution on that floor.

In the spring of 1856, Philemon T. Herbert, a member of Congress from the State of California, killed Thomas Keating, a waiter at Willard's Hotel.

Herbert was at breakfast, and having made some remarks to the waiter of an insulting character, an altercation ensued, the result of which was the shooting of Keating with a pistol. After preliminary proceedings in the case, Secretary of State Marcy addressed a note to Mr. Dubois, the Minister from the Hague, saying that he had received a letter from the United States Attorney for the District of Columbia, in which he represented that the Minister's testimony was important in the investigation, and that if he had no objection to further the ends of justice by giving his testimony, the Attorney would call for him in a carriage. Mr. Dubois interposed a refusal, on the ground of international law, and the Constitution of the United States, as to foreign representatives. He said, in his reply to Mr. Marcy, that he was in fact a witness of the sad occurrence, and the only impartial witness from the beginning to the conclusion of it; for, with the exception of Herbert and Mr. Gardner, his friend, there was no person in the hall at the time besides the comrades of the deceased. Nevertheless, he would have no objection to testify to the truth, and tell all he had seen and heard, if his position of representative of his sovereign did not prevent him from appearing in a court of law. He was, however, ready to go to the Department of State, at any day and hour, and give all the details, leaving the Secretary at entire liberty to have all the persons whose presence he might deem useful and necessary to witness their interview. Mr. Marcy, not satisfied with this proposition, wrote to our Minister at the Hague, Mr. Belmont, saying, he regretted to be under the necessity of requesting him to invite the attention of the Minister of Foreign Affairs to the course of Mr. Dubois, Resident Minister near this Government, with regard to the melancholy affair in a public place in the city of Washington several days previous. It would, Mr. Marcy added, be sufficient to state that while at breakfast, in a room at Willard's Hotel, a difficulty arose between a member of Congress and one of the waiters; a personal conflict ensued between the parties, which resulted in the death of the waiter from a pistol-shot. He (Herbert) appeared before the magistrate for the purpose of a judicial investigation, and the District Attorney, charged with the public prosecution of the offence, invited Mr. Dubois to attend court and give testimony in the case. This he declined to do, and the influence of the Department of State was invoked to induce him to waive his privilege under the law of nations, and appear as a witness. It was not charged that Mr. Dubois had no right to decline, but Mr. Marcy said that he was at perfect liberty to exercise the privilege to the extent requested, and by doing so he would not subject himself to the jurisdiction of this country.

Mr. Belmont, in pursuance of instructions, called on Baron Van Hall, the Minister of Foreign Affairs, who informed Mr. Belmont that Mr. Dubois's conduct had been fully approved by all the members of the diplomatic corps in Washington; and that, in authorizing

Mr. Dubois to give his sworn deposition to the Department of State, the Government of the Netherlands did all that was rational and feasible under the circumstances, and expressed the hope that our Government would appreciate the sentiments of courtesy and friendly disposition which suggested this authority.

Mr. Dubois renewed his proposition to the Secretary of State, to which Mr. Marcy responded that such a declaration made to the Department could not be used on the trial, and that the Government of the Netherlands, by its action, would deprive the United States of important testimony.

And here the correspondence ended. It serves to show the prerogatives of Ministers under international law.

The jury, in the first trial of Herbert, failed to agree, and were, consequently, discharged; but on the second he was acquitted. This announcement was received with manifestations of delight by Herbert's friends, by whom he was surrounded and congratulated. The friends of the deceased were very much incensed, not only against Herbert, but against all who aided in producing the judicial result; and particularly were the Irish loud in their denunciations, for Keating was a fellow-countryman, and had, they said, been shot down like a dog by a drunken member of Congress in a quarrel which the member himself had provoked by infamous language toward the deceased.

Toward the close of the proceedings in this case, Mr. Preston, for the prosecution, wished to reply to some strictures made on the other side, to which Herbert's counsel objected. Ex-Mayor Lenox, who was standing near by, was overheard by Ratcliffe to observe that that was unfair and unjust. Ratcliffe sharply replied they wanted no outside interference there; and in the course of the hurried colloquy, Lenox called Ratcliffe a liar; whereupon Ratcliffe made a dash at Lenox, but Mr. Bradley interposed and prevented a collision. Complaint was made against Ratcliffe and Lenox, and they were both required to give bonds not to fight a duel.

Herbert remained in Congress until the end of his term, but failed to be respected by his fellow-members.

During the proceedings of the House of Representatives in 1856, Mr. Wright, of Tennessee, approached the seat of Mr. Harris, of Maryland, for the purpose, it was said, of speaking to that gentleman; and while there, Mr. Sherman, of Ohio, was of the opinion that Mr. Wright acted in a menacing manner toward himself, in consequence of a personal controversy which had recently occurred in the House. Mr. Sherman endeavored to throw a handful of wafers in Mr. Wright's face, when the latter made an attempt to strike him. Mr. Sherman then put his hand into his side-pocket to pull out, it was supposed, a pistol. Mutual friends immediately interposed. Mr. Watkins and another of Wright's colleagues seized him, and conducted him to his seat, amid the confusion and intense excitement prevalent, but which soon subsided.

Reports of a duel were soon circulated. The parties, however, did not meet for that purpose.

During the year 1856, Mr. Crampton, the Minister of her Majesty, Victoria, near the Government of the United States, undertook to recruit in this country soldiers to engage in the war against Russia, having for his adjuncts the British consuls at New York, Cincinnati, and Philadelphia. President Pierce, on learning the facts in the case, refused to longer recognize Mr. Crampton in his official capacity, and withdrew the exequators of the consuls. The fears of many persons in this country were allayed on the reception, from London, of satisfactory assurances that the dismissal of Mr. Crampton would not be followed by any retaliatory steps of a similar character on the part of the English Government. That Government was duly informed by Mr. Marcy why our own had so acted toward its Minister and consuls. The Earl of Clarendon made the necessary explanations, and Mr. Marcy, in response, said the United States Government was satisfied with the assurances that the charge of having violated the municipal laws of the United States, as well as the general principles of international law, by recruiting within the territory of the United States, was no longer urged against her Majesty's Government as a cause of complaint.

CHAPTER X.

MR. BUCHANAN'S ARRIVAL — THE INAUGURATION — THE CABINET — A GLANCE AT THE KANSAS QUESTION — ENGINEERING THROUGH THE LECOMPTON CONSTITUTION — THE CONDITION OF PARTIES — AN OFFER REJECTED — BUCHANAN'S DENIAL OF THE TRUTH OF A TELEGRAM, WHICH WAS AFTERWARD VERIFIED — AN ANECDOTE ABOUT BUCHANAN — "PETTICOAT GOVERNMENT" — THE PRESIDENT'S KANSAS MESSAGE — FIGHT BETWEEN KEITT AND GROW — A SCENE BETWEEN JEFFERSON DAVIS AND FESSENDEN — "WHO 'S AFRAID"— REMOVAL TO THE NEW SENATE CHAMBER — SPEECHES OF MR. CRITTENDEN AND VICE-PRESIDENT BRECKENRIDGE.

MR. BUCHANAN arrived in Washington several days before the day of inauguration. His room at the National Hotel was overrun with politicians and citizens, who called to see him. Everybody was admitted, without distinction. He called on President Pierce to make arrangements to take possession of the White House. It so happened that it was public reception-day. The President cordially greeted, and the persons present warmly welcomed, him. The President tendered to him the compliment of a dinner with invited guests, as did also Judge Douglas and others, but he declined them all.

The inauguration took place on the 4th of March, 1857, the President elect, seated in a carriage with the retiring President, having been escorted to the Capitol by a procession.

The ceremonies in the Senate Chamber were, as heretofore on similar occasions, deeply interesting. John C. Breckenridge, the Vice-President elect, was sworn into office by Senator James M. Mason, President *pro tempore* of the Senate. He made a brief speech on assuming the chair.

Having delivered his Inaugural Address on the eastern portico of the Capitol, in the presence of thousands of auditors, the President was greeted with cheers and salvos of artillery, and music by the Marine Band.

In honor of the great event, Mr. Elliott made a balloon ascension. For a while the balloon remained nearly stationary over the eastern part of the city, but subsequently passed off toward Bladensburg.

After the President had reached the White House, the doors were thrown open to persons of both sexes, who had assembled in large numbers.

A few days subsequent, the usual visits of courtesy from foreign Ministers, Judges of the Supreme Court, and City Councils, were made.

The following-named gentlemen were appointed members of his Cabinet:

Lewis Cass, Secretary of State; John B. Floyd, Secretary of War; Howell Cobb, Secretary of the Treasury; Isaac Toucey, Secretary of the Navy; Aaron V. Brown, Postmaster-General; Jacob Thompson, Secretary of the Interior; and Jeremiah S. Black, Attorney-General.

About the time of the inauguration, or shortly after, several gentlemen, including the President himself, who had had quarters at the National Hotel, were taken sick. The cause of the disease was difficult to ascertain; but it was believed by some persons that the sickness resulted from decayed kitchen-refuse in the sewer connected with the hotel. Accordingly, the proprietors at once set to work to remove the unhealthy deposits; and since that time there has been no return of the "National Hotel disease." There were others who gave free expression to their suspicion that an attempt had been made to destroy life by poison. Certain it is several persons died, and gentlemen are still living who yet complain of the effects of the "mysterious National Hotel disease."

It may here be remarked that the Democratic National Convention, which nominated Mr. Buchanan, at Cincinnati, declared itself in favor of non-interference by Congress with slavery in the States and Territories, and in the District of Columbia.

Mr. Buchanan, in his Inaugural Address, regarded it as "an evil omen of the times that men had undertaken to calculate the mere material value of the Union," and spoke of the terrific evils which would result from its dissolution.

The Republican Convention which nominated the opposing candidate, General Fremont, was adverse to the repeal of the Missouri Compromise and to the extension of slavery into free territory, and in favor of the admission of Kansas as a free State.

These were the positions of parties at the time of the commencement of Mr. Buchanan's administration.

In March or April, the President appointed Hon. R. J. Walker Governor, and F. P. Stanton Secretary, of the Territory of Kansas.

At that time indictments had been found against many of those who had acted in a military capacity, under the authority of the Territorial Government, for acts and excesses alleged to be wholly illegal and unjustifiable; and similar prosecutions had been instituted against those who resisted the territorial authorities, and who undertook to retaliate for the alleged wrongs committed against them.

Governor Walker, on reaching Kansas, published an address, in which he stated his instructions from the President to be: To sustain the regular legislature in assembling a convention to form a constitution, and when such a constitution should be submitted to the people of the Territory, they must be protected in the exercise of their right of voting for or against that instrument.

Governor Walker earnestly sought to carry out these views, but in a letter to a friend said, that his efforts were directed to bringing Kansas into the Union as "a free Democratic State."

Meantime the "pro-slavery" and "free-soil" inhabitants of the Territory were in stern opposition, and serious personal difficulties resulted. Aid both from the North and the South was sent thither for the benefit of the respective parties.

A convention was about to assemble at Lecompton.

The Southern members of the Cabinet were very anxious to so direct affairs that their section of the country should have the right of carrying their slaves to Kansas. They planted themselves on the principle previously declared by John C. Calhoun and others, that the Territories, as to slavery, were not subject to Federal legislation, and that Southern men could take their property with them into the Territories with as much right as others could remove their horses and oxen, and other like property.

John Calhoun, of Springfield, Illinois, — not, of course, the great Nullifier, — who had been appointed Surveyor-General of Kansas, was a bold and energetic worker in behalf of the Southern men, and he was made president of the convention which met at Lecompton.

The proposition was officially made to me (the author of these pages) to proceed to Lecompton, and engineer through, or assist in the preparation of a constitution with a Southern feature. I was promised letters of confidence "to the aforesaid" John Calhoun, and other prominent personages acting with him. But having neither capacity nor ambition for such work as was suggested, I declined the application. A Mr. Martin, of Mississippi, a clerk in the Department of the Interior, was then the selected agent for such services; and he accordingly went there, and from time to time sent to Washington reports of prospects and progress.

It seemed that Governor Walker's conduct was not approved at Washington headquarters — although he was sedulously carrying out the principles announced in his own inaugural — and therefore an effort was made to induce him either to change his course or to resign his office. Nor was the conduct of the Secretary of the Territory (F. P. Stanton) in better estimation among the Southern members of the Cabinet.

An editorial appeared in the "Union," the official organ of Mr. Buchanan, written by a member of the Cabinet, to the effect that even if the Free-State men should all fail to vote on the Lecompton constitution, and that if the opposite or minority party should vote for and adopt that instrument, it would be recognized by the administration as the embodiment of the popular will. In other words, the friends of the measure were not to be damaged by the neglect of its enemies to attend the polls.

This statement was telegraphed to the Northern press. Mr. Douglas and his friends were incensed; and it was among the first things that placed him in opposition to Mr. Buchanan.

I had intimate private relations particularly with one of the Southern members of the Cabinet, and from him learned nearly every day much intelligence of interest, including the intentions of the Administration with regard to Kansas, which I promptly communicated to the press by medium of the telegraph.

Just see what a large fire the spark of a modest telegram produced. I published something like the following:

"There is reason to believe that if Governor Walker and Secretary Stanton shall not resign, they will be removed."

Directly after this appeared in the newspapers, Mr. Buchanan caused his private secretary and others to send telegrams all over the country, denying its truth; and the President himself wrote a paragraph for the press to the same effect.

I was the subject of much abuse, and was accused in more than one Democratic newspaper with being a "Black Republican," and deserved to have my head broken or to be hung for wilful perversion of the truth, or for hurtful invention. Mr. Greeley was among those who came to my relief. He said:

> "On Friday evening last, the agent of the Associated Press at Washington telegraphed to this city that the removal of Gov. Walker and Secretary Stanton had been resolved on in Cabinet council. That agent is a Southern man by birth and education, and never, so far as we know, suspected of 'Black Republicanism.' We have always understood him to be a Democrat in politics, though we cannot remember that we ever heard him express a political opinion. That he obtained the information on which he based this despatch from a reliable source, and that he had abundant reason for believing it, we have no manner of doubt. That it was substantially true, so far at least as the determination of a large portion of the Cabinet was concerned, we fully believe."

Efforts were at that time made to discover the source of the information on which the telegram was based. Mr. Buchanan sent for me, in order to discover it. His first inquiry was: "Will you tell me from whom you received that information about Gov. Robert J. Walker?" I answered: "I would as soon tell you, Mr. President, as I would any other man, but I do not reveal the sources of my news."—"But you might tell *me*," he rejoined. I then said: "Suppose, Mr. President, you were now to give me an item, and I published it; and that in response to an inquiry of a third party, I were to inform him that I received it from *you*—how would you like to have your name mentioned in that connection?" The President at once said: "I see the point—I withdraw the question."

Still determined to find out who, among his Cabinet officers, were "leaky vessels," he mentioned the circumstances at the council-board, when one of the members unequivocally declared that the information was furnished by himself. He afterward said to me, in reply to the inquiry why he had made the acknowledgment, that he wished to vindicate me against all assaults, and at the same time remind the President of the previous understanding about Robert J. Walker and Frederick P. Stanton.

The telegram was verified in the fact that in six weeks from the date of its publication, Governor Walker resigned, and Mr. Stanton was removed!

Meantime, the troubles in Kansas continued, and the North and South were intensely agitated.

I recollect having a conversation with Mr. Clay, of Alabama, who was as "ardent as a southern sun could make him" in behalf of the pro-slavery cause. He said he had just come from home to attend the session of the Senate. His people, and the Southern people generally, were "resolved to have their rights, even at the expense of a dissolution of the Union."

On the 1st of February, 1858, President Buchanan transmitted a message to Congress, enclosing and indorsing a copy of the Lecompton Constitution, which had been brought to Washington by John Calhoun. He alluded to "the dark and ominous clouds now pending over the Union," and conscientiously believed "they would be dissipated with honor to every portion of it by the admission of Kansas during the present session of Congress; whereas, should she be rejected," he greatly feared "those clouds would become darker and more ominous than ever yet threatened the Constitution and the Union."

The House was thrown into great disorder by this message, and various propositions were made concerning it, including one of reference. During the night-session of Friday, the 5th of February, a gentleman in the crowd asked whether he could move that a daguerreotypist be sent for to take a view of the scenes. (Laughter.)

The Speaker said: "That is not exactly in order at this time." (Much merriment.)

A voice was heard: "How in the devil can they take pictures by gaslight." (Ha! ha! ha!)

Motions to delay action were made, and all questions decided by yeas and nays.

Clerk after clerk broke down, in the exercise of calling the roll.

"Come," said one, "let's adjourn; what is the use

of continuing this farce?" Another replied: "I'll bring my bed and stay here till Monday, before I give way to these Lecomptonites."

The dilatory motions continued.

Mr. Warren, of Arkansas, suggested, as they had been so long engaged on Kansas, they had better do a little for his State of *Ar*-Kansas. (Loud laughter.)

Mr. Warren was called to order from the Republican side.

Mr. James B. Clay, of Kentucky, asked: "Suppose a gentleman occupies another's seat, what then?"

The Speaker replied: "He can be ousted."

Mr. Letcher, of Virginia, asked whether that could be done by legal process. (Laughter.)

Mr. Reuben Davis, of Mississippi, appealed to the Republicans for liberty to speak an hour. He said if this privilege should be denied, his personal popularity would be sacrificed. (Laughter.)

He afterward rose to a privileged question, saying, "that the heat from the gas above was blistering his head, (which was bald,) and he asked unanimous consent to wear his handkerchief on it. (Laughter.)

Mr. Florence (the top of whose head was also bald) objected, causing renewed laughter.

It was now half-past twelve o'clock; the sofas were occupied by fatigued Congressmen, while others slept in their seats. The proceedings became exceedingly dull, one third of the members being asleep, or nodding at their desks; a few were smoking cigars, while others were going to or returning from the restaurant, or "hole in the wall"—a private drinking-place.

Mr. Quitman, of Mississippi, reopened the speaking part of the entertainment, saying, it was now manifest that the present proceedings would come to no practical result. He had no authority to speak for his friends, but he suggested that they come to an understanding that all motions subsequent to the previous question should be withdrawn.

Just at this point the House was thrown into the most violent excitement, and a fearful scene of confusion was presented.

Mr. Grow, of Pennsylvania, was walking down the aisle on the Democratic side of the House, when Mr. Keitt and a friend approached him. A scuffle took place between Grow and Keitt; the latter struck him, when the parties were separated. They then exchanged words in an evidently excited manner, when Keitt again dealt a blow at Grow, who knocked Keitt down. Their respective friends rushed to the rescue.

Various members on each side engaged in a general fight, which took place in the area fronting the Clerk's desk.

Conspicuous among the belligerents were Messrs. Washburne of Illinois, and Potter of Wisconsin. They dealt their blows right and left. The comic feature in the exhibition was: Mr. Covode, of Pennsylvania, seized a heavy spittoon, and raised it to strike Mr. Barksdale, of Mississippi, who had approached him in a menacing attitude. Just at this point, Barksdale's wig fell off. Covode dropped his weapon; he could not strike a man's head which was bald as his hand!

The Speaker, in a loud and imperious manner, demanded order, and excitedly called upon the Sergeant-at-arms to interfere.

That functionary, carrying the mace of office, together with his assistants, hurried to the scene and penetrated the crowd of combatants.

Some minutes elapsed before this beautiful contest was quieted.

A proposition was made that the vote on the Kansas question be postponed till Monday next. There was a general response from the Republicans of "No, no."

The confusion began to break out afresh, when the Speaker said he had directed the Sergeant-at-arms to put under arrest those who disregarded the order of the House.

Mr. Campbell, of Ohio, said he had foreseen that a disagreeable feeling would result here from the exciting questions connected with Kansas.

Mr. Barksdale called the gentleman to order.

Mr. Campbell wished to let the gentleman from Mississippi know that he was his peer.

And thus the proceedings progressed, amid much disorder.

A member on the floor of the House, who was near to Grow and Keitt at the time of the outbreak, kindly furnished me, at my request, with the following particulars, I not having been near enough to ascertain them:

Grow objected to Quitman's making any remarks. Keitt said: "If you are going to object, return to your own side of the House." Grow responded: "This is a free hall; every man has a right to be where he pleases." Keitt then came nearer to Grow, and said: "I want to know what you mean by such an answer as that?" Grow replied: "I mean just what I say; this is a free hall, and a man has a right to be where he pleases." Keitt seized Grow by the throat, saying, "I will let you know that you are a damned Black Republican puppy." Grow knocked up his hand, exclaiming, "I shall occupy such place in this hall as I please, and no negro-driver shall crack his whip over me." Keitt again grasped Grow by the throat, and Grow knocked his hand off. Keitt came at him again, when Grow squarely knocked him down.

The fight took place at twenty minutes to two o'clock in the morning. Of course, all the sleepers were awakened to the combat.

The House continued in session till half-past six o'clock on Saturday morning, and agreed that the vote should be taken on the next Monday, when the message was referred to a committee of fifteen.

Mr. Keitt made a personal explanation. He said it was due to fair-dealing he should assume to himself all the responsibility for violating the order, dignity, and decorum of the House. He was the aggressor; and it was also due to justice he should make whatever reparation it was in his power, to the dignity and decorum of the House thus violated. He acknowledged his profound regret for the disturbance which he had provoked. Personal collisions were always unpleasant, very seldom excusable, and rarely justifiable—never in a deliberative body. In this connection he had but one other remark to make, and that was—whether any blow was directed at him or not was more than he could say; at least he was unconscious of having received one.

Mr. Grow said he had thought in childhood that all fights among men were disgraceful to human nature and to the Christian community, and that this was especially the case when they occurred among lawmakers in the midst of their deliberations. Riper years and the force of education had satisfied him that this lesson was good and true; yet the right of self-defence he recognized as one of the inalienable rights of man, to be exercised on all occasions and under all circumstances, whenever necessary for the protection of life or property. At the last sitting of the House he found himself unexpectedly engaged in the first personal conflict of the session. He tendered to the House most cheerfully whatever apology was due for this violation of order and decorum, and no one regretted more than himself the occasion for this violation of its rules.

There was also a stirring time in the Senate on the 8th of February. The following will serve as a specimen.

Mr. Jefferson Davis, during the debate, said he heartily concurred in the views of Mr. Buchanan's Lecompton message. It breathed the sentiments of a patriot. Its principles stood out in bold relief in contrast with the views of the Senator from Maine.

Mr. Fessenden did not recognize the authority or style of the Senator from Mississippi, who chose to assume to lecture him on the sentiments he thought proper to announce in the Senate. He, in reply to Mr. Davis, expressly disavowed any intention or desire to interfere with slavery in the States where it then existed. The Senator had thought proper to place himself in the attitude of an advocate for disunion. He (Mr. Fessenden) had avowed no disunion sentiments. Could the Senator say as much?

Mr. Davis, excitedly: "Yes, and I have long sought a respectable man who could charge the contrary."

Mr. Fessenden said the newspapers represented the Senator as making a speech in Mississippi, in which he declared that he went into President Pierce's Cabinet a disunion man.

Mr. Davis replied, it was false, and inquired whether the Senator could produce the paper.

Mr. Fessenden said he could produce the paper into which the extract was copied.

Mr. Davis remarked, it was false, no matter where it came from; and if the extract gave such an account of what he had said, it had been falsified.

Mr. Fessenden repeated, he had made no accusation. He had merely put the question to the Senator, who had accused him of seeking to overthrow the Constitution.

Mr. Davis explained, that such attacks as had been made, including that on the Judiciary, would have that effect.

Mr. Fessenden replied, he had not attacked the decision of the Supreme Court, for it had made none of the character indicated, in the Dred Scott case. He believed that such a decision, if carried into effect, would undermine the Constitution of the country.

Mr. Davis did not know whence sprung the habit of accusing him of an attempt to intimidate Senators. He endeavored to intimidate nobody. He did not believe that anybody was afraid of him.

Mr. Fessenden. I am. (Laughter.)

Mr. Davis. I am sorry to hear it. I shall never again reply in a decided and firm tone to the Senator.

Mr. Fessenden. I speak of it only in an intellectual point of view. (Laughter.)

Mr. Davis. Then, sir, the Senator was in a Pickwickian sense when he began. There were no threats and no intimidations, and he is just where he would have been if he had said nothing. (Laughter.)

In conclusion Mr. Davis said he had only sought to carry out good fellowship, and protection where the Government was bound to afford it. Beyond that, he wished to be let alone.

The message was finally referred to the Committee on Territories.

In February, 1858, there was a collision between

Hon. James B. Clay, of Kentucky, and General Cullum, of Tennessee. Cullum entered the bar-room of Brown's Hotel, where Clay, Hawkins, and Mason were standing. He proposed an old-fashioned Kentucky drink, in which all parties participated. Subsequently he commenced a conversation with Clay, stating he had removed from Kentucky to near the Hermitage, in Tennessee, where he bearded the lion in his den. He spoke of his long devotion to and admiration of Mr. Clay's father, Henry Clay. Mr. Clay replied to Gen. Cullum, that General Leslie Coombs had once, as Chickasaw ambassador, also bearded the lion in his den. This expression was supposed by some of the bystanders to be jocular, but was received by Gen. Cullum as an insult. Clay disavowed such an intention. Cullum made a reply, accompanied with a menacing use of his finger, when Clay said he was not accustomed to be addressed in such a threatening manner. Cullum became more excited under the conviction that Clay intended to insult him, and characterized Clay as the apostate son of a noble sire. Clay said his physical condition was such as would prevent him from answering with a blow, but he could not resist proclaiming Cullum a damned scoundrel; whereupon Cullum drew back to strike him. The force of the blow was partially arrested by the spectators, but still reached Clay's nose, and caused it to bleed.

Clay called on Senator Johnson, of Arkansas, to act as his friend, and a preliminary message was communicated to Cullum, of which acceptance was signified as soon as a competent second could be chosen.

Efforts to reconcile the difficulty proving ineffectual, the parties left for the duelling-ground, accompanied by their respective friends. But before they got into fighting position, Senators Crittenden, Toombs, and Kennedy undertook the office of peacemakers, and the quarrel was settled thus: Clay disavowed any intention to insult Cullum, and Cullum apologized for the blow on Clay's nose.

A series of other personal difficulties took place at about the same time. One of them was between General Harney and Colonel Sumner; another between Lieutenant Bell, of the cavalry, and Lieutenant Williams, of the dragoons. They had a fight in the barber-shop at Willard's Hotel, when a cane was broken over the head of one of the combatants. A challenge passed. They went beyond Bladensburg to fight. Bell fired at the word "one." The ball from his pistol penetrated the hat of Williams, who was the assailing party, and having thus given the satisfaction demanded, discharged his pistol in the snow. The belligerents returned to Washington, apparently reconciled.

Lieutenant Rhind and Commander Boutwell, of the Navy, had a "breeze." Lieutenant Rhind and his friend, Captain Corne, of South Carolina, were held to bail for their appearance at the Criminal Court for challenging and posting Commander Boutwell, at whose instance the arrest was made.

The Kansas bill was passed on the 30th of April, 1858, in the Senate, by a vote of yeas 31, nays 22; and in the House by a vote of yeas 112, nays 103.

But the majority of the people of Kansas repudiated the Lecompton Constitution, and made one for themselves, at Wyandot, after previous similar efforts at Topeka and Leavenworth.

It was brought to Washington by Mr. W. F. M. Arny, and presented to the two Houses in February, 1860, through their presiding officers. Mr. Arny, at first, went to the President of the United States, and asked him to transmit it to Congress. Sufficient time was permitted him to look into it. When Mr. Arny again called, Mr. Buchanan said to him there was too much "petticoat government" in the Constitution. Mr. Arny replied that there was nothing of the kind, but it allowed women to vote for superintendents of county schools. The President, however, was stubborn, still objecting to the "petticoat" government feature.

Just after Mr. Arny's interview with the President, several ladies came into the room to pay their respects to him. In the course of conversation, one of them said: "Mr. Buchanan, we have looked all through this House — it is very elegant and well kept; but we have noticed one deficiency." — "What is that, madam?" he blandly said. The lady responded, "That you have no lady of the house." — "That, madam," he said, with a smile, "is my misfortune, not my fault."

Kansas was organized as a territory, May 30th, 1854, and was admitted into the Union as a State, January 29th, 1861, under the Wyandot Constitution.

The reign of bloodshed and disorder for a season was now over; and the sound of cannon in this city announced the act of admission consummated.

There were events of much interest on the 4th of January, 1859, in the old Senate Chamber. The galleries were densely filled, and the floor even much crowded.

Senator Crittenden asked to be indulged in a few words.

"This," [he said in the course of his remarks,] "is to be the last day of our session here, and the place which has known us so long is to know us no more forever as a Senate. The parting is a solemn one. This Chamber has been the scene of great events. Here questions relating to American Constitutional law have been debated, and questions of peace and war decided. Questions of empire, too, have occupied the attention of those assembled in times past. This was the grand theatre upon which these things have been enacted. Great men have been actors here. The illustrious dead that have distinguished this body in times past naturally rise to our view on this interesting occasion. I speak only of what I have seen, and but partially of that, when I say that here, within these walls, I have seen men whose fame is not surpassed, and whose power, and ability and patriotism, are not eclipsed by anything of Grecian or of Roman name. I have seen Clay, Webster, and Calhoun, and Benton, and Leigh, and Wright, and Clayton (last though not least), mingle together in this body at one time, and unite their counsels for the benefit of their country. It seems that they have left their impression on these very walls, and this majestic dome seems almost to echo with the voice of their eloquence. There are hosts of others I might mention, but it would take too long. Their names are in no danger to be forgotten, nor their services unthought of or unhonored. Because we leave this Chamber we shall not leave behind us any sentiment of patriotism, any devotion to country which the illustrious exemplars that have gone before us have set us. These, like our household gods, will be sacred with us and the representatives of the States of this mighty Union, and will, I trust, always be found equal to the emergencies of any time that may come upon our country."

Vice-President Breckenridge delivered a long address, reviewing the formation and history of the Government. He said:

"The Senate has assembled for the last time in this Chamber. Henceforth it will be converted to other uses. Yet it must remain forever consecrated with great events, and sacred to the memories of departed orators and statesmen, who here engaged in high debates, and shaped the policy of their country. There sat Calhoun, *the* Senator, inflammable, austere, but not overwhelmed by his deep sense of the importance of his public functions, seeking the truth, then fearlessly following it. There was Webster's seat; he, too, every inch a Senator. Conscious of his own vast power, he reposed with confidence on himself, and, scorning the contrivances of smaller men, he stood among his peers all the greater for the simple dignity of his Senatorial demeanor. On the outer circle sat Henry Clay, whose imperious and ardent nature, untamed by age, exhibited in the Senate the same vehement patriotism and appreciated eloquence that of yore electrified the House of Representatives and the country. All the States may point with gratified pride to the services in the Senate of their patriotic sons, among whom are the names of Adams, Hayne, Wright, Mason, Otis, Pinckney, and the rest, — I cannot number them, — who, in the record of their acts and utterances, appeal to their successors to give the Union a destiny not unworthy of the past. And now, Senators, we leave this memorable Chamber, bearing with us, unimpaired, the Constitution we received from our forefathers. Let us cherish it with grateful acknowledgments to that Divine Power which controls the destinies of empires, and whose goodness we adore. The day will be when this structure will yield to the corroding tooth of time, and these memorable walls must moulder into ruins, but the principles of Constitutional liberty, guarded by wisdom and virtue, unlike material elements, do not decay. Let us devoutly trust, that another Senate, in another age, shall bear to a new and larger Chamber this Constitution, vigorous and inviolate, and that the last generation of posterity shall witness the deliberations of the representatives of the American States still united, prosperous and free."

After this address, the Senate, preceded by their president, secretary, and sergeant-at-arms, formed a procession and marched to the new chamber.

The Rev. P. D. Gurley delivered a prayer, when the Vice-President took his chair and called to order.

Senator Seward rose and presented a memorial, and moved its reference, and the Senate resumed its regular business.

In the old chamber (now occupied by the Supreme Court) the want of gallery room was a very great defect, which is entirely remedied in the new, which affords gallery room for one thousand persons.

On the removal to the new chamber, the galleries were crowded.

The House had previously removed into their own new Hall, which is far preferable to the old, especially for its acoustic arrangements, but lacks its grandeur and stately proportions. A good many memories also cluster around the "hall deserted;"—it was the scene of many brilliant intellectual conflicts and patriotic demonstrations, and not unfrequently, in the later days of its occupancy, was converted into an arena in which no classic gladiatorial combats delighted, but gross personalities and fisticuff encounters disgusted the spectators.

CHAPTER XI.

DEATH OF COLONEL BENTON — THE ATLANTIC TELEGRAPH — THE CABINET'S TALK UPON THE SUBJECT — THE PRESIDENT'S ANSWER TO QUEEN VICTORIA'S MESSAGE — THE KILLING OF PHILIP BARTON KEY — THE PRYOR AND POTTER DIFFICULTY — "BOWIE-KNIVES, BARBAROUS WEAPONS" — GOVERNOR WALKER AND JUDGE BLACK — A CHALLENGE — VISIT OF THE PRINCE OF WALES — CONTRIVANCES AND PLANS FOR ANNEXING CUBA, ETC.

ON the ninth of April, 1858, Mr. Morris of Pennsylvania, said he thought it proper that the House should now adjourn, to take notice of a fact in the history of the country. A distinguished ex-member of the Senate of the United States, and one who had long enjoyed the confidence of the country, had, within the last few moments, departed this life, (of cancer in the stomach.) He hoped the motion to adjourn would prevail.

Several members asked, "Who is it?"

Mr. Morris responded: "The Hon. Thomas H. Benton."

The Speaker immediately announced the House adjourned.

Mr. Jones, of Tennessee, said:—"Colonel Benton handed me a letter this morning, with a request that if he should die any time soon, and any notice should be taken in the House of his death, I should have it read. I now ask that it be read."

The clerk read the letter as follows:

C STREET, WASHINGTON, April 8, 1858.

To you, as old Tennessee friends, I address myself to say that, in the event of my death here, I desire that there shall not be any notice of it in Congress. There is no rule of either House that will authorize the announcement of my death; and if there were such a rule, I should not wish it to be applied in my case, as being contrary to my feelings and convictions, long entertained, as shown in a note to a speech of Mr. Randolph on the occasion of the death of Mr. David Walker, published in the Abridgment of Debates, volume vi. 566. The request of Mr. Walker, there recorded, and the remarks of Mr. Randolph, express entirely my sentiments and convictions. Should therefore any of my kind friends, in either House, make it necessary to do so, I intrust to you to make known, by means of this note, my express wish and desire that the event remain unnoticed in Congress. Your old Tennessee friend,

THOMAS H. BENTON.

To SAMUEL HOUSTON, Esq.,
Senator in Congress from the State of Texas, and
GEORGE W. JONES, Esq.,
Representative in Congress from Tennessee.

In the Senate, Mr. Polk, of Missouri, said, he did not think it would be consonant to the wishes of Colonel Benton, as expressed just before his death, that any public demonstration should be made in consequence of his death; but in order to give to each individual member of the Senate, as a citizen, an opportunity of attending his funeral, which was to take place on the 12th of April, on his motion the Senate adjourned. The funeral was largely attended by members of Congress and other prominent persons.

On the 6th of August, 1858, Cyrus W. Field addressed a telegram to President Buchanan, dated Halifax, the tenor of which is shown from the reply of Mr. Buchanan, which is as follows:

WASHINGTON, August 3th.

MY DEAR SIR:—I congratulate you with all my heart on the success of the great enterprise with which your name is honorably connected. Under the blessing of Providence, I trust it may prove instrumental in promoting perpetual peace and friendship between two kindred nations. I have not yet received the Queen's speech. Yours, respectfully,

JAMES BUCHANAN.

The Queen's speech did afterward come, a part of it at least. This was sent to Mr. Buchanan from the "New York Associated Press" office in this city. A short time after it was delivered to him, he requested Mr. Thompson, the Secretary of the Interior, to call at the office, and ascertain its authenticity. There were doubts on the subject, owing to what was considered bungled phraseology, or its inelegant diction; but having been satisfied that Her Majesty had actually caused the message in question to be telegraphed to the President, the latter proceeded to frame a reply. He sent for me, and I repaired to the White House, where I found all the members of the Cabinet talking over the matter and speculating as to whether telegrams *could* be sent by cable!

Secretary Cobb, lying on a sofa, disbelieved everything of the kind; but the majority of them were less incredulous. Mr. Buchanan asked a number of questions, wanting to be *certain* that the Queen had sent him the message. He was properly exercised as to its truth, not wishing to show his gallantry in the absence of a proper invitation to do so; in other words, he was afraid of being "hoaxed." I satisfied him that he ran no risk in responding to the lady. Then he showed me what he had written, and read it to me, placing a candle between the manuscript and his face, in order to have more light than the gas afforded. He then asked me how I liked it, and I replied in terms that pleased him. Mr. Appleton, the Assistant Secretary of State, was present, and to him Mr. Buchanan handed the manuscript to "look over." Mr. Appleton struck out two lines of the message. Mr. Buchanan again read it, and finally he handed it to me, to be telegraphed to Her Majesty. "It is yours," he said. "I'll make a copy, and keep the original," I responded. "No, no," exclaimed Mr. Cobb; "let the original be deposited in the public archives." I frankly told Mr. Cobb that I was a good custodian, and would keep the document until the President should call for it. "It is yours, sir," repeated Mr. Buchanan, and I carried away the document and filed a copy of it.

Mr. Buchanan never called for the message. I kept it a long time. It was of no use to me, and I gave it to a gentleman who has one of the finest collections of autographs in the country, and it now is safe in his custody, and treasured according to its value, perhaps beyond its actual worth.

It was said by the late veteran editor of the "National Intelligencer"—Joseph Gales—at that time:

"It remains for us to hope, in all the varied capabilities of the Atlantic telegraph, which more than a year ago rose upon the vision of one of New England's most gifted orators, under the similitude of a gigantic ocean-harp, it may evermore continue to swell its 'deep diapason,' producing melody on the sea more magical than old mythology, or modern fable ever ascribed to siren or mermaid — a melody which, taking its key-note from that of the angels heard of old on the plains of Bethlehem, shall inaugurate the dream of the poet:

'The Parliament of man, the fraternity of the world.'"

In February, 1859, the country was startled by the intelligence of the killing of Philip Barton Key, by the Hon. Daniel E. Sickles, a member of Congress from the State of New York. The offence of the former was of a grave character, and closely affected the latter's family-peace. The circumstances are still familiar to the people, and need not, therefore, be repeated in this book. The trial of Mr. Sickles took place at the March term of the Criminal Court, commencing on the 7th, and ending on the 26th of April, 1859, in his acquittal. Robert Ould was District Attorney, and conducted the case for the Government. The prisoner was defended by Messrs. Stanton, Graham, Brady, Ratcliffe, Chilton, Magruder, and several others. Previous to this trial — on the 1st of January of that year — Mr. Key came into the office of the Clerk of the Court, and presented Mr. Erasmus Middleton, the assistant clerk, with a large gold pen, saying, "Here's a New Year's gift for you." Mr. Middleton thanked him, and laid it carefully aside; but, after the homicide, on looking into his private drawer, he was reminded of the present, and the first use he made of the pen was to write with it the indictment against Sickles.

On the 5th of April, 1860, a disgraceful scene was enacted in the House, and on the 11th of that month, Mr. Roger Pryor rose to a "personal explanation." He caused to be read a report of a "scene" on the floor a few days previous. Pryor said, on recurring to the manuscript of the reporters, Potter had interpolated the record of proceedings in a matter touching personal relations, affecting that record in a most material regard. "We listened to them quietly, and heard them through; and now, sir, this side shall be heard." "There," Mr. Pryor said, "stopped the manuscript of the reporter. The member from Wisconsin then added in his own handwriting, "let the consequences be what they may." Again I am reported as having said: "You shall not come here, gesticulating in a menacing and ruffianly manner." Mr. Potter was reported to have made no response. The reporter heard no response, and accordingly reported none. The member from Wisconsin here interpolated in his own handwriting, "You are doing the same thing." Again, following a remark made by Mr. John Cochrane, the member from Wisconsin is made by the reporter to say: "I do not believe that side of the House can say where a member shall speak." There the official report terminated, but the member from Wisconsin has added: "and they shall not say it." With this statement of facts, repeating that the newspapers of the country have not reported his presence in the House at all on that occasion, and that the official report of our proceedings exhibits the fact that he did not say that which he represents himself to have said, I resume my seat."

Mr. Potter said he *was* present on that occasion. He did no more than Pryor did, — he corrected his remarks to make them conform to the language actually used by himself.

Mr. Pryor replied: "I understand the gentleman, then, to remark, that he did say, on that occasion, that I had, in a ruffianly and violent manner, approached and gesticulated towards the gentleman from Illinois, (Mr. Lovejoy.) Now, I wish to know if I am to understand further that he intends by that any menace or offence to myself individually?"

Mr. Potter, in the course of his response, said that he considered that a member had the right, not only to correct his remarks as taken by the reporters, but if a remark had, in the excitement and confusion of the occasion, been left out, he had a perfect right to put it in. He did put in this remark, because he wanted the report to be correct. "But," he added, "that remark of mine, put in its proper place, as I uttered it, was entirely wiped out by the member from Virginia. He erased it in such a way that neither the reporters, the printers, nor anybody else could have told what were the words which had been written."

Mr. Pryor. One word, and then I am done with this matter. The gentleman from Wisconsin wants to know by what authority — for he impeaches the act —

I erased matter which he had interpolated there. I erased no word which the reporter had written upon his manuscript, but I felt myself authorized to erase an unwarrantable and impertinent interjection in the gentleman's own handwriting. He says that before he would have done that thing — erased that which somebody else had put upon the manuscript — he would have his arm cut off, and yet he could interject into the manuscript that which the reporter did not write down and report him to have said. [There was laughter from the Republican side.] The gentleman says he stands by his language. I am very glad to hear it. I understand him then to give me the liberty of construing his remark as I please. I will put what construction I please upon it, and whether or not he stands by it, the sequel will demonstrate. [Derisive laughter from the Republican side.]

Mr. Potter. Let it demonstrate. Thus ended the dialogue in the House.

Pryor sent Potter a note, asking him whether he would accept a challenge; to which Potter replied he would inform him whenever a challenge should reach him. Pryor then sent a challenge. Potter replied, referring him to General Lander to make the necessary arrangements. The latter informed the friend of Pryor, Colonel T. P. Cheeseman, that while Potter disclaimed allegiance to the code, he would fight Pryor in any place, in-doors or out, in the District, with bowie-knives. This was declined by Pryor, on the ground that the weapons were barbarous, inhuman, and not used among gentlemen. To this, Lander replied that Potter detested the whole system of duelling as barbarous and unchristian, but, being called on to account for the exercise of free speech on the floor of the House, he consented, not being accustomed to the weapons of the duellist, to meet him in a way that would place them on equal terms; and to name the time and place. As bowie-knives were objected to by Pryor, Lander, without Potter's knowledge, tendered himself to Pryor, without restriction. This was also declined, on the ground that he had no quarrel with Lander.

Pryor, on the day of the challenge, left Washington for Alexandria, and was joined there by Messrs. Miles and Keitt, of South Carolina.

While these things were in progress, it was difficult to command the attention of the House, so general were the feeling and interest on the subject, and there was, besides, much excitement in the city.

The result was that both Pryor and Potter were required to give bonds to keep the peace.

Mr. John Covode introduced a resolution, which was adopted, providing for the appointment of a committee to inquire into certain alleged corruptions and abuses on the part of officers of the Government, and as to the employment of money to carry elections. A large number of witnesses were examined, one of whom testified that he had a conversation with Hon. Jeremiah S. Black, a member of Mr. Buchanan's Cabinet, and that Judge Black said that Hon. Robert J.

Walker, who had been Governor of Kansas, had no such instructions as the latter alleged from President Buchanan, respecting that Territory.

This reported testimony having gained publicity, Mr. Walker sent, by Senator Brown, of Mississippi, a challenge to Judge Black. Mr. Brown asked whether Judge Black would reply to it. The Judge said he did not know whether he would do so or not. He then asked Jacob Thompson, of Mississippi, and Senator Gwin, of California, what he ought to do; and they said he ought to keep perfectly quiet. The Judge did so. Some time afterward, Mr. Thompson informed Judge Black that he wanted a note from him to Mr. Brown on the subject. Mr. Thompson and President Buchanan dictated the note, which Judge Black signed; and it was sent to Mr. Brown through Mr. Thompson.

The truth was, that the witness either did not testify truthfully, or was misrepresented; and this was shown by the testimony of Judge Black and General Bowman before the Committee. Governor Walker felt himself injured by the alleged conversation between the witness and Judge Black; and acting from these feelings, had sent the challenge.

It was a long time before Judge Black and Governor Walker met — it was on professional business — when Governor Walker said he was exceedingly sorry for their quarrel; and Judge Black met him in a like friendly spirit. The disagreement had grown out of a misapprehension, and left no sting behind.

In October, 1860, the Prince of Wales visited the city of Washington, and was, together with his suite, the guest of the President of the United States. On the fourth of that month there was a grand reception in his honor, and thousands of persons availed themselves of the opportunity to see the royal personage, and heir to the British throne. There was a pyrotechnic display at night on the President's grounds, which "his Majesty graciously witnessed!"

On the 5th, at eleven in the morning, the Prince, accompanied by the President, Lord Lyons, Sir George Holland (the Queen's physician), the Heads of the Departments, and their families and others, in all about forty persons, visited Mount Vernon. The Marine Band played a dirge at the tomb of Washington.

By request of the Mount Vernon Association, the Prince planted, with but trifling formality, a young horse-chestnut-tree, to commemorate his visit to the place. The tree was planted on a mound, not far from the tomb.

The Prince was the recipient of marked attentions everywhere. When he had visited other cities in the United States, he returned home.

Lord Lyons, by direction of her Majesty, communicated to President Buchanan her expressions of thanks for the kind and hospitable manner in which her son had been treated; and to this communication Mr. Buchanan made a graceful reply.

Aaron V. Brown, the Postmaster-General, died about March, 1859, and was succeeded by Joseph Holt,

Esq., of Kentucky. His funeral took place from the White House.

As Mr. Buchanan for many years had been anxious to annex Cuba, the following scraps of history may prove interesting in that connection.

President Fillmore (in July, 1852) communicated to the House of Representatives a mass of interesting correspondence on the subject. Among this was a letter from Mr. Buchanan, Secretary of State, dated June 17, 1848, to Mr. Saunders, our Minister to the Court of Spain, in which, by direction of President Polk, he called his attention to the present general and future prospects of Cuba. "The fate of that island," he said, "must ever be of deep interest to the people of the United States. We are content that she shall be a colony of Spain. Whilst in her possession we have nothing to apprehend; besides, we are bound to her by the ties of ancient friendship, and we certainly desire to render this perpetual; but we can never consent that the island shall become the colony of any other European power. In possession of Great Britain, or any other strong naval power, it might prove ruinous to both our domestic and foreign commerce, and even endanger the Union of the States."

Mr. Saunders, in responding to the Secretary of State, said that difficulties surrounded the subject, which met us at the threshold. He was not a little embarrassed as to the person to whom he should open the subject. He had learned that the Duke of Sotomayer was unfriendly to the United States, though of this he had no personal evidence. General Narvaez, the President of the Council, was a bold, true man, and the soul of the Cabinet, yet he was difficult to approach. Another difficulty was the influence of the Queen, who had great control over her daughter, and was feared by the ministry, and he thought was decidedly against the cession. It further appeared from the correspondence, that in Secretary Forsyth's instructions to Minister Vail, in 1840, the latter was authorized to assure the Spanish Government that in case of any attempt from whatever quarter to wrest from her any portion of her territory of Cuba, she might surely depend upon the military and naval resources of the United States to aid her in preserving or recovering it. The assurances were again repeated by Washington Irving, under instructions from Secretary Webster. With this guarantee for the safety of the island the Spanish Government rested in perfect security. All of these Ministers were satisfied, and so informed our Government, that Spain would not sanction a cession of Cuba to the United States.

Much opposition was made by statesmen of that day to the measure; Mr. Calhoun declaring that Cuba was "forbidden fruit to the United States."

When Mr. Buchanan became President, he renewed the cession scheme, and asked Congress for an appropriation of one hundred thousand dollars, with which to open negotiations. Congress, however, did not sanction the proposition.

About that time the island was in a feverish condition, and it was ascertained that some of the leading men there were anxious for annexation. A Southern gentleman, whose name I have forgotten, came to Washington, with documents professing to have been written by General Concha and other prominent men of the island, in furtherance of the scheme. He exhibited these to a Southern member of the Cabinet, who informed me that the documents appeared to be right enough, but that they had no signatures, which he accounted for by saying the Cubans were cautious not to compromise themselves by signing them. Apart from this, they were satisfactory. And the same member informed me that the hundred thousand dollars asked for by Mr. Buchanan were intended to be spent on the prominent Cubans to whom reference was made. Furthermore, as represented by the Southern agent, the scheme was to declare the island of Cuba independent of Spain, erect it into a State, and then ask for its admission into the Union. Whatever truth or falsehood there was in the statement, it is certain that such representations were made to the member of the Cabinet. I cannot say, for I am not aware that Mr. Buchanan knew anything of this scheme. I made inquiry of the Spanish Minister "near this government" as to whether there was serious disaffection in the island. He assured me there was not, but notwithstanding the denial, a short time afterward the Captain-General was removed, and a fleet of war-vessels anchored off Havana.

CHAPTER XII.

JOHN BROWN'S RAID — THE PARTICULARS — HIS EXECUTION — SENATORIAL INVESTIGATION INTO THE FACTS — PRESIDENTIAL ELECTION — ANXIETY OF THE CABINET TO HEAR THE RESULT — JEFFERSON DAVIS A FALSE PROPHET — A SCENE AT THE WHITE HOUSE — SAMUEL F. GLEN THERE — HIS TELEGRAM — DISGUST OF THE PRESIDENT, ETC.

ON the 18th of October, 1859, the entire country was startled by the intelligence of John Brown's raid into Virginia. The facts, so far as can be recollected, are as follows:

On Sunday night, the 17th of that month, John Brown and Captain J. E. Cook, with a party numbering nineteen men, white and black, marched into the town of Harper's Ferry, and took possession of the arsenal. They seized and imprisoned the watchman on duty, and also Colonel Washington and other citizens of the vicinity. The invaders established their quarters in the engine-house, where they kept all their prisoners. The news soon spread, exciting much alarm, especially in Virginia and the bordering counties of Maryland. Meantime, a party of United States marines from Washington, and several military companies, together with Governor Wise, had arrived at the scene of action. The marines commenced an attack on the arsenal, for the purpose of dislodging Brown and his men. The latter offered a stubborn resistance, firing briskly from the portholes on the soldiers. Colonel Shutt approached with a flag of truce, and demanded a surrender. After expostulating some time, the invaders refused to surrender. The marines advanced to the charge, and endeavored to break the door down with sledge-hammers; but the door resisted all their efforts. A ladder was then used as a battering-ram, and the door gave way. The invaders fired briskly, and shot three men. The marines fired through the broken door, and in a few minutes resistance was at an end. The surviving invaders were brought out amid the most intense excitement, and it was with difficulty some of the spectators were restrained from shooting them on the spot.

With the exception of John Brown and three or four others, all the invaders were either killed or wounded in their attempt to escape, while several citizens outside were shot down by the fire of Brown's men.

Brown and his surviving companions were tried at Charlestown, Virginia, for their offence.

Governor Wise had received numerous letters informing him of the existence of secret societies in various portions of Ohio and elsewhere, the members of which, it was alleged, were bound by horrid oaths, not only to rescue Brown, but to take revenge on those who were instrumental in the conviction of himself and his associates, for their offence at Harper's Ferry. Governor Packer, of Pennsylvania, tendered him the services of ten thousand men, and offers of aid also reached the Governor from South Carolina and other Southern States. There was feverish excitement everywhere, for no one knew the extent of the preparations for the reported invasion of the entire South, and the gathering of negroes to aid in the work of the emancipation of the slaves.

Under these circumstances, ample arrangements were made to guard against all danger, and troops in large number were concentrated near the scene of John Brown's late operations.

Although the public property had been seized and the offence committed on United States soil, President Buchanan, in behalf of the Government, waived the right to try the invaders in a Federal court, and handed them over to the authorities of the State of Virginia.

After John Brown had been convicted and sentenced to be hung, he wrote a letter to his wife, dated Charlestown prison, November 30th, 1859, in which he said:

> "I am waiting for the hour of my public murder, with great composure of mind, in the strong assurance that in no other possible way could I be used to such advantage to the cause of God and of humanity. I have no doubt, that our serious disaster will ultimately result in most glorious successes; so, my dear, shattered, broken family, be of good cheer, and believe and trust in God with your heart, and with all you have, for He doeth all things well."

John Brown was hung on the 1st of December, 1859. Governor Wise ordered that no civilian be admitted within the military lines around the gallows. But the reporters, with their usual enterprise, furnished full and graphic accounts of the execution to the press.

On the first day of the December session of Congress, Senator Mason, of Virginia, offered a resolution —

"That a Committee be appointed to inquire into the facts attending the late invasion and seizure of the armory and arsenal of the United States at Harper's Ferry, in Virginia, by a band of armed men, and report whether the same was attended by armed resistance to the authorities and public force of the United States, and by the murder of any of the citizens of Virginia, or of any troops sent there to protect the public property; whether such invasion and seizure was made under color of any organization intended to subvert the Government of any of the States of the Union; what was the character and extent of such organization; and whether any citizens of the United States, not present, were implicated therein, or accessory thereto, by contribution of money, arms, munitions, or otherwise; what was the character and extent of the military equipment in the hands, or under the control, of said armed band, and where and how and when the same was obtained and transported to the place so invaded. — And that said Committee report whether any and what legislation may, in their opinion, be necessary, on the part of the United States, for the future preservation of the peace of the country, or for the safety of the public property; and that the same Committee have power to send for persons and papers."

This occasioned a debate. Senator Trumbull expressed the hope that the investigation would be thorough and complete. He believed it would do good by disabusing the public mind in that portion of the Union which felt most sensitive upon the subject, of the idea that the outbreak at Harper's Ferry received any countenance or support from any considerable number of persons in any portion of this Union. No

18

man who is not prepared to subvert the Constitution, destroy the Government, and resolve society into its original elements, could justify such an act. He concluded his speech by moving an amendment to extend the investigation to the facts regarding the invasion, seizure, and robbery, in December, 1855, of the United States Arsenal at Liberty, Missouri, by a mob or body of armed men, and report whether such seizure and robbery was attended by resistance to the authorities of the United States, and followed by an invasion of the Territory of Kansas, and the plunder and murder of any of its inhabitants, or of any citizen of the United States, by the persons who thus seized the arms and ammunition of the Government, or others combined with them, etc.

Mr. Mason fired up at Mr. Trumbull's amendment. He should like to know when that honorable Senator heard any "shrieks" from Virginia. He should like to know if that honorable Senator conceived he could be sustained by any, even of his constituents, in speaking in that manner of one of the States of the Union. "Shrieks from Virginia!" "Sir," he continued, "I do not know what sort of people, what sort of population are represented in the Senate of the United States by one who spoke there of shrieks from one of the States of this Union."

Mr. Trumbull explained, he used the word "shriek" as it was used in regard to the people of Kansas. The example which was followed at Harper's Ferry, was set in Missouri. In one case the object was to extend slavery; in the other, to extinguish it. In one case, the persons engaged had been brought to the gallows and suffered for their act; in the other case, the men engaged had been rewarded with office. He thought the Harper's Ferry affair owed its origin to the overlooking of the outrages which had occurred in the West, and to which honorable Senators paid very little attention at the time. Now he trusted they might get that attention which they deserved, and that all might deal impartially and alike by all violaters of the law, whether their object was to introduce or extinguish slavery. He would stand by the Senator equally in maintaining the Constitution of his country and the constitutional rights of all, as well in Virginia as in Illinois.

Mr. Hale remarked that it had been said upon pretty high authority, that there was documentary evidence — a carpet-bag full of it — which, when it was laid before the country would produce a tremendous excitement, and convince the community that men in high places and high station in this land were concerned in this affair. He wanted to see that carpet-bag turned inside out. If this matter was to be pushed, — and he was perfectly willing to have it go on just as far as it might, — not only in reference to the particular acts which were the subject of investigation as proposed by the resolution, but to the ultimate results which were supposed to come out of this anti-slavery agitation, or rather this pro-slavery agitation, — for the agitation all came from that side,— and he thought he might say that, ever since he had been a member of that body, every time the action of that body had been invoked on this subject, it had not been by those who are opposed to, but by those who are in favor of slavery.

Mr. Hunter, of Virginia, expressed his surprise at the manner in which the resolution offered by his colleague had been received. He charged that Mr. Trumbull proposed to stifle inquiry, while Mr. Hale treated the subject with unbecoming levity.

Mr. Davis, of Mississippi, was comparatively temperate in his views. "The Senator from Illinois might have any committee he pleased for the purpose of investigating the Liberty Arsenal affair; but let the inquiries be separate. "Let us," he said, "not look back so far to stir up subjects of irritation, to increase the discord, to magnify the ill feeling that unfortunately already exists. In the case before us the object undeniably was to incite to insurrection the ignorant slaves who were peacefully living in the relation of domestics to their Southern masters. Apologetically, it would seem, for the crime thus described, we have had cited to us the language of the Declaration of Independence,—miserable prostitution of the ideas of noble men announced in support of the noblest cause."

Mr. Chandler said he believed this investigation, "if fairly and ably and honestly conducted, would show that if there was any political party in the United States responsible for the action of John Brown, it was the Democratic party, and that alone."

Mr. Wilson, of Massachusetts, said: "The conduct

of Governor Wise throughout the whole affair, carried to the people of the country the idea that he wanted to act a part, to create an excitement, to get up a panic, to arouse and alarm the people of the South, and to redeem his fallen fortunes. The Governor never supposed that the encampment of three thousand men at Charlestown was required; he clutched at the opportunity to make a parade, to get up a bill of expenses, which he hoped to pay out of the national treasury. He told us in 1856, that they "would hew their bright way through all opposing legions," and the Charlestown telegraphers said that "he had no sort of fear of a rescue," that in reply to a gentleman he remarked he never had the least fear on the subject, but considered it the finest opportunity ever offered to put the State in military training. "I can now," he said, "teach my boys how to carry biscuits in their knapsacks and to arrange bullets in their cartridge-boxes.'"

Mr. Bigler, of Pennsylvania, called Mr. Iverson, of Georgia, to account for a portion of his remarks.

Mr. Iverson explained that he referred, when he spoke of the rottenness of a portion of the Democratic party, "to that portion of that party which, under the lead of Stephen A. Douglas, had denied to the Southern people their rights in the Territories of the Union."

Mr. Bigler exclaimed: "Rottenness of the Democratic party on the slavery question! Sir, the Senator can hardly realize the offensiveness of the term. I know he does not intend to apply it to r yself, but it is unjust when applied to any portion of the Democratic party. Why, sir, thousands of witnesses will spring up in every Northern State, on every hill-top and in every valley, on every rostrum, and on the corners of the streets, daily and hourly, contradicting every statement he has made. The opposition of every shade contradict him. They call us doughfaces of the North, yielding constantly to Southern dictation and Southern aggressions."

Mr. Johnson, of Tennessee, in his speech said: "There does seem to be providential interposition in the affair. Brown murdered Doyle and his two sons. Doyle left a widow and four helpless children. Justice seemed to be a little tardy, but it kept constantly in pursuit of its victim, and but a short time since the man who murdered Doyle and his two sons fell a victim with his two sons at Harper's Ferry. I do not say this was a stroke of Providence, but it was a singular coincidence. He whose hands were red, crimson with the blood of a father and two sons, fell a victim at Harper's Ferry with his own two sons. It seems that Divine Providence intended it as a rebuke, an illustration that justice will not only overtake its victim, but will mete out justice in a similar manner."

Mr. Wade, of Ohio, said in reply to Southern senators: "There is no way by which either one section or the other can get out of the Union; I do not say whether it is desirable or not. There is no way by which it can be effected, but least of all on the contingency that has been spoken of. Said the Senator from

Georgia, (Mr. Iverson,) if you wait until a Republican President is elected, you will wait a day too late. Why do you not do it now, when I say again you have the government in your own hands. Why tell us that it is to be done when our man is elected? I say to you, Mr. President, he would be but a sorry Republican who, elected by the majority of the voters of the American people, and consequently backed by them, should fail to vindicate his right to the Presidential chair. He will do it! No man at the North is to be intimidated by these threats of dissolution that are thrown into our teeth daily; and I ask Senators on the other side, why do you do it? I know not what motive you can have in preaching the dissolution of the Union day by day. If you are going to do it, is it necessary to give us notice of it? There is no law that you should notify us that you are going to dissolve the Union, [laughter,] and I should think it would be better to do it at once, and to do it without alarming our vigilance on the subject. It grates harshly on my ears; and I say to gentlemen that if a Republican President shall be constitutionally elected to preside for the next four years over this people, my word for it, preside he will. Who will prevent him?"

The above is a mere glance at the irritating and exciting debate which continued some weeks.

Mr. Trumbull's amendment was rejected — 22 against 32, and the resolution introduced by Mr. Mason was adopted unanimously.

In June he made a report, concluding as follows:

"Upon the whole testimony, there can be no doubt that Brown's plan was to commence a servile war on the border of Virginia, which he expected to extend, and which he believed his means and resources were sufficient to extend through that State, and throughout the whole South. Upon being questioned soon after his capture, by the Governor of Virginia, as to his plans, he rather indignantly repelled the idea that it was to be limited to collecting and protecting the slaves until they could be sent out of the State as fugitives. On the contrary, he vehemently insisted that his purpose was to retain them on the soil, to put arms in their hands, with which he came provided for the purpose, and to use them as his soldiery. The point chosen for the attack seems to have been selected from the twofold inducement of the security afforded the invaders by a mountain country, and the large deposit of arms in the arsenal of the United States there situated. It resulted in the murder of three most respectable citizens of the State of Virginia without cause, and in the like murder of an unoffending free negro. Of the military force brought against them, one marine was killed and one wounded, whilst eight of the militia and other forces of the neighborhood were wounded with more or less severity, in the several assaults made by them. Of the list of 'Insurgents' given in Colonel Lee's report, (fourteen whites and five negroes,) Brown, Stevens, and Coppie, of the whites, with Shields, Green, and Copeland of the negroes, captured at the storming of the engine-house, were subsequently executed in Virginia, after judicial trial, as were also John E. Cook and Albert Hazlett, who at first escaped, but were captured in Pennsylvania and delivered up for trial to the authorities of Virginia, making in all seven thus executed. It does not seem to have been very clearly ascertained how many of the party escaped. Brown stated that his party consisted of twenty-two in number. Seven were executed, ten were killed at the Ferry, thus leaving five to be accounted for. Four of these five, it is believed, were left on the Maryland side in charge of the arms when Brown crossed the river, and who could not afterward join him; leaving but one, who, as it would appear, is the only survivor of the party who accompanied Brown across the bridge, and whose escape is not accounted for. The Committee, after much consideration, are not prepared to suggest any legislation which in their opinion would be adequate to prevent like occurrences in the future. The only provisions in the Constitution of the United States which would seem to import any authority in the Government of the United States to interfere on occasions affecting the peace or safety of the States, are found in the eighth section of the first article, among the powers of Congress, 'to provide for calling forth the militia to execute the laws of the Union, to suppress insurrections, and to repel invasions,' and in the fourth section of the fourth article, in the following words: 'The United States shall guarantee to every State in this Union a republican form of government, and shall protect each of them against invasion, and on the application of the Legislature, or of the Executive, (when the Legislature cannot be convened,) against domestic violence. The 'invasion' here spoken of would seem to import an invasion by the force of a foreign power, or, (if so limited and equally referable to an invasion by one State of another,) still it would seem that public force, or force exercised under the sanction of acknowledged political power, is there meant. The invasion (to call it so) by Brown and his followers at Harper's Ferry, was in no sense of that character. It was simply the act of lawless ruffians, under the sanction of no public or political authority—distinguishable only from ordinary felonies by the ulterior ends in contemplation by them, and by the fact that the money to maintain the expedition, and the large armament they brought with them, had been contributed and furnished by the citizens of other States of the Union, under circumstances that must continue to jeopard the safety and peace of the Southern States, and against which Congress has no power to legislate. If the several States, whether from motives of policy or a desire to preserve the peace of the Union, if not from fraternal feeling, do not hold it incumbent on them, after the experience of the country, to guard in future, by appropriate legislation, against occurrences similar to the one here inquired into, the Committee can find no guarantee elsewhere for the security of peace between the States of the Union.—So far, however, as the safety of the public property is involved, the Committee would earnestly recommend that provision should be made by the Executive, or, if necessary, by law, to keep under adequate military guard the public armories and arsenals of the United States, in some way after the manner now practised at the Navy-Yard and forts."

NOVEMBER 6, 1860.—The election had taken place for President and Vice-President of the United States. The ultra Southerners occupied an extreme position on the slavery question. The moderate Democrats of the North could not sustain them. The party split, and the ultraists nominated Breckinridge, and the *moderados* Douglas. The Republican Convention nominated Lincoln, and the Constitutional Union men Bell, of Tennessee. The campaign was exciting and hard-fought. In the result, Lincoln received one hundred and eighty; Douglas, twelve; Bell, thirty-nine; and Breckenridge, seventy-two electoral votes. The Republican candidate was consequently elected. The popular vote was: Lincoln, 1,866,452; Douglas, 992,139; Breckenridge, 669,082; Fusion Democrat, in Connecticut, New Jersey, New York, Pennsylvania, and Rhode Island, 563,741; Bell, 588,799.

On the night of the election, Jefferson Davis, Jacob Thompson, and other members of Mr. Buchanan's Cabinet, not satisfied with such returns as the President had received, proceeded to the "Constitution" office,—the editor, Browne, as he was called, having changed the name of the paper from the "Union" to the "Constitution,"—and there sought for further election news. I happened to be passing that locality at midnight. They hailed me at the door, to learn the "latest," but seemed to be disappointed with the vote Breckinridge had received, acknowledged he had no chance, and immediately started for their respective homes. Jefferson Davis had previously declared in a public speech, delivered on the steps of Breckinridge's residence, that the Democracy were certain to triumph with Breckenridge and Lane!

On the morning of the 21st of November, entering the reception-room of President Buchanan, I there saw Senator Joe Lane, of Oregon, on a chair near the fire, while in front sat the President, in his slippers and morning-gown. He and Lane were engaged in earnest conversation, loud enough for the fifteen or twenty persons present to hear. It was not secret between them. Lane was insisting on "the rights of the South," and what the President ought to do to secure them. During this conversation, Sam. R. Glen, of the "New York Herald," came in, and wished for some information or facilities in aid of his professional business. Mr. Buchanan did not give him much encouragement. It was not his character to help the press. Samuel informed the President that the prospects were gloomy in the South,—he knew this from personal observation,—he had made the circuit of that section. "How long ago?" asked the President. "A month," Mr.

Glen replied. "Oh," the President said, "we have later news than that."

The President did not ask Mr. Glen his name, and perhaps had never before seen him. But he *heard* from him the next night, in the following telegram, which appeared in the "New York Herald:"

"WASHINGTON, November 22d.

"In an interview this afternoon between the President and some ardent secessionists, Mr. Buchanan took strong grounds against secession, without resorting first to conciliatory measures. He could not believe that the mighty West would permit the mouths of the Mississippi to be held by a foreign power, which both Louisiana and Arkansas would become, in case of their withdrawal from the Union. 'South Carolina,' he said, 'wishes to enter into a conflict with me — a conflict with myself — and upon the drawing of the first drop of blood, to drag other Southern States into the secession movement.' The President did not intimate what he would do in that event. He admitted that the South had suffered great wrongs at the hands of the North; but the Federal compact was not to be broken up precipitately, and without reasoning and reflection. He would first appeal to the North for justice to the South, and if that was denied them, 'then,' said the President, emphatically, 'I am with them.'

"All the reports received by the President from the South are of the gloomiest description. He says: 'I see no gleam of sunshine yet.' He denied that Mr. Keitt had authority for declaring that he (Mr. Buchanan) was committed to the Secessionists; and he also denied the declaration of Mr. Yancy to the same effect."

When Mr. Buchanan saw this despatch he was very much disgusted, and inquired and found out the name of the enterprising correspondent. The revelations in this telegram troubled him not a little. I can attest to the general correctness of "Samuel's" statement.

President Buchanan, in his annual message of December, 1860, announced, that, while our country was eminently prosperous in all material interests, the long-continued and intemperate interference of the Northern people with the question of slavery in the Southern States had at length produced its natural effects. He also asserted that no power was delegated by the framers of the Constitution to Congress or any other Department of the Federal Government to coerce a State. On the contrary, it was expressly refused.

Attorney-General Black had sustained this view of the President in an elaborate opinion, dated the 20th of November. He concluded it as follows:

"The right of the General Government to preserve itself in its whole constitutional vigor by repelling a direct and positive aggression upon its property or its officers cannot be denied; but this is a totally different thing from an offensive war, to punish the people for the political misdeeds of their State government, or to prevent a threatened violation of the Constitution, or to enforce an acknowledgment that the Government of the United States is supreme. The States are colleagues of one another, and if some of them shall conquer the rest and hold them as subjugated provinces, it would totally destroy the whole theory upon which they are now connected. If this view of the subject be correct, and I think it is, then the Union must utterly perish at the moment when Congress shall arm one part of the people against another for any purpose beyond that of merely protecting the General Government in the exercise of its proper constitutional functions."

Events in connection with secession began to thicken.

CHAPTER XIII.

THE NEW SESSION OF CONGRESS — A FIREBRAND THROWN AMONG THE MEMBERS — "THE HELPER BOOK," THE "IMPENDING CRISIS" — THE GREAT CONTEST FOR THE SPEAKERSHIP — JOHN B. HASKIN AND HORACE F. CLARK — ANOTHER PISTOL SCENE — AN EXCITED DEBATE BETWEEN SENATORS DOUGLAS, GREEN, AND JEFFERSON DAVIS.

THE first session of the 36th Congress — December 7, 1859 — was, to say the least, stormy. John Brown had been hung, and the excitement growing out of slavery was at its height.

James C. Allen, the Clerk of the last House, called the members to order, when a vote was taken for Speaker. Thomas S. Bocock, of Virginia, received 86 votes; John Sherman, of Ohio, 66; Galusha A. Grow, of Pennsylvania, 43; Alexander R. Boteler, of Virginia, 14. Twelve others were voted for, receiving each, one or two votes.

Mr. Clark, of Missouri, rose to give his views on the questions of the day, but met with much opposition. He expressed the hope that gentlemen on the other side of the House (the Republicans) would bear with him and not get unhappy before he had had an opportunity to deliver his sentiments, and placed upon the political record of the country facts as to deeds which struck at the peace of the people of this Union, and at the perpetuity of the Union itself. No wonder they were unhappy and wanted to stop debate, when the constituents of members upon that floor had been incited by their representatives, and by their advice, to insurrection, to treason, to bloodshed, and to murder. He then offered the following resolution :

"Whereas, certain members of this House, now in nomination for Speaker, (John Sherman and Galusha A. Grow,) did indorse and recommend the book hereinafter mentioned,

"*Resolved*, That the doctrines and sentiments of a certain book, called 'The Impending Crisis — how to meet it,' purporting to have been written by one Hinton R. Helper, are insurrectionary and hostile to the domestic peace and tranquillity of the country, and that no member of this House who has indorsed and recommended it, or the Compend from it, is fit to be Speaker of this House."

(Applause in the galleries, accompanied with hissing.)

Mr. Stevens, of Pennsylvania, rose to a question of order. It seemed to him that, in the present condition of the House, there were but two things in order — one was, a motion to adjourn, and the other, to proceed to a second vote.

Mr. Palmer hoped the gentleman from Missouri would not be interrupted. If the negro was to be thrust upon them the first day of the Congress, let them go to work as speedily as possible, and put him out.

Mr. Clark replied, the negro would not have been thrust into the House but for the action of that gentleman's party; nor would any occasion have arisen except for the advice which they gave to the country;

but if gentlemen would make themselves equal to the negro, by saying that the negro shall be free, and equal in all things, at the polls and otherwise, it was rather a strange sentiment for the gentleman now to wish to drive the negro out of the House the first day of the session. He proceeded to demonstrate the unfitness for the Speakership of certain gentlemen on the other side of the House, and caused to be read a circular, signed by sixty-eight members of the House, and twenty-four other prominent persons, recommending the circulation of Helper's book. They said that Helper was a native of North Carolina, and it was believed that the testimony of a Southern man, born and reared under the influence of slavery, would be more generally listened to and profoundly heeded, whether in the Slave or in the Free States, than an equally able and conclusive work written by a Northern man.

Mr. Clark said, in the course of his speech: "Are we to have these appeals made to the baser passions of our nature, and is the country to be crushed and degraded by having placed in the chair, filled by the great Clay and Winthrop, and other lights whose political science and intelligence have radiated over this whole Union, a man who signed such an incendiary commendation? Do these gentlemen suppose that slaveholders, who have won the confidence of their constituents, and who have been sent here to assist in making laws and preserving the Constitution, and keeping the Government, in fact, feel themselves honored by their association? If they do, they are greatly deceived." He afterward said, that such advice as was in the book was treason: such advice was rebellion, and the men who gave it, understanding the scope and purport of their advice, and who design to carry that treason and rebellion into effect, deserve a fate which it would not be respectful for him to announce to the House.

Mr. Gilmer, of North Carolina, did not rise to make a speech, but to offer the following as a substitute for Mr. Clark's resolution:

"Whereas, the circumstances and condition of the country require that the asperities and animosities which, for the last few years, have been rapidly alienating one section of the country from another, and destroying those fraternal sentiments which are the strongest supports of the Constitution, should be allayed. Whereas, inasmuch as the history of the Government furnishes instances of success in giving quiet to the country by the united exertions of conservative national men, irrespective of party, there is reason to hope for a like result from similar labors. Whereas, in 1851, when the minds of the people of the North and of the South were inflamed on the subject of slavery, national men appealed to the country as follows, to wit: —

"'The undersigned, members of the thirty-first Congress of the United States, believing that a renewal of sectional controversy upon the subject of slavery would be both dangerous to the Union and destructive of its objects, and seeing no mode by which such controversy can be avoided, except by a strict adherence to the settlement thereof effected by the compromise acts passed at the last session of Congress, do hereby declare their intention to maintain the said settlement inviolate, and to resist all attempts to repeal or alter the acts aforesaid, unless by the general consent of the friends of the measure, and to remedy such evils, if any, as time and experience may develop.

"'And for the purpose of making this resolution effectual, they further declare that they will not support for office of President or Vice-President, or of Senator or Representative in Congress, or as member of a State Legislature, any man, of whatever party, who is not known to be opposed to the disturbance of the settlement aforesaid, and to the renewal, in any form, of agitation upon the subject of slavery.

"'Henry Clay, Howell Cobb, C. S. Morehead, William Duer, Robert L. Rose, H. S. Foot, William C. Dawson, James Brooks, Thomas J. Rusk, Alexander H. Stephens, Jeremiah Clemens, Robert Toombs, James Cooper, M. P. Gentry, Thomas G. Pratt, Henry W. Hilliard, William M. Gwin, F. E. M'Lean, Samuel Eliot, A. G. Watkins, David Outlaw, Alexander Evans, H. A. Bullard, C. H. Williams, T. S. Haymond, J. Phillips Phœnix, A. H. Sheppard, A. M. Schermerhorn, David Breck, John R. Thurman, James L. Johnson, D. A. Bokee, J. B. Thompson, George R. Andrews, J. M. Anderson, W. P. Mangum, John B. Kerr, Jeremiah Morton, J. P. Caldwell, R. I. Bowie, Edmund Deberry, E. C. Cabell, Humphrey Marshall, and Allen F. Owen.'"

The preamble further recited that the Democratic and Whig National Conventions in 1852 pledged themselves to the same effect; and concluded with the resolution:

"That, fully indorsing these national sentiments, it is the duty of every good citizen of this Union to resist all attempts at renewing, in Congress or out of it, the slavery agitation, under whatever shape and color the attempt may be made."

Mr. Washburne, of Illinois, moved, but the House refused to lay the whole subject on the table—yeas 116, nays 116.

Mr. Barksdale, of Mississippi, asked Mr. Gilmer if his resolution referred either directly or indirectly to the election of Speaker, or to the qualification of any member of the House for the Speakership.

Mr. Gilmer considered it did. "It shows," he said, "that we want the Speaker who may be elected, to understand that we will expect him to act in accordance with the sentiments of the House, as expressed in my resolution."

The debate was continued from day to day.

Mr. Sherman said he did not recollect signing the paper referred to, but presumed, from his name appearing in the printed list, that he did sign it. He had never read Helper's book, or the compendium founded upon it. He had never seen a copy of either. As many harsh things had been uttered against him, he desired to say, that, since he had been a member of the House, he had always endeavored to cultivate the courtesies and kind relations that were due from one gentleman to another. He never addressed to any member such language as he had heard that day. He never desired such language to be addressed to him, if he could avoid it. It was the intention of his friends to organize the House quietly, decently, in order, without vituperation; and they trusted to show to members on all sides of the House that the party with which he had the honor to act could administer the House, and administer the government (applause from the galleries and the Republican seats) without trespassing on the rights of any one.

Mr. Keitt, (in his seat.) "Only one half of it."

Mr. Sherman. "I say then, that I, for one, would

not trespass on a right of a single Southern citizen; and I defy any man to show anywhere a word that I have uttered, that would lead to a different conclusion. The signing of that paper, and the book, every member of the House can appreciate without my saying a word about them."

Mr. Leake, of Virginia, wanted to know from Mr. Sherman, of Ohio, whom he called "the candidate of the Abolition party in this hall," if he said he is opposed to any interference with the subject of slavery outside of the halls of Congress, as well as in them.

Mr. Sherman. Allow me to say, once for all, (and I have said it five times on this floor,) that I am opposed to any interference whatever, by the people of the Free States, with the relations of master and slave in the Slave States, (applause in the hall and galleries.)

Mr. Stevens, of Pennsylvania, said: I do not blame the gentlemen from the South for taking the course they do, although I deem it untimely and irregular, and although I deem it withholding from the public creditors, who are needing the means which we are bound as honest men to give them speedily; nor do I blame them for the language of intimidation, for using this threat of rending God's creation from the turret to the foundation. (Laughter.) All this is right in them, for they have tried it fifty times, and fifty times they have found weak and recreant tremblers in the North who have been affected by it, and who have acted from those intimidations. (Applause.) They are right, therefore, and I give them credit for repeating with grave countenances, that which they have so often found to be effective when operating upon timid men.

Mr. Crawford, of Georgia. Will you keep down your Union meetings at the North, and not deceive the South by pretending to respect our rights, whilst you never intend to give us peace? (Shouts of "Order! order!")

Mr. Stevens. I am not to be provoked by interruptions.

Mr. Crawford. I do not desire to provoke you; but desire to say that you will have your Union meetings all over the North. (Cries of "Order! order!")

Mr. Stevens. I am not to be provoked by interruptions. Interruptions have no effect on me.

Mr. Crawford, (amid continued interruptions, and cries of "Order!") I do not mean to interrupt the gentleman. My object is only to make a single remark, and it is, that I hope that the Black Republican party will not undertake to deceive the South by a pretended friendship for our Constitutional rights now, and when our apprehensions are gone, then renew their warfare on slavery. . . . . All we want is a square and manly avowal of your sentiments, that our people may not be deceived. Do this, and, my life upon it, you will see no cowardly shrinking upon our parts from the maintenance of every Constitutional right to which our people are entitled.

Mr. Stevens. That is right. That is the way that they frightened us before. (Applause.) Now you see exactly what it is, and what it has always been.

P

During the above colloquy, members from the benches upon both sides crowded down into the area, and there was for a time great confusion and excitement in the hall.

Mr. Morris, of Pennsylvania, objected to Mr. Stevens' proceeding until gentlemen resumed their seats.

The Clerk. Gentlemen will please be seated.

Mr. Stevens. This was a mere momentary breeze, sir; nothing else. (Laughter.) I do not believe anybody meant anything by it. If they did, I do not think their meaning reached this side of the House. As I said before, I do not wish to delay the organization of the House, for I wish its business to proceed. I therefore distinctly make the point of order that no business is in order until the House is organized, except balloting for Speaker and moving to adjourn, and upon that I call the previous question.

Mr. John Cochrane, of New York. I move that this body do now adjourn, and upon that I demand the yeas and nays.

Mr. Garnett, of Virginia. I wish to give notice, for one — and I am sure I speak the sentiment of this part of the House—that this discussion shall not be stopped, and there is no power in this Assembly to stop it. (Applause in the galleries.) I speak the sentiments of gentlemen around me, when I say that this discussion must and shall be exhausted. (Renewed applause.)

Mr. John Cochrane. I have made a motion to adjourn. The motion to adjourn is not intended to cut off or arrest this debate. It having been launched, I for one am willing to sail over this stormy sea. Let it go on to-morrow.

The House refused to adjourn.

A second ballot for Speaker was not taken until the 7th of December. It resulted: for Sherman, 107; Bocock, 88; Gilmer, 22; the "Americans" for the last named. Fourteen votes were scattered among others.

On the 8th the debate was resumed, involving the John Brown raid, the slavery question, and Helper's book. During the discussion, Mr Corwin, of Ohio, said: "I had the pleasure of introducing my colleague (Mr. Sherman) as a candidate for the office of Speaker. I know he was charged with indorsing that book. I looked into 'Chitty on Bills,' to see how far he might be liable. (Laughter.) I did not know but that I might be held liable as second indorser. (Renewed laughter.) Chitty tells us about the liability of indorsers of bills of exchange, but does not touch upon the indorsement of books. You all know, that gentlemen who are honored with a seat in Congress are supposed to have a remarkable taste for literature, and a gentleman handed me this book; but the book had little in it besides dry tables of statistics, and hence I dismissed it without knowing anything about it.

"Had it related to polite literature, and not followed in the footsteps of Adam Smith, these gentlemen would have read it before they indorsed it. They did not, and so they did not know what they did. 'Father, forgive them, for they knew not what they did.'

(Laughter.) . . . The eloquent gentleman from South Carolina (Mr. Keitt) who spoke with such fervid eloquence yesterday, believes our Constitution, our temple of liberty, can be rent 'from turret to foundation-stone,' to use his own language, by Helper's book, or any book. If it can be done that way, better go to work and pull it down ourselves and go home.

"A very religious man and a great ruler, in a period of great peril, was told that a Quaker had written a pamphlet against his Government. He asked: 'What does he say in it?' 'He denounces you for being a man of blood and war.' 'Very well,' said the great Protector, 'if my Government cannot stand paper bullets, let it fall.'

"Oliver Cromwell was a man who always 'looked to the Lord,' to use his own words; but nevertheless advised his people to 'keep their powder dry,' showing that, while he had great confidence in the great Ruler of the Universe, he had a certain confidence in 'charcoal and saltpetre, when it was kept dry.'"

[It may here be repeated that the "Americans" concentrated their strength, and sought to select a Speaker of their own political persuasion.]

During a speech made by Mr. Etheridge, he said: "If any gentlemen are resolved to keep up the discussion, I presume they may do so forever; but I can make the gratifying announcement that the Democratic party is agreed to any proposition. This, Mr. Clerk, you will acknowledge is the greatest triumph that any gentleman upon this floor has yet achieved. This is the first time, during the session, that this body has been a unit. I appeal to the Republican party, to the Democratic party — "

Mr. Bouligny, of Louisiana. I should like my friend to tell me who he calls his friends. He says the Democratic party are his friends, that the Republican party are his friends, and so he goes through all the parties here.

Mr. Etheridge. I am glad the gentleman has asked me the question. I call every man my friend who wears an honest face, speaks the English language, swears by the Holy Bible, and does not spell Constitution with a K. (Laughter.)

Mr. Bouligny. I hope my friend has not left me out of his remarks, because I do not speak the English language. I do not, however, spell "Constitution" with a K. [Mr. Bouligny had a strong French accent.]

Mr. Etheridge. The gentleman from Louisiana is embraced among my friends.

A little colloquy between Mr. Florence, of Pennsylvania, and his colleague, Mr. Stevens, is as follows:

Mr. Florence. I wish to ask my colleague a question.

Mr. Stevens. I shall be glad to hear any questions from my friend from the Navy Yard. (Laughter.)

Mr. Burnett. I must object to further interruptions.

Mr. Etheridge. The gentleman from Pennsylvania is a brief and pertinent man, and I will yield to him to ask his question. I hope there will be no objection.

Mr. Florence. My question is mathematical, one of figures; and I put it to my colleague, because I know he was once a schoolmaster.

Mr. Stevens. Yes, I am proud to say that I have taught several hopeful boys. I wish I had taught you too. (Laughter.)

Mr. Florence. I am afraid I would have been an incorrigible pupil. My colleague seemed to speak intelligently of the White House, and of the opinions of the President in reference to the organization of the House of Representatives. He spoke of the power of the Administration over the members on this side, who range themselves under the Democratic banner. I want to ask him a mathematical question. How is it possible, with even all the power of the Administration, that ninety-three, or eighty-nine, or ninety members can organize this House, when it takes one hundred and nineteen to elect a Speaker?

Mr. Stevens. Oh, I do not think those eighty-nine, or ninety, or ninety-three, ever will elect a Speaker. (Laughter.)

Mr. Florence. I submit the problem to him; and if he can, mathematically, let him deduce the solution by which ninety men can organize this House, when one hundred and nineteen votes are required to elect a Speaker. How is that possible, with all the power of the administration?

Mr. Stevens. If my friend and about five more would step out some day during the voting—get a little sick, or go out to get something to eat, or anything — we could then elect a Speaker. (Laughter.) As to my intelligence of the White House affairs, the gentleman must remember that the President is one of my constituents. (Renewed laughter.)

Mr. Florence. If the gentleman represents his other constituents no better than he does the President, I have little hope for him. (Laughter.)

The House, on the 25th of January, took the 35th ballot for Speaker, which resulted: for Sherman, 105; Bocock, 51; William N. H. Smith, ("American,") 26. And on the 27th of that month, the 39th ballot, Mr. Smith received 112; Mr. Sherman, 106; Mr. Pennington, 1; the other votes were scattered. The Democrats joined their force with the "Americans," for Smith.

Before the 40th ballot was taken, Mr. Sherman said that eight weeks ago he was honored by the votes of a large plurality of his fellow-members, for the high office of Speaker. Since that time they had adhered to their choice with a fidelity that had won his devotion and respect, and, as he believed, the approbation of their constituents. They had stood undismayed, amid threats of disunion and disorganization, conscious of the rectitude of their purposes; warm in their attachment to the Constitution and Union, and obedient to the Rules of Order and the laws. They had been silent, firm, manly. On the other hand, they had seen their ancient adversary, and their only natural adversary, reviving anew the fires of sectional discord, and broken into fragments. They had seen some of them shielding themselves behind a written combination to prevent the majority of the House from prescribing rules for its organization. They had heard others openly pronounce threats of disunion; proclaim that if a Republican be duly elected President of the United States, they would tear down this fair fabric of our rights and liberties, and break up the Union of these States. And now they had seen their ancient adversary, broken, dispersed, and disorganized, unite in supporting a gentleman, (Mr. Smith,) who was elected to Congress as an "American," in open, avowed opposition to the Democratic organization. Mr. Sherman said he should regret exceedingly, and believed it would be a national calamity, to have any one who was a supporter, directly or indirectly, of the Administration, or who owed it any allegiance, favor, or affection, occupying a position of importance or prominence in the House. He would regard it as a public calamity to have the power of the House placed, directly or indirectly, under the control of this Administration. It seemed to him a fatal policy to trust the power of the House to the control of gentlemen who had proclaimed that under any circumstances, or in any event, they would dissolve the Union of the States. "For this reason," he said, "we would be wanting in our duty to our God and our country, if we did not avert such a result of this contest. I regard it as the highest duty of patriotism to submerge personal feelings, to sacrifice all personal preferences, and all private interests, to the good of our common country. I said here a few days ago, and I always stood in the position, that when I became convinced that any of my political friends or associates could receive further support outside of the Republican organization, I would retire from the field, and yield to him the honor of the position that the partiality of friends has assigned me. I believe that that time has now arrived. I believe that a greater concentration can now be made on another gentleman, who, from the beginning, has acted with me." Mr. Sherman then formally withdrew his name as a candidate. (There was suppressed applause.)

The House proceeded to the 40th ballot with the following result: William Pennington, of New Jersey, 115; Mr. Smith, 113; and 6 scattering. The next two trials exhibited the same distribution of figures.

An appeal was made to the few Democrats who had thrown away their votes on other gentlemen, to change them for Mr. Smith, which they did, after explanation, to the effect, that although he acted with the "Americans," he was not in affiliation with Knownothings, and was an old-line Whig, and was far more preferable than a Republican.

Mr. Smith withdrew from the canvass in a graceful speech. He was satisfied that the presentation of his name longer before this body would not contribute to the desired success, or accord with the wishes of the gentlemen who had so cordially and steadily sustained him; and he begged leave now, before another ballot was taken, to withdraw his name, and to say that he hoped the indications which were presenting themselves might be harbingers of returning good-will among all the States of this Confederacy; that they might in the preservation of an intact and inviolate Constitution find a guarantee of the rights of every part of our Confederacy, and that our glorious and blessed Union might be perpetuated to the remotest period of time. (Applause on the floor and in the galleries.)

Mr. Reagan, of Texas, said the elements of the House who stood opposed to the Republican party had tried a number of combinations for the purpose of securing for Speaker a man of national and conservative character. When the name of the gentleman from North Carolina (Mr. Smith) was presented, although he differed with the great body of the Democrats in his political opinions, yet satisfied that it was his purpose to maintain the Constitution and the integrity of the Government, they agreed, without a dissenting voice, to give him their support, with the sincere hope that they might succeed in securing his election. He concluded his remarks by saying: "I present the name of a gentleman whose record, as a member of this House in years past, is one of which any Democrat, in any part of this Union, might justly be proud — a gentleman who is capable of presiding with dignity, and of conducting successfully the business of the House in that Speaker's chair. I present the name of John A. McClernand, of Illinois."

Much debate of an explanatory character between

Republicans, Democrats, anti-Lecompton Democrats, and Americans followed.

Mr. Moorhead, of Pennsylvania, said: "I rise, Mr. Clerk, for the purpose of congratulating this House and the country upon the fact that we are now ready to proceed to elect a Speaker of this House. And why? We were informed at an early stage of the session, by the gentleman from Missouri, (Mr. Clark,) that a certain smoking-out process would have to be gone through with before we could elect a Speaker. That has been gone through with this morning, and we are now ready to elect a Speaker." (Cries of "Call the roll!" from all sides of the House.)

Mr. Clark. The gentleman from Pennsylvania says that at the beginning of this session I said there was to be a smoking-out process. I did make that assertion, and that gentleman now feels the effects of that process I have no doubt. Sir, that resolution of mine has worked its effect, so far at least, that it has smoked out before the American people the fact that an indorser of the Helper book cannot be Speaker of this House. I want to tell an anecdote just here, which the gentleman will enjoy, perhaps. I heard of a hunter once who went out turkey-hunting. He found a turkey roosting upon one of the highest trees of the forest. He fired, the turkey fell, and he started for the purpose of catching him; but the turkey got up and ran off with a broken wing. The hunter pursued until he got tired, and ceased his pursuit with the exclamation, "There is one consolation; you will have to roost lower the rest of your life." (Laughter and cries of "Call the roll!" "Call the roll!")

Another ballot was taken, with the result: Pennington, 116; McClernand, 91. The other votes were scattered.

The remainder of the session was consumed in explanations. The next day, amid much excitement, and after the changing of votes, Mr. Pennington was — on the 44th ballot — elected Speaker.

He received 117 votes; Mr. Riggs, anti-Lecompton Democrat, and Mr. Briggs, American, going over to his support; Mr. McClernand, 85; Mr. Gilmer, 16, (of the Americans.) The other votes were scattered. There were numerous explanations of an excited character.

[Mr. Haskin, anti-Lecompton Democrat, had voted for Sherman and afterward for Pennington. When Henry Winter Davis, American, changed his vote for Pennington, there was considerable applause from the Republican seats, followed by mingled applause and hisses from the galleries.]

The tellers reported the result of the ballot, whereupon the Clerk announced that William Pennington, a representative from the State of New Jersey, having received a majority of all the votes cast, was duly elected Speaker of the House of Representatives for the 36th Congress.

The announcement was received with the waving of handkerchiefs, and prolonged and enthusiastic cheering in the galleries and on the floor, accompanied by slight hisses.

Mr. Hindman, of Arkansas. I rise to call the attention of the House and the country to the fact that a Black Republican Speaker—(Cries of "oh! oh!" and deafening shouts of "order!" from the Republican side.)

Mr. Adrian, of New Jersey. I call the gentleman to order.

The Clerk. The Clerk will state to the gentleman from Arkansas, that in pursuance of the vote of the House—

Mr. Hindman. I am in order. But if a point of order is made, I will speak to that point. (Cries of "order!" and great confusion.) I have a right to be heard upon the point of order. Now, what point of order have you raised?

Mr. Adrian. That debate is out of order.

Mr. Grow. My point of order is, that a Speaker has just been elected by the House, and that until he has been conducted to the chair, nothing is in order, nothing can be in order.

The Clerk. The Clerk begs leave respectfully to suggest to the gentleman from Arkansas, that this House has just declared a Speaker elect, and the first thing in order is to conduct that Speaker to the chair. The Clerk has no power further to preserve order. Until the Speaker has been conducted to the chair, the House is without an organ or any person having authority to entertain motions or questions of order.

Mr. Hindman. All I proposed to say was, that a Black Republican Speaker—(Shouts of "order!")

— has been elected by the votes of two members of the Knownothing party. (Vehement shouts of "order! order!")

The Clerk appointed Messrs. Bocock and Sherman a committee to conduct the Speaker elect to the chair; which duty was immediately performed by those gentlemen.

The Speaker, on taking the chair, delivered an address returning his grateful acknowledgments for the distinguished honor conferred upon him. His friends would do him the justice to say that he had not sought the position, as certainly he never desired it. He concluded as follows: "A representative from the State of New Jersey, upon whose soil so many brilliant achievements were accomplished in the Revolutionary War, and whose people have ever been distinguished for their devotion to the Constitution and the Union, I pray the great Arbiter of our destinies that I may do no act to impair the integrity of either; that by wise and prudent counsels, peace and order may yet reign in our midst, and our free institutions be perpetuated to our descendants. I feel that I have a national heart, embracing all parts of our blessed Union."

Mr. Phelps of Missouri, being the oldest consecutive member of the House, then administered the usual oath to support the Constitution of the United States, to the Speaker elect; after which the oath was administered by the Speaker to the members and delegates present.

The new Speaker was at once involved in trouble,

numerous questions of order having been raised. The House was in the utmost confusion, twenty members on the floor at the same time, shouting "Mr. Speaker."

In the course of a few days there was a better state of feeling, and the business proceeded with as much order as could be expected, considering the bitterness of political parties.

During the struggle for the speakership, there was a quarrel between Horace F. Clark, of New York, and John B. Haskin, of the same State.

Mr. McRae, of Mississippi, was making a speech about a conference on the subject of the speakership.

Mr. Haskin wished to ask the gentleman a question.

Mr. McRae replied: "When I get through, then the gentleman can ask the question.

Mr. Haskin. I desire to know if your anti-Lecompton friend from New York (Mr. Clark) agreed to this proposition.

Mr. McRae. I tell the gentleman when I get through, I will answer the question.

Mr. Clark. I hope the gentleman from Mississippi will not answer the question. I do not know that it is any of his (Haskin's) business.

Mr. McRae continued his remarks; and when he finished them,

Mr. Haskin said: The gentleman from Mississippi has refused to answer a question which I put, to know whether my colleague, who claims to be an anti-Lecompton Democrat, favored the proposition before this self-constituted Sabbath Conference Committee to vote down the proposition of the gentleman from Pennsylvania (Mr. Hickman) to correct the Journal. I want to know whether that had been approved by my colleague?

Mr. McRae. I put it to the sense of the House, whether I was bound to answer.

Mr. Haskin, still speaking in a loud voice, said: The gentleman refused to answer.

Mr. McRae repeated. I had no right to answer. I referred the gentleman to his colleague.

Mr. Haskin. My colleague, sir, having impertinently said that it was none of my business, I desire now to make an explanation personal to myself, and personal to that colleague, for the purpose of showing to the House and the country in what a circus-riding aspect that colleague stands in the House. (Loud and excited calls to order.) Now, sir, I desire to make a personal explanation (cries of "Order! order!") for the purpose of satisfying the House—(continued calls to order from the Democratic side)—for the purpose of satisfying the House that my colleague, who claims to be an anti-Lecompton Democrat, has on this and on other questions acted with—"

Mr. Barr, (amid much confusion and excitement.) I call the gentleman to order, (cries of "Order! order!") I call on the clerk to direct the Sergeant-at-arms to make gentlemen take their places.

Many members had risen from their seats, and some rushed to the main aisle, where Mr. Haskin was standing.

Mr. Keitt (elevating his voice to the highest pitch)

said: "Where personal difficulties exist among gentlemen, it is their business to settle them outside of this hall." ("Order! order!")

Mr. Haskin. I rose to make a general explanation, and I have a right to do so.

Mr. Keitt repeated this remark, which was now scarcely audible, from the noise and confusion.

Mr. McClernand. The gentleman from New York has no right to bully the House.

Mr. Harris, of Maryland. I am entitled to the floor, and I demand it at your hands, Mr. Clerk.

The Clerk. The Sergeant-at-arms will go into the House, and insist that members shall resume their seats. The Clerk calls upon members to preserve the order of the House.

The excitement was at its height — every one seemed apprehensive of a personal collision, and made preparation accordingly. One of the members armed himself with a spittoon!

Mr. Keitt. I want to say a word.

The Clerk. No member will be recognized until order is restored.

Mr. Taylor took the Clerk's desk, and endeavored to address the House; but the confusion among the members, who still crowded into the area, and the constant cries from all sides of "Order!" "Sit down!" together with excited conversations, prevented him from proceeding.

The Clerk again appealed to members to preserve order.

The Sergeant-at-arms carried the mace of the House of Representatives through the hall, and compelled members to disperse to their seats.

Mr. Davidson desired to say that if these things were to continue in the future, he must bring a double-barrelled shot-gun into the House with him. (Laughter.)

Mr. Harris, of Maryland. I am sorry to find that my friend from Louisiana is disposed to make game of the House. (Renewed laughter.)

He then deprecated these disturbances. Members should show by their conduct now that these temporary excitements could be quieted as speedily as they were raised, and they should determine that never again would they permit such a scene to be renewed upon this floor. (Applause in the galleries.) They all ought to be decorous and dignified representatives of a great nation. (Applause in the galleries.)

Mr. Clemens, of Virginia, said he had witnessed here to-day what he trusted it might never be his fortune to witness again, whether in public or private life. Standing about four feet from the gentleman from New York — referring to Mr. Haskin — and when he replied to the remark made by his colleague that "it was none of his business," and said that he had impertinently said something which he ought not to have said, he put his hand upon his breast, his coat buttoned by two brass buttons — (Loud cries of "Order! order!" all over the House.)

Mr. Morris, of Illinois, thought the remarks of the gentleman from Virginia had a tendency to add fuel to the fire, and to increase the excitement and personal feeling which prevailed. He objected to them. (Cries of "Order! order!")

Mr. Clemens said, the gentleman ought to be held politically responsible to his constituents, and he should do it. (Loud cries of "Order," — and great confusion in the hall.)

Mr. Haskin explained that his having the pistol with him was an accident arising from the fact that he was out last night until twelve o'clock, and he lived in a neighborhood where outrages had been committed. Any gentleman of the other side, who asserted, if any would do so, that he either drew, or attempted to draw, that pistol in the House, asserted that which was not within the pale of truth. "God knows," he said, "I would not, under any circumstances, draw that pistol upon any in this House, unless I was unjustly assaulted, and had to do it in my own self-defence."

Mr. Clark explained. He said he understood his colleague to address an inquiry to his friend from Mississippi, touching what was said on that occasion beyond the scope of the subject-matter of their action, and the revelations which gentlemen had been pleased to make. He ought simply to have suggested to his colleague the idea that he was wandering beyond the scope of the subject-matter before the House. He regretted that he was thus led into an error, and made this explanation to the House, and to his colleague. He also acknowledged that the remark made by him, which was, at least, uncourtly, led to the excitement of his colleague; therefore he had to remark that he ought not to have used the language he employed.

The excitement was thus calmed.

A "breeze" occurred in the Senate, between Messrs. Douglas and Green, on the same day. They were talking about the Kansas-Nebraska Act.

Mr. Green said it was distinctly understood when that bill was passed, by the Senator from Illinois and others, that the question as to the power of Congress was to be determined by the court, and they all not only agreed to abide by the decision, but provided facilities for bringing the question before the court; but—he asserted this in his presence this hour—neither he nor any other man pretended that if Congress did not have that power, the Territory could have it. Never in the history of this Government, up to that time, had it been asserted.

Mr. Douglas replied: He always contended that the territorial legislature had this power. He did not go into the argument as to where they got it generally, but whenever he expressed an opinion, it was that it was recognized by the Constitution of the United States in its amendments, as being reserved to the people.

Mr. Green. I mean exactly what I say, and he dare not controvert me. Neither he, nor any other man, ever contended that if Congress did not have this power, the Territory could have it.

Mr. Douglas. Mr. President, the word "dare" is

unnecessary in this body. It is unnecessary to bandy words. I dare assert the truth always.

Mr. Green. But no more.

Mr. Douglas. No, sir; I trust the Senator from Missouri does not intimate that I would.

Mr. Green. No, sir; not at all.

Mr. Douglas. I think I know what my opinions are, and have been, as well as he. I am willing that he shall make his assault, and that every other man who desires to do it shall make his, and when they get through, I will fire at the lump, and vindicate every word that I have said. I will not go into a controversy with each man separately, my health will not permit it; but if there is a disposition to impeach my record, let them all get through with their impeachments, and I will reply to the whole.

Mr. Green. I say the Senator from Illinois may fire at the lump whenever it suits his convenience; it makes no difference to me, and he will find not only a lump, but he will find an individual who will meet him at Philippi.

Mr. Douglas remarked, that anything he had to say in future would be purely in self-defence; but as he saw a disposition, as he thought, to "double teams" on him, as they did last year, when a debate grew up, five or six to one, and as the state of his health did not enable him to take each one in turn, he simply said, "Gentlemen, when you get through with your assaults on my record, or my political character, I will reply to you in general; but I have made no assault on any one."

Mr. Green. That is exactly my condition. My health is worse than that of the Senator from Illinois, for I am hardly able to sit here in my seat through the day; but if he fires at the lump, he will find a Roland for his Oliver.

Mr. Jefferson Davis then took part in the debate. He thought the Senator from Illinois magnified himself when he supposed that there was any combination against him. As to his firing at the lump, he had better get through with one before he takes the lump.

Mr. Douglas explained: I have no arraignment to make. In regard to the statement of the Senator from Mississippi that I overrate myself, I shall institute no comparison between him and me, or the modesty of my bearing and his in this body. The Senate and the country could judge of our respective bearing toward our brother Senators.

There was some movement toward a duel between Douglas and Green. Notes had passed, but friends intervened to prevent a hostile meeting.

CHAPTER XIV.

THE EVENTS OF DECEMBER, 1860 — SECESSION INAUGURATED — NEW CABINET APPOINTMENTS IN PLACE OF THE RETIRING MEMBERS — PEACE CONVENTION — COMPROMISE MEASURES — MR. LINCOLN FORMALLY ACCEPTS THE PRESIDENCY — STIRRING DEBATE ON THE VOLUNTEER BILL — THE "IRREPRESSIBLE CONFLICT" — CLOSE OF THE MEMORABLE CONGRESS, ETC.

THE following, among other events, had taken place in December, namely: Resignation of Howell Cobb, of Georgia, as Secretary of the Treasury; resignation of General Cass, as Secretary of State; South Carolina passed an ordinance of secession; Major Anderson transferred the United States garrison of Fort Moultrie to Fort Sumter; South Carolina authorities seized Fort Moultrie and other United States property; John B. Floyd, of Virginia, resigned as Secretary of War, owing to the refusal of the President to withdraw the Federal troops from the forts of Charleston; and, on the 8th of January, Jacob Thompson resigned his office as Secretary of the Interior, on learning that the *Star of the West* had sailed from New York with troops and supplies for Fort Sumter.

In relation to the resignation of General Cass, Mr. Buchanan's official paper said:

"To avoid all misconstruction or misstatement of the reason which caused the event, we have taken pains to ascertain the true cause. It is not that General Cass differed from the President in regard to any portion of the late message. On the great question of coercing a State to remain in the Union by military force, the President and General Cass were perfectly united in opinion. The difficulty rose from the fact that General Cass insisted that a naval and military force should be sent immediately to Charleston to reinforce the forts in the harbor. The President was of opinion that there was no necessity for any such measure, in order to secure the forts against attack. This being the President's conviction, he would not sanction a movement which might lead to quarrel and bloodshed in the present excited state of feeling in South Carolina and other Southern States, and at a time when every friend of the Union is using his best efforts to prevent its dissolution, or if that be not possible, to avert the adoption of any measure which would render its reconstruction hopeless."

Owing to these resignations, the President appointed Philip Frank Thomas, of Maryland, (who was at the time Commissioner of Patents,) to the office of Secretary of the Treasury; transferred Joseph Holt from the Post-Office Department to the War Department; appointed Horatio King Postmaster-General; and transferred Mr. Black from the Attorney-General's office to the State Department, and E. M. Stanton was appointed Attorney-General. Mr. Toucey continued to be Secretary of the Navy, and Moses Kelly, chief clerk of the Department of the Interior, acted as Secretary of that Department. Mr. Thomas, not agreeing with the President's policy, resigned, and General Dix was appointed Secretary of the Treasury in his place.

I recollect calling upon Mr. Holt after he had taken possession of the War Department, and said to him: "Mr. Holt, I see that you have, for the first time in our history, hoisted the National flag over your Department." — "Yes," he responded, "I did not feel as if I could work for the country without the old flag flying over my head."

In January, the following, among other events, occurred: Forts Pulaski and Jackson, Savannah, seized by order of Governor Brown, of Georgia; the demand of South Carolina's Commissioners refused by the President of the United States; a National Fast observed; Fort Morgan, Mobile, seized by the authorities of Alabama; the steamer *Star of the West* fired into by Rebel batteries; Mississippi passed an Ordinance of Secession, and seized the United States Forts and property in that State the next day; Alabama passed an Ordinance of Secession; Florida passed an Ordinance of Secession; the forts and property at Pensacola were seized by the Rebels, excepting only Fort Pickens, which was defended by Lieutenant Slemmer; Georgia passed an Ordinance of Secession; the Mississippi, Alabama, and Florida Senators of the United States, resigned; Louisiana passed an Ordinance of Secession, and seized revenue cutters and other property and moneys of the United States; on the 1st of February, Texas passed an Ordinance of Secession; the Louisiana delegation, with the exception of Mr. Bouligny, withdrew from the Congress of the United States; on the 9th of February, the Congress of the seceding States, at Montgomery, Alabama, elected Jefferson Davis President, and Alexander H. Stephens Vice-President of "the Confederate States of America." On that same day, Tennessee voted against secession. On the 1st of March, General Twiggs, of Georgia, having surrendered and abandoned the United States property in Texas, was dismissed from the army as a traitor. Missouri voted against secession. Various representatives of the seceding States. withdrew from Congress, thus severing their connection with "the agency."

On the 10th of December, 1860, the House of Representatives appointed a Committee of thirty-three on the state of the Union, who immediately proceeded to the consideration of the great questions affecting the National integrity.

In the meantime, various propositions were offered and rejected. Some of the members advocated the calling of a National Convention, with a view to adjust sectional difficulties; others said they would favor a Convention when satisfied the present Constitution, as it was, could not be sustained. Toward the close of February, Senator Crittenden's plan of compromise was voted down — yeas 80, nays 112.

The Committee had reported two series of resolutions, and the question now occurred on ordering the first series to be engrossed and read a third time.

Mr. Branch, of North Carolina, as the only mode of expressing his dissent from a certain portion of the resolutions in the series, moved to lay on the table the one following, namely: "That it is the duty of the Federal Government to enforce the Federal laws, protect the public property, and preserve the Union of these States."

The Speaker decided that the gentleman could not select from the resolutions, which must be voted upon as an entirety.

The resolutions were then passed — yeas 136, nays 53.

The House next voted on the joint resolution reported from the Committee, but amended by the House, proposing to the legislatures of the several States the following amendment to the Constitution of the United States, to be valid to all intents and purposes, as a part of the Constitution, when ratified by three fourths of the States.

"No amendment shall be made to the Constitution which will authorize or give to Congress power to abolish or interfere, within any State, with the domestic institutions thereof, including that of persons held to labor or service by the laws of said State."

The vote on the passage of this joint resolution was yeas 133, nays 65. Two thirds voting in the affirmative, it was passed.

The announcement was received with deafening and prolonged applause, both on the floor and in the galleries.

The House also passed, yeas 92, nays 83, a bill supplemental to the Acts for the rendition of fugitives from labor.

Mr. Washburne, of Illinois, rose to a question of

privilege. The Committee appointed to wait upon the President and Vice-President of the United States elect, and inform them of their election, had discharged that duty, and directed him to submit a report, namely:

Mr. Lincoln said, in reply to the Committee:-

"Gentlemen: With deep gratitude to my countrymen for this mark of their confidence, with a distrust of my own ability to perform the required duty under the most favorable circumstances, now rendered doubly difficult by existing national perils, yet with a firm reliance on the strength of our free government, and the ultimate loyalty of the people to the just principles upon which it is founded, and, above all, an unshaken faith in the Supreme Ruler of nations, I accept the trust. Be pleased to signify my acceptance to the respective Houses of Congress."

Mr. Hamlin said, in response to the Committee:

"Gentlemen: You will please communicate to the respective Houses of Congress my acceptance of the trust confided to me by a generous people. And while it is a position which I neither sought nor desired, I am truly grateful for the confidence reposed in me, and, deeply sensible of the obligations it imposes, it shall be my earnest effort to discharge my duty in that manner which shall subserve the interests of the whole country."

On the 18th of February, 1861, Mr. Stanton, of Ohio, rose to a privileged question, and reported from the Committee on Military Affairs a bill providing that the President, in any case in which it may be lawful to use either the militia or the military and naval force of the United States, may accept the services of such volunteers as may offer their services as cavalry, infantry, or artillery, to continue in employment until discharged.

A motion was made to reject the bill.

Mr. Bocock said, if there be any hope of a restoration of peace, it must be in the defeat of the force bills. The House refused to reject the bill, 68 against 110. It went over.

The next day Mr. Stanton, of Ohio, made a speech in support of that measure.

Mr. Bocock, of Virginia, would tell the gentleman, as the Duke of Argyle told George the Third, that "if you intend to convert this country into a great hunting-ground, give us an opportunity to lift up our voices, that our people may hear and prepare for the change. As the Duke of Argyle said to George the Third, when he proposed to make Scotland a great hunting-ground, so I say to him, that our people may be ready for the change."

Mr. Stanton. If gentlemen intend to interpose factious opposition to this bill, I must ask that the rules be enforced. Discussion is not in order.

Mr. Hindman, of Arkansas. I am not only willing, but I desire, that the members upon the other side of the House shall force the bill through under the previous question in whatever haste they may wish, so that the country may know their determination.

Mr. Stanton. Let us have the previous question then.

Mr. Boteler, of Virginia, had but a word to say. At every stage of the progress through the Committee on Military Affairs of this most ill-timed, unwise, and iniquitous measure, he had warred against it; and only

22

this morning he took occasion to warn the Chairman of the Committee that he could not devise a more efficient method by which to destroy the Union, than to persist in pressing it in this way, and at this particular time, through the House.

The question was then taken on the motion to lay the bill upon the table. Before the vote was announced,

Mr. Cox, of Ohio, said: As this is a disunion measure, I vote to lay the bill on the table.

Mr. Hindman. It is with great reluctance that I vote for the motion to lay upon the table, recognizing the measure as one of the best disunion propositions ever made in this Congress.

Mr. Sickles, of New York. The people of the North will regard this as the substitution of coercion for justice, as the abandonment of conciliation for war. (Cries of "Order.") I vote aye.

The House refused to lay the bill on the table — yeas 68, nays 105.

Mr. Stanton proposed to postpone the further consideration of the bill till the next day.

During a debate on the naval appropriation bill, which intervened, Mr. Garnett, of Virginia, who had the floor, gave way to Mr. Anderson, of Kentucky, who said, in the course of the colloquy, "I am still for the Union; and I ask that gentleman whether he is or not?"

Mr. Garnett. I am in favor of the State of Virginia seceding from this Union at the earliest possible moment. (Great applause on the floor and in the galleries, mingled with hisses.)

Mr. Barr, of New York. I hope order will be preserved here. If this occurs again, I shall ask that the galleries be cleared.

Mr. Hindman. It is the first time there has been a patriotic demonstration here for two or three weeks.

Mr. Barr. I think the gentleman himself has made a great many patriotic demonstrations.

Mr. Hindman. I make one now for your instruction.

The Chairman. The Chair would say that gentlemen upon the floor ought not to set the example of applause.

Mr. John Young Brown, of Kentucky. My colleague says that he is for the Union. Will he sustain the incoming Administration in the event it commences a coercive policy against the States which have withdrawn?

Mr. Anderson. If my colleague will respond to a question that I shall propound to him, I will then answer him. (Laughter, and cries of "No Yankee.") I desire to know if my colleague said the other day, [during the debate upon the bill of the gentleman from Indiana (Mr. Colfax) in reference to mail-service in the seceding States,] that a State has the right to secede? It has been reported that he said so; but the Louisville "Democrat" says that he did not say it. I ask my colleague now if he believes that a State has a right to secede?

Several members. Answer the question.

Mr. Anderson. I say I do not believe a State has. (Cries of "That is no answer to the question.") I am for the Union, the Constitution, and for the enforcement of the laws, as long as I am a member of this Union. (Great applause in the galleries.)

The Chairman. The Chair will order the galleries to be cleared if applause or disapproval is again manifested. The Chair will arrest this whole debate. It is all out of order.

Mr. Leake, of Virginia. I demand that the galleries be cleared. (Cries of "No, no!")

Mr. Adrian. All except the ladies' gallery.

Mr. John Cochrane. I think the galleries behave better than we do.

Mr. Hindman. So do I.

Mr. Brown replied to his colleague: that as one of Kentucky's sons and representatives in this Congress, inspired by the spirit of her elevated love for what our fathers gave us, he was now, as he always had been, for the Union; a Union of equality, justice, fraternity, and amity between its members, wherein the rights and honor of his fellow-citizens would be preserved. . . . If an effort be made to coerce her sister Slave States, the moment that rings the echo of the first gun of that conflict over her hills and valleys, will find her unerring riflemen gathering for the rescue of the South, and in battle will she meet the forces of this Government, which she is now doing most to preserve. Such an unholy, fratricidal and causeless war would precipitate his State to the bosom of the Southern Confederacy; and as she might be the last to join, once the partner of its fortunes, she would be the last to leave it, come weal or woe.

The debate on the Militia Bill was resumed on the 21st of February.

Mr. Wm. A. Howard, of Michigan, made a speech in its support. He said:

"The Constitution provides that Congress shall call forth the militia to suppress insurrection and repel invasion, and to execute the laws of the Union. *This is our duty.* And that is all that is proposed to be done, unless it may be necessary to execute that power of the Government which is higher than all law, above all law, before all law — the power to preserve its own existence until it shall be dissolved by the power which made it. And protecting the public property is exercising this very right. We need no legislation about that. It becomes at once the question of the existence of the Republic, and the Republic is bound to exist until it is regularly dissolved; not only for its own sake, but to discharge the high trust which has been placed in its hands by the people of the United States."

Mr. Pryor, of Virginia, made a speech in which he said he knew — and no man on the other side of the House would dare gainsay the asseveration — that the Republican party were resolved never to recognize the independence of the seceding States; never to surrender the dominion of the captured forts; never to relinquish the Federal authority over any locality where it might have prevailed,— in short, were resolved to permit the South no other alternative than submission or subjugation. He dared proclaim to the country that it was the policy of the dominant party and the incoming Administration to carry slaughter and the sword into the bosom of the Republic, sooner than to tolerate the independent existence of the Southern Confederacy. The bill before the House was proof of their purpose. He concluded as follows: "Pass your bills of coercion. Pass them with whatever of indecent haste and aggravating circumstance. Collect the materials of war, so that when your leader descends upon the scene, he may draw the curtain from the bloody drama — so that when he assumes the reins of power, he may precipitate his legions into the bosom of the South. I do not say they will be 'welcomed with bloody hands to hospitable graves,' but this I will adventure, that the people of the South will not surrender their rights without a struggle; and that for whatsoever may be wrested from them by the grasp of superior force, they will indemnify their posterity by bequeathing them the legacy of an unstained name."

Mr. Curtis, of Iowa, replied. The gentleman who last addressed the House had disclosed his purpose. He commended him for his frankness. He had been surprised at the arguments of his predecessors, because they seemed to be addressed to the fears or the prejudices of somebody. He did not see why they should address such arguments to their peers in this House. He thought, possibly, they were intended for the galleries. They cried "War!" They constantly declared the purpose of the Republicans was coercion; while everything they did and said had a different bearing. The gentleman (Pryor) hoped they would pass this bill, and had defiantly challenged them to pass it, *in order that it might arouse the people of Virginia and the South.* He did not address the reason of the House, but spoke to the conventions and assemblages of the South, which were prepared to take action against his own mother-country — our nursing mother who was assailed — alas! assailed by her own ungrateful and unnatural children. She had borne much and suffered long. She had been assailed in the Executive chambers. Traitors had been skulking behind Executive robes, and they had stabbed her in the Senate Chamber. They had drawn their murderous weapons upon her, and stabbed her in her own national halls. In this House, too, she had been assailed with the same ruthless, matricidal ferocity. With tears and anguish she appealed in vain to her children, who, instead of clasping her in affection, come into this hall and show their bloody daggers, reeking with the blood drawn from their own mother's bosom — from that bosom which sustained and nourished them — and vaunt the glory of their achievement! To say that we have not the constitutional power to protect ourselves, is an absurdity; and to say that we are going to revolutionize ourselves, is to say that we are going to commit suicide, and conclude our career as a *felo de se.*

Mr. Simms, of Kentucky, wished to ask the gentleman whether he and his party, upon this floor, whose intent and purpose against these seceding States were so plain that the wayfaring man, though a fool, could not be deceived in reference to their designs, could here, in this House, in broad daylight, and before the world, be guilty of the moral cowardice of skulking the logical effect of that policy and that intent which had thus far marked their every vote in the House? "Sir," he said, "a brave man may sometimes err, but he never seeks to shun the results of his own conduct, or the responsibilities that attach to his acts. If you mean war, have the manliness to avow it. If you mean peace, you cannot expect to convince the world that such is your purpose by calling around the Executive of the nation a million of armed men, to be supported out of the public treasury, and to obey his behest. This is a war measure, not only mad and desperate in its designs, but a measure in direct violation of the Constitution. I shall expect a frank answer from the gentleman. I shall expect him to meet boldly and manfully the logical consequences of the policy which he and his party are seeking, by this bill, and others now pending in this House, to inaugurate.

Mr. Curtis replied: All this declamation against his party was gratuitous, and had no place in the gentleman's interrogation but to lead him from his argument. In one sense he abhorred the doctrine of coercion. He did not wish to see our armies marched into the Southern or Northern States, and our countrymen subdued by force of arms. The gentleman knew he had no concealments, and he had no right to impute sinister motives to the Republican side of the House. This Government was never going to subjugate and degrade mankind anywhere, but it was going to secure to all who came within its influence the equal rights we enjoy. The object of the bill was to send our eagles to protect our citizens, and shield them against revolution, and against all the ills of anarchy, civil war, and oppression. It was designed as a defence for all those who seek shelter under our flag, all who desire peace and protection under the Constitution and Laws. This bill was not intended to coerce sovereign States, as such; but it was intended to secure the execution of the laws, to maintain our common government, to protect and shelter all citizens of all sections, wherever they were, and wherever they claimed protection under the stars and stripes.

Mr. Hughes, of Indiana, desired to ask the gentleman whether he considered the seceding States in a state of insurrection.

Mr. Curtis replied: Every open hostile act committed against the laws of the United States is, of course, an act of rebellion against the laws, and so far insurrection. I am not talking about States, but about individuals who are in rebellion against the laws, wherever they may be, few or many.

Mr. Hughes. Do you consider the seceding States in a state of insurrection?

Mr. Curtis replied, he regarded every man who was in arms against the Government as an enemy of his country. The gentleman might call it war. He called it insurrection and war, and be they many or few, counties or states, all who are in arms against the United States are in a state of insurrection.

Mr. Hughes replied: This law, then, of course, applies to the seceding States.

Mr. Curtis. It applies to all who are in rebellion against the Government of the United States.

Mr. Burnett, of Kentucky. We want to know what your objects are. You deal in generalities, but you will not come to the point. You talk about enforcing the laws and executing the laws. Now, as a frank man, I desire you to tell us whether that is your purpose, and that of the Republican party, or not.

Mr. Curtis. My purpose is to support the Constitution of the United States as it is, until some power shall be vested in me to do otherwise. I am sworn to support it, and God knows I have no desire to avoid that obligation.

Mr. Burnett. Do you hold that, in order to execute the laws, it is necessary to reinforce the forts now in the possession of the Federal Government, and to recapture the property of the Federal Government, now in possession of the seceded States?

Mr. Curtis. Mr. Speaker, I am not going to say in an open hall, in a public assemblage, what will be the duty of my country in the event of further development of aggressive war against us. I will not speak of measures that ought to be spoken of only in a secret session, if a purpose of that kind were entertained.

Mr. Simms exclaimed, "Murder!"

Mr. Curtis. No, sir; murder comes from the other side. The murderous acts are committed against this Government. The murderers have been skulking behind Executive robes, in the Executive Chamber, and in the Senate of the United States; and they strike at their own mother country, and vaunt their parricidal achievements. And when your mother-country comes with tears in her eyes, and, with supplicating hands, and a lacerated bosom, raises her voice or her hands to avert these disasters, and shield herself from further afflictions, you clamor about war.

The House failed to secure a vote on the bill, other business intervening.

On the 1st of March, a motion was made to receive a communication from the Peace Conference, which, on that day, had agreed on proposals for compromise, and adjourned *sine die.*

Mr. Bocock, of Virginia, said, as the Peace Conference was called by his State, he would vote to receive the report; but unless the report, as it appeared in the papers, could be amended, it could not receive his approval.

Mr. Sherman, of Ohio, would vote against suspending the rules, because they had no time to consider the report.

Mr. Hindman, of Arkansas, would vote against suspending the rules, because he desired to defeat the proposition of the Peace Conference, believing it to be unworthy of the vote of any Southern man.

Mr. Garnett, of Virginia, intended and desired to express his abhorrence of this insidious proposition, conceived in fraud, and born of cowardice, by giving a direct vote against it; yet, from respect for the Convention, he was willing to receive it.

Mr. Maynard, of Tennessee, believed the Peace proposition was eminently wise and just.

The House refused to suspend the Rules — 93 against 67 — not two thirds.

Mr. McClernand, of Illinois, said, "This vote defeats the Republican party, and sounds its death-knell."

Mr. Howard, of Michigan, made a final report from the Special Committee of Five, in which they discussed the question of secession, and showed the unconstitutionality of the whole proceeding.

The remaining time of the session was occupied with other matters of public business. An adjournment *sine die* took place on the morning of the 4th of March.

The closing scenes of the Senate were unusually interesting. On the 21st of February, resolutions reported by the Select Committee were taken up, when

Mr. Wilson, of Massachusetts, opposed them, regarding them as not intended to encourage emancipation, but to perpetuate slavery; and making an earnest speech against the efforts to disrupt the Government.

The subsequent proceedings are epitomized as follows: —

Mr. Seward, of New York, who with Mr. Trumbull constituted the minority of the Committee, submitted a substitute for the Crittenden proposition, as follows:

Whereas, The Legislatures of the States of Kentucky, New Jersey, and Illinois, have applied to Congress, to call a Convention, proposing amendments to the Constitution of the United States, therefore,

"*Be it resolved, etc.*, That the Legislatures of the other States be invited to take the subject into consideration, and to express their will on that subject to Congress, in pursuance of the fifth Article of the Constitution."

Mr. Seward said this joint resolution was one single, complete proposition. If they should adopt it, they would simply do this: they should submit these amendments to the people of the United States for their acceptance, for the reason that the Peace Convention, as it was called, had considered the subject, and thought it grave enough to solicit them to invest it with the legislative or congressional sanction, and so submit it to the legislatures and conventions of the States; but whenever they had made a single alteration in it, such as was proposed by the Senator from Virginia (Mr. Hunter), it was not then the proposition of the States of "Maine, New Hampshire, Vermont, Massachusetts," or any other States; but it was a recommendation of the Congress of the United States. The whole character was changed. The convention was swept out of existence in the history of Congress. The resolutions then adopted became the deliberate conviction of the majority of the Congress of the United States, who substitute their own judgment, and their own wisdom, and their own will, for the wishes, the opinions, respectfully submitted to them by the representatives of those States, and take the responsibility of saying that this was what the Peace

Convention should have submitted, instead of the proposition which it had sent there.

Mr. Hunter, in discussing the proposition from the Peace Conference, said it would put the Southern States in a far worse position than they then occupied under the present Constitution and the Dred Scott decision.

Mr. Crittenden said, he should vote for the proposition of the Peace Conference to amend the Constitution, and there he would stand. He preferred this proposition because he had no hope for his own. He hoped that the Senate, rather than see the country fall into ruin, fall into dismemberment, limb from limb, and blood flowing at the plucking out of every limb, would supply the remedy which was proposed. It seemed to him proper and just.

Mr. Mason, of Virginia, opposed the peace proposition — it would be obnoxious to the South. He said he had expressed himself "temperately and without heat."

Mr. Baker, of Oregon, concluded a speech by saying: "Sir, there is other business to be done here besides the mere ordinary business of the Government; besides the voting of supplies, and the raising of means with which to buy them. We have questions here to-day, as I believe, of peace and war, and I have waited long to see some mode of their solution. I repeat, I go for this proposition, and agree to submit it to the vote of the people, not because I believe it to be the best that can be done, but because that to-day, being two days from the close of this session, it is all I can do. When my people ask me, on my return, 'Sir, have not States gone out?' I will say, 'Yes.' 'Do not more threaten it?' if that is the word, (I trust it is not the best one,) I say, 'Yes.' They say, 'Sir, do you believe they will do it?' 'On my honor and on my conscience,' I say, 'if something is not done, YES!' They then ask, 'What have *you* done?' Mr. President, what have we done? I believe that is the question the country will ask of us, and I for one will vote for this proposition, that I may be able to respond."

Mr. Green, of Missouri, said this proposition presented by the Peace Conference, as it was called, was the merest twaddle — and he used the term with entire respect to the members — the merest twaddle that ever was presented to a thinking people. There was no guarantee for slavery.

Mr. Lane, of Oregon, said: The resolutions proposed by Mr. Crittenden were as low down as he could go. They did not secure to every State that right they have under the Constitution; but the resolution now before the Senate, to speak modestly, as he looked at it, with all due respect to the great men who met here to consider this matter, who deliberated for many days, and presented this as the result of their deliberations, was a cheat, a deception, a humbug — nothing that any State could take as a final settlement of the questions which were giving trouble to the country, nothing that could permanently settle these difficulties.

"We must," he said, "have something more definite, something more certain, or there can be no union even of the States that now remain in the Union, as I believe." He referred to the withdrawal of several of the States, and declared that Virginia would also go out, if nothing were done, and join the great Southern Confederacy. He argued at length in favor of the right of secession, and said that the Republican party would not let the slave States go into the Territories with their property, and would not let the Southern States stay in the Union, nor yet allow them to go out, and concluded as follows: "I can only now repeat, that neither the Senator from Tennessee, nor any other Senator, nor can any man, tell the truth and say that I have, by any vote, word or act of mine, at any time or on any occasion, refused protection to all property alike in the Territories. . . . With this remark I part with him, who, in imitation of Esau, seeks to sell his birthright."

Mr. Johnson, of Tennessee, rose to reply, when Mr. Bigler, of Pennsylvania, said he had no desire to interpose against a fair opportunity to respond on the part of the Senator from Tennessee, but he thought if it would be agreeable to him, it would be important to the Senate and the country to know precisely what position they were to occupy on this great question. Now, a single Senator had it in his power to prevent the final passage of any one of the propositions pending before the Senate. If that was the determination, the Senator from Tennessee might talk as long as he saw proper to do so.

Mr. Johnson replied, so far as he was concerned, it was his intention to occupy the attention of the Senate but for a very short time. He would not do so did he not feel that it was a duty to himself and a duty to his country. (Cries of "Go on.") He asked, "Why is it that no one in the Senate, or out of it, who is *in favor* of the Union of these States, has made an attack upon me? Why has it been left to those who have taken both open and secret ground in violation of the Constitution, for the disruption of the Government? Why has there been a concerted attack upon me from the beginning of this discussion to the present moment, not even confined to the ordinary courtesies of debate and of senatorial decorum? It is a question which lifts itself above personalities. I care not from what direction the Senator comes who indulges in such personalities toward me: in that, I feel that I am above him, and that he is my inferior." (Applause in the galleries.)

The presiding officer (Mr. Polk, of Missouri) rapped with his mallet, and said that if disturbance should be repeated in the galleries, they must be cleared.

Mr. Doolittle remarked, that when applause was given on the expression of Union sentiments, in which he concurred, he desired that the order should be enforced, and there could then be no exception taken, if they enforced the rules when applause might be given for any other sentiments uttered on the floor.

Mr. Johnson resumed. "Why," he asked, "abandon the great issues before the country, and go into personal allusions and personal attacks? Cowper has well said,—

> 'A truly sensible, well-bred man
> Will not insult me, and no other can.'

But there are men who talk about cowards, courage, and all that description of thing; and in this connection I want to say, not boastingly, with no anger in my bosom, that these two eyes of mine never looked upon anything in the shape of mortal man that this heart feared. Sir, have we reached a point at which we cannot talk about treason? Our forefathers talked about it; they spoke of it in the Constitution of the country, they have defined what treason is;—is it an offence, is it a crime, is it an insult to recite the Constitution that was made by Washington and his compatriots? What does the Constitution say? 'Treason against the United States shall consist only in levying war against them, or in adhering to their enemies, giving them aid and comfort.' There it is defined clearly that treason shall consist only in levying war against the United States, and adhering to and giving aid and comfort to their enemies. Who is it that has been engaged in conspiracies? Who is it that has been engaged in making war upon the United States? Who is it that has fired upon our flag? Who is it that has given instructions to take our arsenals, to take our forts, to take our dockyards, to take the public property? In the language of the Constitution of the United States, are not those who have been engaged in it guilty of treason? We make a fair issue. Show me who has been engaged in these conspiracies, who has fired upon our flag, has given instructions to take our forts and our custom-houses, our arsenals and our dockyards, and I will show you a traitor. (Applause in the galleries.)

The presiding officer gave orders to the Sergeant-at arms to immediately clear the galleries on the right of the Chair.

Mr. Douglas suggested, as that was not a very loud noise, the order for this time be dispensed with.

The presiding officer said he would not dispense with it except by a vote of the Senate.

Some debate took place on this motion, when Mr. Johnson expressed the hope that the execution of the order would be suspended, and he would go security for the galleries that they would not applaud any more.

Mr. Lane said he hoped the gentlemen in the galleries would be permitted to remain, and applaud as much as they pleased. It did not make any difference to him, for he was standing up for the right.

Mr. Hale, of New Hampshire, said those in the galleries were probably new-comers, and got their ideas of the Senate from the newspapers. He thought it were better to excuse them. The discussion lasted for nearly an hour; several motions were made and withdrawn; and, at last, Mr. Douglas withdrew the one which he had offered, it being considered out of order.

The Chair then suspended the order to clear the galleries.

Mr. Johnson resumed, "I was going on to remark, in reference to a general allusion to treason, that if individuals were pointed out to me who were engaged in nightly conspiracies, in secret conclaves, and issuing orders directing the capture of our forts and the taking of our custom-houses, I would show who were the traitors: and that being done, the persons pointed out coming within the purview and scope of the Constitution, which I have read, were I President of the United States, I would do as Thomas Jefferson did, in 1806, with Aaron Burr. I would have them arrested, and if convicted, within the meaning and scope of the Constitution, by the Eternal God! I would execute them. Sir, treason must be punished. Its enormity, and the extent and depth of the offence, must be made known. The time is not distant, if this Government is preserved, its Constitution obeyed, and its laws executed in every department, when something of this kind must be done." He further said: "The Senator from Oregon (Mr. Lane) is more Southern than the South itself. He has taken under his wing of protection the peculiar guardianship of the Southern States, and his every utterance is upon the equality of the States, their rights in the Union, or their independence out of it. I think Dr. Johnson advised that when a man comes to your house, and makes great professions of his purity, his uprightness of purpose, his exalted character, of being far above suspicion and imputation, if you have any silverware, hide it. When Northern senators and Northern gentlemen make greater professions of devotion to our institutions than we do ourselves, our suspicions are somewhat excited." In conclusion he said : " The serpent's wile and the serpent's wickedness, in the garden of Eden, first started secession ; and now, secession brought about a return of the serpent. The people of the country ought to be aroused to this condition of things ; they ought to buckle on their armor, and, as Tennessee has done, (God bless her !) by the exercise of the elective franchise, by going to the ballot-box under a new set of leaders, they will repudiate and put down those men who have carried these States out, and usurped a government over their heads. I trust in God that the old flag of the Union will never be struck; I hope it may long wave, and that we may long hear the national air sung,—

> 'The Star-Spangled Banner, oh, long may it wave
> O'er the land of the free and the home of the brave.'

Long may we hear old Hail Columbia, that good old national air, played on all our martial instruments! Long may we hear, and never repudiate, the old tune of Yankee Doodle! Long may wave that gallant old flag which went through the Revolution, and which was borne by Tennessee and Kentucky at the battle of New Orleans,—upon that soil the right to navigate the Mississippi near which they are now denied,—upon that bloody field the stars and stripes waved in triumph ; and, in the language of another, the Goddess of Liberty hovered around when 'the rocket's red glare,' went forth, indicating that the battle was raging, and watched the issue, when the conflict grew fierce, and the issue was doubtful; but when at length victory perched upon your stars and your stripes, it was then on the plains of New Orleans that the Goddess of Liberty made her loftiest flight, and proclaimed victory in strains of exultation. Will Tennessee ever desert the grave of him who bore it in triumph, or desert the flag that he waved with success? No! We were in the Union before some of these States were spoken into existence; and we intend to remain in, and insist upon — as we have the confident belief we shall get — all our constitutional rights and protection in the Union, and under the Constitution of the country."

As Mr. Johnson concluded, applause again broke forth from the galleries.

The presiding officer (Mr. Fitch in the chair) said, it would become the unpleasant but imperative duty of the Chair to clear the galleries.

Mr. Johnson. I have done

The entire audience rose. The applause was renewed, and was louder and more general than before. Hisses were succeeded by applause, and cheers were given and reiterated, with three more cheers for Johnson and the Union.

The presiding officer said: The Sergeant-at-arms will immediately clear the galleries, and the order will not be rescinded.

As the assistants of the Sergeant-at-arms proceeded to execute the order, many of the spectators hissed and clapped their hands, stamped their feet, and indulged in other expressions of feeling.

The presiding officer said: The Sergeant-at-arms will arrest every man he can find who is guilty of this disorderly conduct; and after the galleries are cleared, the doors will be locked.

Mr. Kennedy. I should like to know if it is in order to move that the doors be locked.

Mr. Wilson. I hope the eastern (the ladies') gallery will also be cleared.

The presiding officer. The order is general; all will be cleared.

After an interval of ten minutes, during which the gentlemen's gallery had been cleared, many spectators still remained in the ladies' gallery.

Mr. Pugh wanted to know if the Sergeant-at-arms had executed the order of the Senate.

The Chair hoped that Senators would preserve order on the floor while the galleries were being cleared.

The order having been executed by clearing the galleries and locking the doors leading to them, the presiding officer announced that the business of the Senate would be proceeded with.

Mr. Crittenden thought the circumstances which surrounded them required a meeting on the next day, Sunday as it was. He accordingly made a motion to adjourn till Sunday, at eleven o'clock.

Mr. Trumbull, to save the scruples of some gentlemen, suggested an adjournment until seven o'clock Sunday evening.

Mr. Rice suggested that proper officers be stationed at the doors, and no more persons admitted than could be comfortably seated; and then the disturbers of the peace could be pointed out.

Mr. Kennedy should like, for the residue of the session, to have the doors of the galleries locked. He thought the insult just offered to the dignity of the body had been the most glaring insult ever offered to the dignity of the Senate since the Government had been formed.

Mr. Polk did not see the necessity for a Sunday session. For one he would not come here, unless it were a matter of overruling necessity.

After debate on the subject of adjournment, Mr. King said: "I think there is no business that we need do to-morrow. I voted against the second reading of the resolution referred to by the Senator, and I shall vote against the third reading, but I do not look upon these little matters as things calculated to save this Union."

Mr. Crittenden. Very "little matters!" very small matters, Mr. President!

Mr. King. The Union rests in the affections and the hearts of the people. That is its security. I will not violate the Sabbath.

Mr. Crittenden. "Violate the Sabbath!" You are keeping the Sabbath holy, holier than you have kept any day in the week, by serving your country on that day, endeavoring to save it from bloodshed and ruin. (Applause.)

Further proceedings took place, when the motion of Mr. Crittenden was voted down.

Mr. Bigler had offered a resolution, that the twenty-sixth rule of the Senate be suspended, so far as it might affect joint resolutions of the Senate or House of Representatives, proposing, or providing for, or relating to amendments to the Constitution of the United States. This was agreed to.

Mr. Douglas moved that the Senate proceed to the consideration of the joint resolution of the House, to amend the Constitution of the United States.

Mr. Mason objected. He thought it was due not only to those honorable gentlemen who came here and submitted to the Senate the result of the Peace Conference, that they should give to that the precedence, but he felt that it was due to the State of Virginia, who invited that conference, that no precedence should be given over it.

Mr. Douglas was glad to find that the Senator from Virginia had become such a warm advocate of the report of the Peace Conference. How many hours was it since they heard him denounce it as unworthy the consideration of Southern men or of this country? How long was it since these denunciations were ringing in their ears? They did not hear the praises of the Peace Conference sounded until they were about to get a vote on another proposition to pacify the country; and for fear they *might* have a vote that would quiet the apprehensions of the Southern States in respect to the designs of the North to change the Constitution so as to interfere with slavery in the

States, we find now that the Peace Conference was to be pushed forward to defeat this.

Mr. Mason said the Senator would not find him taking back one word that he had said of objection to the resolutions which came from the Peace Conference, but he protested against their precedence being taken from them — a matter which had engaged the attention of the Senate for the last two hours to effect it.

Finally, the motion to take up the joint resolution of the House was agreed to — 25 against 11. It proposed an amendment to the Constitution of the United States. It had passed that body by a vote of yeas 133, nays 65, and was intended as an "olive branch" to the South.

It was as follows:

"That no amendment shall be made to the Constitution of the United States, which will authorize or give Congress power to abolish or interfere in any State with the domestic institutions thereof, including that of persons held to labor or servitude, by the laws of said State."

Mr. King moved that the doors on the right be now opened.

Mr. Latham, of California, wanted to admit ladies only.

Mr. Pugh, of Ohio, protested against the admission of any gentlemen, after the insult received to-day.

Mr. Kennedy, of Maryland, said the Senate had been insulted in a manner unprecedented, and he would not sit here and be insulted any more. He protested against the admission of any men.

The motion of Mr. King, of New York, was laid on the table.

Mr. Wilkinson, of Minnesota, said he was opposed to all subterfuges and compromises. The people had risen and hurled from power a corrupt and debauched administration, whose officers, to avoid the indignation of an outraged people, had taken refuge under the black flag of treason.

Mr. Chandler, of Michigan, referred to the remarks of the Senator from Kentucky, (Mr. Powell,) and asked if a compromise were made would he go for the enforcement of the laws in all the States.

Mr. Powell replied he would enforce the laws in all the States of the Union, but he was opposed to every form of coercion. He thought that war would destroy all our hopes.

Mr. Chandler replied, denouncing all compromises with traitors. The question was, whether we had a government or not. If we had no government, he would emigrate to some place where there was a government, even to the Comanches. He was willing to yield anything to true Union men, but nothing to traitors.

Mr. Wigfall, of Texas, said it was strange that men declared they meant nothing personal, while they made wholesale charges of theft and treason against the opposite party. Unfortunately, the North did not always send here men who were either gentlemen or Christians. When he called a man a scoundrel, he meant what he said, and held himself responsible for the epithet. He hoped the Senator from Michigan would not turn himself over to the Comanches. They suffered a great deal already by contact with the whites. (Laughter.) He declared that the navigation of the Mississippi River would never be impeded by the seceding States.

Mr. Rice, of Minnesota, said the people of the Northwest knew their own rights too well to suppose that the navigation of that great river would ever be impeded by anything except ice.

Mr. Wigfall. "And low water. (Laughter.) If the Senator will put this in, I will accept his amendment." After further remarks, he predicted that Lincoln would leave the Chicago platform and go for peace, and receive the commissioner from the Confederate States. Instead of making war, he would withdraw the Federal forces from the forts. He did not think there would now be war.

Mr. Rice was sorry the discussion had taken place, and expressed his belief that the people of the Northwest would not vote one dollar for coercion.

Mr. Wigfall, resuming, said he believed that nothing short of the acknowledgment of the right of secession would satisfy the South. As to the propositions of the Peace Conference, all the States which had not gone out would immediately go out if they were adopted.

The Senate took a recess till Sunday evening at seven o'clock.

On that occasion the galleries were crowded, and many persons had to leave the premises, being unable to obtain admission. The floor, too, was thronged with strangers, but those who were not privileged to remain were forced to retire.

The joint resolution of the House was taken up.

Mr. Crittenden, of Kentucky, made a long speech, in which he declared the country was in danger. "We are," he remarked, "one people of the same blood, and one family. As we compromise family troubles, so should we those pertaining to the Union." His remarks were, as usual, earnest and patriotic throughout, and he concluded them by saying, as he was about to part with friends, he had spoken what he believed in truth and soberness.

Mr. Trumbull, of Illinois, said President Buchanan had received the Southern Commissioners; for this, under any other government, he would have been hung for treason. The President should not have waited till the last moment, when he found it necessary, either to take sides or join the Secessionists, and let Major Anderson perish. He had just spoken, though feebly, for the integrity of the Union, but allowed the Secessionists to do as they pleased until they had taken our forts and other property to a great amount. He was opposed to compromising with traitors.

Mr. Wigfall asked, whether the succeeding Administration would pursue the same policy, or whether it would attempt to recapture the forts and other property.

Mr. Trumbull replied, the Senator would find out his principles before he got through with his remarks, and trusted he would learn the opinions of the incoming Administration to-morrow, from the eastern portico of the Capitol.

Mr. Wigfall. I hope we shall.

Mr. Trumbull, resuming, said, that secession never would have reached such a height, if we had had a government. Let it be known that the people of the North are determined to maintain the Union, and there will be Union men in the South.

Mr. Pugh offered a substitute for the pending House resolution, namely, the Crittenden Compromise.

Mr. Mason, of Virginia, characterized the resolution from the House as delusive to the South, and spoke at some length against it.

Mr. Morrill, of Maine, contended that the act of Virginia was a menace, and said that all this terrible agitation came from the trifling administration of head-pills, and was to end in a dissolution of the Union. He wanted no more such dosing as had been proposed, to compromise with traitors.

Mr. Wade, of Ohio, had heard of revolutions in this and other countries; but the present one was more extraordinary than them all; for it was conducted against the best government in the world. All the troubles had grown out of the repeal of the old compromises, which had brought the Union to the verge of dissolution and destruction.

Mr. Wigfall said, he felt that this was positively the last time he should appear on these boards. The Senator from Ohio was the real author of the "irrepressible conflict," and he and his friends were responsible for the dissolution of the Union.

Mr. Doolittle, of Wisconsin, rose to a point of order, and asked, if the Senator from Texas was really "a foreigner," whether he had any right to speak as a Senator of the United States.

Mr. Wigfall said, if the Senate would not call his name from the roll, and would acknowledge the secession of his State, then he would cease his remarks; but so long as his name was called, he would continue here.

Mr. Pugh wanted a test-vote, and desired to stop discussion.

Various propositions were offered. The Crittenden Compromise, as an amendment, was lost, and the House resolution was passed — yeas 24, nays 12.

A distinctive vote was taken on the Crittenden plan of adjustment, and the question determined in the negative — yeas 19, nays 20.

The Senate continued in session until late on the morning of the 4th of March, and adjourned *sine die*, without conclusive action on the Peace Conference proposition.

The House, on Saturday night, adjourned till Monday, at 10 o'clock A. M. There were no persons in the galleries, excepting the reporters. Spectators had been excluded by direction of the Committee of Arrangements for the Inauguration. No business of particular importance was transacted; and an adjournment *sine die* took place.

The author, it will be thus far seen, has only glanced at current events; and, following out this arrangement, to make a very long story very short, it may be added to this closing chapter in the history of Mr. Buchanan's administration, that, while the compromise measures were pending before Congress, the ardent Secessionists, such as Toombs, telegraphed South that there was no hope for their passage, and everything was lost. Crittenden and Douglas were appealed to by conservatives of that section, and telegraphed them to the effect that they trusted the rights of the South and of every State and section could be protected within the Union. "Don't give up the ship — don't despair of the Republic!" etc. The Senators and Representatives of the seceding States had taken their farewell of Congress: a few of them in set speeches. The rebellion had fairly been inaugurated, and Mr. Buchanan retired at the rumbling of the storm of battle, leaving his successor to combat all its formidable appliances, though unprepared for the now "irrepressible conflict."

CHAPTER XV.

ARRIVAL OF MR. LINCOLN — HIS CALL ON PRESIDENT BUCHANAN — EXPOSITION OF HIS VIEWS — THE INAUGURATION — LIEUTENANT-GENERAL SCOTT — PRECAUTIONARY MEASURES — TAKING POSSESSION OF THE WHITE HOUSE — THE CABINET — THE INAUGURAL — EXTRAORDINARY SESSION OF THE SENATE — INTERESTING DISCUSSION AS TO THE MEANING OF THE INAUGURAL, ETC.

ABRAHAM LINCOLN arrived in Washington, at half-past six o'clock on the morning of the 23d of February, 1861, having secretly left Harrisburg, in a special train, the night before; it having been understood that a conspiracy had been formed to prevent his reaching this city, by taking his life. He was accompanied by Col. Ward H. Lamon, of Illinois, who was subsequently appointed Marshal for the District of Columbia.

He was met at the railroad station by Hon. E. B. Washburne, of Illinois, whence he was conveyed in a hack to Willard's Hotel, where Senator Seward was in readiness to receive him. In the course of the morning he paid a visit to President Buchanan, with whom he had a long interview.

On the 27th of February, the City Councils, in company with the Mayor of Washington, took their farewell of Mr. Buchanan. They then proceeded to Willard's Hotel to pay their respects to Mr. Lincoln. The Mayor having delivered a brief address, Mr. Lincoln replied:

"Mr. Mayor: I thank you, and through you the municipal authorities, by whom you are accompanied, for this welcome; and as it is the first time in my life since the present phase of politics has presented itself in this country that I have said anything publicly within a region of country where the institution of slavery exists, I will take this occasion to say, I think very much of the ill-feeling that has existed, and still exists, between the people of the section from which I came, and the people here, is owing to the misunderstanding between each other, which unhappily prevails. I therefore avail myself of this opportunity to assure you, Mr. Mayor, and all the gentlemen present, that I have not now, and never have had, any other than as kindly feelings toward you as to the people of my own section. I have not now, and never have had, any disposition to treat you in any respect otherwise than as my own neighbors. I have not now any purpose to withhold from you any of the constitutional rights, under any circumstances, that I would not feel myself constrained to withhold from my own neighbors; and I hope, in a word, when we shall become better acquainted,—and I say it with great confidence,—we shall like each other the more. Again I thank you for the kindness of this reception."

Before and about this time, companies of men were openly drilling in this city. They were strongly tinctured with secessionism, in fact, had passed resolutions to that effect, and looked for a favorable opportunity to strike a blow at the Government. Finding that they would not have the gratification of doing so, now that stringent measures were being taken for the protection of the public property and the preservation of the public peace, they disbanded—some of them going South, and a compartively few remaining in Washington.

Before the inauguration of President Lincoln, extensive preparations were made, under the direction of Lieutenant-General Scott, to prevent the interruption of the procession at any point. A temporary fence was placed round the space immediately in front of the platform, from which the President was to deliver his Inaugural Address. To guard against surprise, an enclosed avenue of stout boards was constructed, from the point where the President elect would leave his carriage until he passed into the Capitol, a distance of about one hundred feet.

The day for the inauguration arrived. Senators Baker and Pearce rode in the procession, in the same carriage with the retiring President and the President elect. Mr. Buchanan looked very grave, and conversed but little on the way. Mr. Lincoln appeared calm, and slightly affected by the excitement around him. The military arrangements showed that apprehensions existed of a murderous plot against the President elect. His carriage was closely surrounded on all sides by marshals and cavalry, so as almost to hide it from view. A shot could not have possibly reached him, owing to the denseness of the military enclosure. The guard of honor was selected from the most efficient companies of regular troops and marines. One of the notable features of the procession was a large car, supplied by the Republican Association, to allegorize the Constitution and the Union. The States and Territories were represented by a corresponding number of little girls, dressed in white, and displaying miniature flags; the whole drawn by two horses, on the covering of which the word "Union" was printed in large letters. Besides this there were numerous delegations on foot from the several States and Territories, accompanied by citizens of Washington, of the same political sentiments as those of the President elect.

Mr. Lincoln, on arriving at the Capitol, was escorted to the Senate, and took the seat assigned to him. The chamber was crowded, as usual on such occasions, with the most prominent officers of the Government in all its branches, with senators and representatives, and foreign ministers. The oath was administered to Hannibal Hamlin, as Vice-President, by Mr. Breckenridge, when he made an address, and assumed the duties of the chair as presiding officer of the Senate.

The procession was then re-formed, and having, with Mr. Lincoln, reached the platform on the east side of the Capitol, Senator Baker said: "Fellow-citizens, I introduce to you Abraham Lincoln, President elect of the United States."

This was greeted with repeated cheers.

Mr. Lincoln, after a short pause, laid down his manuscript for a few moments on the table; then thrusting his hand into his pocket, took from it a pair of steel-bowed spectacles, which he placed carefully and deliberately on his nose, and used his goldheaded cane as a paper-weight during the reading of the Inaugural.

Mr. Lincoln, before he came to Washington, had had

an address for the occasion printed at the office of the "Springfield Journal," but that which he delivered, was somewhat different, being extensively interlined, in accordance with new developments, after the first draft. An exact copy of this was furnished to the "Associated Press" to be telegraphed.

The President read his Inaugural Address in a clear, distinct voice, concluding as follows:

"I am loth to close. We are not enemies, but friends. We must not be enemies. Though passion may have strained, it must not break our bonds of affection. The mystic cords of memory, stretching from every battle-field and patriot grave to every living heart and hearthstone all over this broad land, will yet swell the chorus of the Union, when again touched, as surely they will be, by the better angels of our nature."

He was applauded when he concluded the reading of his Address.

Never was there a more solemn spectacle. The thirty thousand auditors who listened attentively to his words, were evidently most deeply impressed with the momentous character of the occasion. There was no noise, no confusion, no thoughtless nor indecent scenes of applause or disapprobation. All seemed to be moved with the deep conviction, that their own fate and that of their country, depended on the developments of that memorable day.

In taking the oath, as administered to him by the venerable Chief-Justice Taney, the President placed his hand upon the Bible, and responded in a firm and decided tone. At the conclusion, he bowed reverently, and kissed the Book.

The firing of cannon and the playing of music announced the ceremonies ended.

It may here be stated, that Mr. Lincoln kissed the thirty-four States of the Union, as represented by the thirty-four young ladies.

The President was escorted to the Executive Mansion in the same order that he was attended to the Capitol. Mr. Buchanan accompanied him to the White House, and there took his leave, expressing the hope, in kindly terms, that his administration might prove to be happy and prosperous.

A line had been formed at the Mansion, when there was a great rush into it, thousands of persons offering their congratulations to the new President.

Not only were arrangements made to defend the Capitol, but troops were stationed in different parts of the city, to be used in case of necessity. A report prevailed that a gunpowder plot had been arranged to blow up the Capitol, and I well remember that the Chief of the Capitol Police, Captain C. W. Dunnington, a Southern sympathizer, and who subsequently joined his fortunes with the rebellion, examined all the sewers and secret places on the premises, and made a report that there was no cause for alarm. There were so many rumors of a probable serious difficulty, that every precaution was taken by General Scott and the public authorities, to guard against all disturbance.

Everybody rejoiced that the inauguration had passed without any event to regret.

The New York delegation called upon Mr. Seward

on the morning of the 4th of March. In response to their greeting he made a touching and impressive address, in the course of which he said: "I have been a representative of my native State in the Senate for twelve years, and there is no living being who can look in my face and say that in all that time I have not done my duty toward all — the high and the low, the rich and the poor, the bond and the free." The scene was impressive in the highest degree, and its interest was heightened by the fact that in the interval between his resignation as a senator, and his acceptance of the office of Secretary of State, he was for the first time in many years simply a private citizen.

On the night after the inauguration, the New York delegation called to pay their respects to the President. He said to them he was rejoiced to see the good feeling manifested by them, and hoped that "our friends South" would, when they read his Inaugural, be satisfied. He had made it as near right as it was possible for him to make it, in accordance with the Constitution; which he thought was as good for the people who lived south of Mason and Dixon's line, as those who lived north of it.

The President called an extra session of the Senate, for executive business, and he nominated as his Cabinet, Secretary of State, William H. Seward; Secretary of the Treasury, Salmon P. Chase; Secretary of War, Simon Cameron; Secretary of the Navy, Gideon Welles; Postmaster-General, Montgomery Blair; Secretary of the Interior, Caleb B. Smith; Attorney-General, Edward Bates.

There was a great pressure of office-seekers from all sections, excepting the South; and many removals and appointments were made. Mr. Taylor, a messenger at the Post-Office Department, tells a truthful story of a man from the country seeking a "little place." He had made several visits to the Department, during which he innocently asked that venerable and worthy gentleman, "When will the hiring time begin?"—a question that others may ask, though not in that precise form, on the accession of the next President.

The Senate met in extraordinary session on the 4th of March. Nearly all the Southern States had "seceded," leaving in the Senate only Bragg and Clingman, from North Carolina; Andrew Johnson and Nicholson, from Tennessee; Hemphill and Wigfall, from Texas, and Mason and Hunter, from Virginia.

An interesting debate took place concerning the drift and meaning of the Inaugural Address. It was based on a resolution offered by Mr. Dixon, of Connecticut, that there be printed, for the use of the Senate, the usual number of copies of the Inaugural Address of the President of the United States.

Mr. Clingman, of North Carolina, reviewed the Address. He had no objection to printing it, as a matter of course; but he must say he did not wish to be understood, for one Senator, that, in assenting to the printing of it, he indorsed its positions. If he understood it aright, the purpose which seemed to stand out clearly and directly, was one which he thought would lead to war—war against the Confederate or seceding States; and as he thought that policy would be very unwise for the United States, he must frankly say to gentlemen on the other side, that he did not see, if they adopted the principles of the Inaugural, how that was to be avoided.

Mr. Wigfall, of Texas, commenced a speech, but gave way to

Mr. Douglas, who said that in the remarks which he had submitted the day before, he (Mr. Douglas) reviewed the Inaugural with a view of ascertaining distinctly and certainly what was to be the policy of the new Administration, and he came to the conclusion that it was the wish and purpose of the President to pursue a peaceful policy and to avoid war. He was rejoiced in being able to arrive at that conclusion.

Mr. Wigfall asked the Senator to say explicitly whether he would advise the withdrawal of the troops from Fort Sumter and Fort Pickens, the removal of the flag of the United States from the borders of the Confederate States, and that no effort should be made to levy tribute upon a foreign people.

Mr. Douglas answered: "I do not choose to proclaim what my policy would be, in view of the fact that the Senator does not regard himself as the guardian of the honor and interests of my country, but he is looking to the interests of another, which he thinks is in hostility to this country. It would hardly be good policy or wisdom for me to reveal what I think ought to be our policy, to one who may so soon be in the counsels of the enemy, and the command of its armies." (Laughter and applause in the galleries.)

The Vice-President called to order.

Mr. Wigfall hoped the galleries would not be interrupted. This was a public meeting, and he trusted they should be permitted to continue it after that fashion. He then reviewed Mr. Douglas's Norfolk speech, and concluded by saying he sincerely desired "this matter may be solved peaceably." It was not for them to say whether it should be by the sword or by treaty, but what he wanted to say was that he did not desire that Texas, which he still represented here, should be put in a false position.

Mr. Mason challenged the President for not explicitly telling them what he meant to do, leaving them to inference, to construction, to interpretation, that might possibly mislead these people as to his actual purpose. The Republican party were in the ascendant; they had got the political power of the country in their hands; the Chicago platform had laid down the law by which that power was to be administered, and the President declared that the platform was law to him. It was due that this message should be clearly understood, not only in its purpose, but in the time that purpose was to be executed, in order that the proper preparation should be made to meet the great occasion.

Mr. Foster, of Connecticut, offered a resolution —

"Whereas, L. T. Wigfall, now a Senator of the United States from the State of Texas, has declared in debate that he is a foreigner; that he owes no allegiance to this Government; but that he belongs to, and owes allegiance to, another and foreign government, therefore

"*Resolved*, That the said L. T. Wigfall be, and he hereby is, expelled from this body."

Mr. Clingman moved as a substitute: —

"Whereas, it is understood that the State of Texas has seceded from the Union, and is no longer one of the United States; therefore

"*Resolved*, That she is not entitled to be represented in this body."

Mr. Foster differed with the Senator from North Carolina. He could not admit that any State of this Union had any right, any power, under the Constitution, to secede — to take itself out of the Union of these States, which go to make up the United States of America. He knew of no right that they had to say here that the State of Texas had seceded from the Confederacy of States and no longer belonged to the United States of America.

Mr. Clingman replied, as to the question of secession, gentlemen might take it either way. If Texas had not seceded, the Senator was entitled to be here, notwithstanding the opinions he had expressed; if Texas had seceded, and had the right to secede, his resolution was the proper one.

Mr. Mason, of Virginia, in opposing Mr. Foster's resolution, said, "I aver it here, as a Senator from Virginia, in the face of the country, that I owe and recognize no allegiance to the Government of the United States — none whatever; and there I take my position alongside of the Senator from Texas, and I should be unworthy of my true relation to my sovereign State if I did not."

Mr. Hunter, of Virginia, regarded the movement as one which was calculated to be very dangerous in its effects and consequences. It was a motion to visit with the highest censure of the Senate — to wit, expulsion — the mere expression of an opinion which might happen to be different from that of a majority. The Senator from Texas had done nothing more than to declare his belief in the doctrine of secession.

The Senate disposed of the pending resolution and amendment, by referring the subject to the Committee on the Judiciary.

Mr. Fessenden, of Maine, offered the following resolution: —

"*Resolved,* That Albert G. Brown and Jefferson Davis, of Mississippi; Stephen R. Mallory, of Florida; Clement C. Clay, Jr., of Alabama; Robert Toombs, of Georgia; and Judah P. Benjamin, of Louisiana, having announced that they are no longer members of the Senate, and having withdrawn therefrom, their seats in this body have thereby become vacant; and the Secretary is directed to strike their names from the roll of members."

Mr. Fessenden said, it was perfectly obvious that there must be some period when the Senate shall act on questions of this description.

Mr. Bayard, of Delaware, offered, as a substitute, that the persons mentioned, "having announced that by the secession of their respective States they were no longer members of the Senate, and withdrawn therefrom, the Secretary is directed to omit their names in calling the roll of the Senate."

Mr. Bayard submitted to senators, that there was no necessity for the decision of this question, in any way whatever. It could reach no practical result. He did not desire them to admit the right of secession, or to recognize the effect of secession. All he asked of them was, to leave the question undisturbed.

Mr. Mason opposed Mr. Fessenden's resolution, and Mr. Fessenden accepted Mr. Mason's suggestion, that his resolution be amended so as to read, that the names mentioned be "omitted," instead of "stricken," from the roll.

Mr. Bayard's amendment was rejected — 12 against 26.

The original resolution was modified, and passed in the following form: —

"Whereas, The seats of Albert G. Brown and Jefferson Davis, of Mississippi; Stephen R. Mallory, of Florida; Clement C. Clay, Jr., of Alabama; Robert Toombs, of Georgia; and Judah P. Benjamin, of Louisiana, as members of the Senate, have become vacant, therefore,

"*Resolved*, That the Secretary be directed to omit their names respectively from the roll."

Mr. Douglas offered a resolution, calling on the Secretary of War to inform the Senate what forts, navy yards, and other public works, within the limits of the States of South Carolina, Georgia, Florida, Alabama, Mississippi, Louisiana, and Texas, are now within the actual possession and occupation of the United States; and by what number of men each is garrisoned and held; and whether reinforcements are necessary to retain the same; and, if so, whether the Government has the power and means, under existing laws, to supply such reinforcements within such time, as the exigencies and necessities of the case may demand; and whether the defence and protection of the United States and their interests make it necessary and wise to retain military possession of such forts, places, and other property, except at Key West and Tortugas, and to recapture and reoccupy such others, as the United States have been deprived of by seizure or surrender for any other purpose, and with a view to any other end than the subjugation and occupation of those States, which have assumed the right to secede from the Union, and within whose limits such forts and other public property are situated; and if such be the motives for recapturing and holding the forts and other public property, what military force, including regulars and volunteers, would be necessary to enable the United States to reduce the States aforesaid, and such others as are supposed to sympathize with them, to subjection and obedience to the laws of the Union, and to protect the Federal Capital.

Mr. Douglas thought the information which it was proposed to elicit was very important to the quiet and the peace of the country. The public mind was greatly disturbed by the apprehensions of civil war. The Inaugural Address of the President was understood by many in both sections of the Union as indicating a war policy. If they allow these apprehensions to ripen into a conviction that the Administration did meditate a war policy to reduce to subjection the seceded States by military force, he apprehended that they should find a terrific issue precipitated upon them in a shorter time than many of them imagined. But he did not believe such to be the policy of the President; he did not so understand his Inaugural. It was in this speech that Mr. Douglas said, they must choose, and that promptly, between one of these lines of policy:—1. THE RESTORATION AND PRESERVATION OF THE UNION by such amendments to the Constitution as will insure the domestic tranquillity, safety, and equality of all the States, and thus restore peace, unity, and fraternity to the whole country. 2. A PEACEFUL DISSOLUTION of the Union, by recognizing the independence of such States as refuse to remain in the Union without such constitutional amendments, and the establishment of a liberal system of commercial and social intercourse with them by treaties of commerce and amity. 3. WAR, with a view to the subjugation and military occupation of those States which have seceded or may secede from the Union.

Mr. Wilson, of Massachusetts, said the Senator from Illinois, was certainly a man of anxieties. Hardly had the inaugural address been flashed over the country, before the Senator stepped forth, unasked, to give an interpretation of it. Nobody on the Republican side of the chamber had undertaken either to sanction or disavow that interpretation. "The Senator struts up before the Senate and the country, and talks about what he will not permit — what he will do. I beg leave to say to that Senator, that in the Senate and in the country he is clothed with no power to dictate to us, or to any considerable body of men. He has not a Senate at his heels. He stands here alone, and he is hardly more powerful before the nation. I say to that Senator — and I want him and his friends in the country to understand it — that the Administration which has just come into power will take its own time to deliberate, to act, to declare its policy; that it does not select him as its exponent; that it will speak in due and proper time its own sentiments, and declare its own policy, and will do it through the men in whom it has confidence, who have a right to speak for it. The Senator made here to-day, what I say to the Senator I regard as a mischievous, a wicked, and in the present condition of the country, an unpatriotic speech. He talks about the alarm that pervades the country. Sir, that Senator, by the course he has chosen to take during the last few days, assumes to be the alarmist of the country, and he is the only man I see alarmed. The great portion of the country at this day, and this hour, are coming to look at these questions that have distracted and divided the country, as they are. There is to-day less excitement, ill will, and anxiety in the country. Matters are clearing up. The skies brighten. The sober judgment and patriotism of this nation are rising to meet the wants of the time and the occasion."

Mr. Douglas said: I can pardon the petulant remarks and personal attacks of the Senator from Massachusetts, for it only shows that he had been hurt. He winced under what I had said. I had not said a word disrespectful or unkind to any Senator. He talks about strutting, about dictating, about assuming a leadership uninvited. He merely shows that he thought it was wise to make a personal attack upon me instead of answering the argument that I advanced. I pay no attention to those things, sir. I am rejoiced at what he has said, so far as it relates to the policy of the Administration. I am glad that he has spoken. I think the country will thank him for what he has said, although it is not as much as I would like. He has told us that ten days was too short a time to determine what the policy of the Administration was to be; that they are going to wait and act calmly, and determine hereafter when they have the leisure and the time to investigate what their policy will be. Here we are told that I was right in my construction of the Inaugural; that those general clauses about enforcing the laws, and collecting the revenue, and possessing forts, did not indicate what Mr. Lincoln was going to do. Here is a confession that my construction of the Inaugural was right, when I said that his policy was going to depend upon the necessities of the case, and be changed from time to time with a view to preserve the peace of the country. He concluded by saying: "Now, sir, my object has been to demonstrate that the wing of the party to which the

Senator from Massachusetts belongs, the war wing, the disunion wing, were not authorized to speak for the President in regard to his policy. I take it for granted that the Senator has a line of policy very different from mine. Mine is to preserve the Union. I do not understand that to be his. Mine is to preserve peace. I do not understand that to be his. I know there are union men on that side of the chamber, and I know there are disunionists on that side of the chamber; hence I do not expect to be in harmony on the union question with the whole of that side of the chamber. I will act and harmonize with every union man in America, no matter what his politics or where he comes from, who will forget party, and act with reference to the country. But I will not detain the Senate. I take no exception to the petulant, irritable, irritating personal attacks the Senator from Maine may make.

[Mr. Douglas called in question the accuracy of this report. He said his remark was: "I take no exception to these petulant and personal attacks, considering whence they came."]

Mr. Fessenden. What State did the Senator say?

Mr. Douglas. I did not call any State at all. No, sir; I said irritating, personal remarks, from where-ever they came. I said nothing about Maine. I was not thinking of him. I am sure I did not use the word.

Mr. Fessenden. The Senator is entirely mistaken. He said the Senator from Maine. We all so understood you.

Mr. Douglas. Yes, I know; but you cannot understand the truth when it is told to you. If there is any one parliamentary law and law of courtesy more clear than any other, it is that when a Senator utters a remark and is misunderstood, and corrects the misunderstanding, every gentleman accepts the correction. The Senator attaches more importance to himself than I do to him. He is a very respectable man, of very respectable talent, and debates well; I listen to him with a great deal of pleasure, but I assure him there are other people in the Senate than himself; and hence it does not necessarily follow that I allude to him when I do not call his name or his State, or say anything that will be applicable to him.

Mr. Fessenden. I rise merely for the purpose of making a personal explanation, which I very seldom do. When I interrupted the Senator, it was merely with a view to call his attention to the fact that, unwillingly, as I supposed, he had said the Senator from Maine, when he meant the Senator from Massachusetts.

Mr. Douglas. No; I said "wherever they came." That was what you understood to be Maine.

Mr. Fessenden. The Senator is mistaken. It is impossible for him to admit his mistake; but if he asks his own friends about him, I think he will be satisfied he made the mistake. I took no exception to it in any way, but it has resulted in the Senator, speaking precisely as he has with reference to the matter, and the intimation about what a gentleman would do and what a gentleman would not do. Now, sir, I do not pretend to be very much more of a gentleman than other people, nor very much less. My idea is that a gentleman does not make pretensions in one shape or another.

Mr. Douglas. Well, I will ask the Senator, does he not recognize the rule, that if he misunderstood me, or whether he did not, if I correct him, is he not bound by every courtesy of a gentleman to accept the correction? Is not that the invariable rule, I ask him?

Mr. Fessenden. If the Senator had admitted that by a slip of the tongue he said one thing when he meant another —

Mr. Douglas. I did not admit it, because I say now the statement is false.

The Vice-President. The Senator is out of order.

Mr. Douglas. And he knows it is false.

The Vice-President. The Senator from Illinois is out of order.

Mr. Fessenden. The Senator wants to have a personal quarrel with me on that subject, but I assure him he will fail here, at any rate. If it is his deliberate design to use language unbecoming a senator, unbecoming a gentleman, which no man here uses unless he has proper provocation for using it, he will not elicit from me a reply of the same description, I assure him — here, at any rate, in this place.

Mr. Fessenden then replied at length to Mr. Douglas's speech, the object of which, he said, was to inflame the suspicions of the people; to arouse their spirit, and the anxieties which were now about being lulled to sleep, and which would soon be utterly destroyed and exterminated by the peaceful yet firm course of the Administration.

Messrs. Douglas and Fessenden further prosecuted their quarrel.

Mr. Hale, of New Hampshire, remarked: "As I intended to say something in reply to the Senator from Illinois, it occurred to me that there was, in an old book I used to read, an answer to his speech. It is very short, and I will read it. It is written in the fifteenth chapter of second Samuel, fourth verse. (Laughter.) 'Absalom said, moreover, Oh, that I were made judge in the land, that every man which hath any suit or cause might come unto me, and I would do him justice." (Laughter in the galleries.)

Mr. Douglas. Mr. President —

Mr. Baker. If the Senator will allow me, I want to have the galleries cleared.

Mr. Douglas. Oh, no; I will not give way for that. Mr. President, I presume that there was great wit in the quotation of the Senator from New Hampshire. It only shows, as I intimated before, an attempt on that side to avoid argument by seeking to make personal points on an individual. You could not desire a better proof that there is a fixed purpose to avoid the issue, and avoid argument by making personal points on the individual. Hence, I say to that combination, Come on! attack after attack; get your quotations in advance, make a pre-arrangement, and bring them in here, and I am ready to meet you in this discussion.

The Senator has furnished the evidence of the truth of what I said of this combination. The Senator from Massachusetts led off in that miserable personal attack; the Senator from Maine follows; and then the Senator from New Hampshire comes in with his written speech to fit the occasion. Now, sir, I expect to give these gentlemen some trouble during this Congress. I know their scheme. I do not mean that they shall break up this Union. I do not mean that they shall plunge this country into war. (Applause in the galleries.)

The Vice-President called to order.

Mr. Douglas. As the galleries cannot keep quiet, I will say no more.

Mr. Breckinridge, of Kentucky, addressed the Senate. He regretted that he had not been able to construe the Inaugural Address as it had been construed by other Senators. Instead of peace, it meant war. The only mode on earth to preserve the peace of this country was for the Administration, with or without the advice of the Senate, immediately to remove the Federal troops from within the borders of the Confederate States. It would be a bold act, but it would be the act of a patriot and statesman; it would be an act that all good men would approve and justify; it would be an act that would be hailed from one end of this country to the other as the harbinger of peace, as the true test of a peace policy. If he should do it, opinions would be various; some would brand him as a false and faltering statesman; but more, and far more, and history would approve their voice, would declare him to be a patriot, who nobly refused to plunge his country into the calamity of civil war.

Mr. Hale, of New Hampshire, made a speech. The difficulty was, that those who were *ins* are *outs* — nothing else on this earth. He could not appreciate it; he did not see how it was that it stirred men up so. He had been out in the cold a long time, (laughter,) and he had borne himself with such equanimity that it was astonishing to him to see how it affected gentlemen stepping out.

Mr. Clingman, of North Carolina, said he could not adopt the view of the Senator from Illinois; all the tracks now pointed in one direction, and that was toward collision and war.

Mr. Chandler, of Michigan, said the Senator from Kentucky (Mr. Breckinridge) did him the honor to allude to a remark that he had made upon the subject of blood-letting, and called it his (Mr. Chandler's) doctrine. He said the Senator was evidently not present when he made those remarks, because, if he had been present, he would have seen that he was not entitled to the origination of that doctrine. Thomas Jefferson, in a letter from Paris, on the 13th of November, 1787, said: "The tree of liberty must be refreshed from time to time with the blood of patriots and tyrants. It is its natural manure." He trusted the Senator was satisfied that that great statesman, that patriot, that honored son of Virginia and Kentucky, Thomas Jefferson, knew precisely what he meant when he penned that letter to which attention had been called. He trusted that the Senator from Kentucky would read and re-read it with profit.

Mr. Breckinridge replied, if the expression was not original with the gentleman, he certainly misled him and the public by failing to put it in quotation-marks.

Mr. Simmons, of Rhode Island, proposed a substitute for the pending resolution, the object of which was to ascertain the character of the members of the Senate, and their constitutional position, and whether any of them were elected by legislatures the members of which were not competent to vote for a Senator.

Mr. Bayard, of Delaware, made a despondent speech, and offered a resolution, declaring that "the President, with the advice and consent of the Senate, has full power and authority to accept the declaration of the seceding States, that they constitute hereafter an alien people, and to negotiate and conclude a treaty with 'the Confederate States of America,' acknowledging their independence as a separate nation; and that humanity and the principle avowed in the Declaration of Independence, that the only just basis of government is 'the consent of the governed,' alike require that the otherwise inevitable alternative of civil war, with all its evils and devastation, should be thus avoided."

Mr. Howe, of Wisconsin, opposed the pending resolution, and said in the course of his speech, they had a new Administration, just come into power. It had proclaimed its earnest desire, its fixed purpose, to maintain the authority of the United States — not the authority simply of this Administration, or of that, but the authority of the people of the United States — by peaceable means, if peaceable means would suffice.

Mr. Douglas replied to such portion of Mr. Howe's remarks as applied to him, reiterating his opinion that the Inaugural meant peace.

Mr. Breckinridge made a speech, to show that the Inaugural meant war, and concluded by earnestly giving as his opinion, that the best thing the Senate could do for a distracted and anxious country would be, by resolution, to advise the President to withdraw the troops from the Confederate States, and thus render bloodshed impossible.

Mr. Douglas replied, his object having been to correct the misapprehension under which a portion of the Southern people were laboring in regard to the true condition of the Territories, he wanted the facts known to the people of Kentucky, not to injure the Senator, as he supposed, but to enable him to rally the Union men, and vote down and crush out every disunionist in Kentucky. (Applause in the galleries.) He was not willing that disunionists should cut his throat, and get his State out of the Union, depriving him of his seat for the next six years in this chamber.

Mr. Douglas's resolution was laid upon the table by a vote of yeas 23, nays 11.

Mr. Breckinridge offered a resolution, that the Senate recommend and advise the removal of the United States troops from the limits of the Confederate States; but no quorum voted.

Mr. Trumbull offered the following resolution: —

"*Resolved,* That, in the opinion of the Senate, the true way to preserve the Union, is to enforce the laws of the Union; that resistance to their enforcement, whether under the name of 'anti-coercion,' or any other name, is encouragement to disunion; and that it is the duty of the President to use all the means in his power to hold and protect the public property of the United States, and enforce the laws thereof, as well in the States of South Carolina, Georgia, Florida, Mississippi, Alabama, Louisiana, and Texas, as within other States of the Union."

Mr. Trumbull said: As we were unable to obtain a vote, yesterday, on the propositions then pending, I have offered this resolution, as expressive of the views which I entertain as to the duty of the Government. I desire that the resolution may be printed, and I should be very glad, indeed, if we could get a vote on it.

The yeas and nays were ordered on the passage of the resolution, but they were not taken. The Senate closed its extraordinary session on the 28th of March, 1861.

CHAPTER XVI.

FIRST PUBLIC RECEPTION AT THE WHITE HOUSE — MILITARY GUARDS — THE NEW INSTITUTION, THE PRESS CENSORSHIP — HUMORS OF THE CENSOR — HOW THE "GREAT" MEN ACTED — DEATH OF DOUGLAS — MAJOR-GENERAL McCLELLAN AND THE NEWSPAPER MEN, ETC.

THE first public reception at the White House was largely attended. Near the door stood President Lincoln, uninterruptedly engaged in hand-shaking. He was dressed in a plain black suit, with a frock coat, a turn-over collar, and white gloves. A happy, genial smile illumined his face. His color was good, and his demeanor dignified and calm. Mrs. Lincoln stood near her husband, accompanied by Mrs. Kellogg, a sister of Mrs. Lincoln, Mrs. Grimsley, a cousin of Mrs. Lincoln; Mrs. Edwards, Mrs. Julia E. Baker, and Miss Lizzie Edwards, of Springfield, Illinois. There were present persons from all sections of the country, and from foreign lands, and Senators Douglas, and King, of New York, and other members of Congress.

The secession events continued. The Southern Congress had met at Montgomery, Alabama, and elected Jefferson Davis President of the Southern Confederacy, and Alexander H. Stephens Vice-President. They were inaugurated on the 18th of February; and on the 9th of March, that Congress passed an Act for the establishment and organization of the army of the Confederate States.

On the 9th of April, Secretary of State Seward replied to the Confederate Peace Commissioners, declining to receive them in their official capacity, but expressing deference for them as gentlemen. He announced a peaceful policy on the part of the Government, declaring a purpose to defend only when assailed. The Commissioners wanted "a divide" of public property, and to make a treaty of peace and commerce.

The fires of resistance were kindled everywhere in the South. The Confederacy promised, in effect, not to make war on the Union, if our Government would let it have its own way!

The Administration had taken no active measures up to the 9th of February. I had conversed with numerous prominent gentlemen in official positions, and thought I understood their views very well, no matter what might be their future action. Early on that day, I wrote what I supposed was, or ought to be, the policy of the Administration. I inclosed this in an envelope, and addressed it to a Cabinet officer, with a line, "Important — not an Application for Office." I delivered it to him in person, and requested, if he disapproved of the "notes for a telegram," to destroy the manuscript; but, if he approved, to return the manuscript to me. This he did in the evening of the same day. Being thus supported, and having official indorsement, I re-wrote carefully the article, and telegraphed it as "the general despatch," in the following form:

"WASHINGTON, April 9, 1861.

"POLICY OF THE ADMINISTRATION.—Extensive as the military and naval preparations are, it is persistently stated in Administration quarters that they are for defensive purposes only, and that nothing is intended not strictly justified by the laws, which it is the duty of the President to enforce to the extent of his ability. If resistance be made to his efforts in this particular, and bloodshed be the result, the responsibility must fall on those who provoke hostilities; and the assurance of the Inaugural is repeated, that the Administration will not be the aggressor.

"Various theories or reasons have been given for the present military demonstrations; among others, that they were only recently stimulated by the result of certain state or municipal elections; but this is known to be an error, for at the very commencement of the Administration, the President and Cabinet entertained the idea of reinforcing both Forts Sumter and Pickens, but, owing to the condition of the country at the time, and a non-acquaintance with the means at the command of the Government, the prosecution of the plans now progressing was impracticable; in other words, it was necessary first to ascertain the extent of the effects bequeathed to the present by the late Administration. As to the secrecy of the objects of the military movement, this was deemed absolutely necessary, especially the sailing of vessels with sealed orders.

"Under the late Administration were persons who clandestinely communicated its purposes, from time to time, to the secessionists, and, as frequently occurred, before they were reduced to official form; and, according to a remark of an ex-Secretary, the Administration thus always found itself embarrassed at the threshold. The present Administration, however, with a full appreciation of this obstruction, has limited an actual knowledge of its purposes to the members of the Cabinet, and perhaps several other trusty officers, and taken such precautionary measures as will render it next to impossible to improperly acquire the forbidden information.

"The Administration, while constantly declaring its policy to be peace, claims that it can only be held to a strict accountability by the people; and that however variant and speculative may be the public respecting its movements, it is under no obligation to announce its purposes and plans; in other words, the Administration should be judged by its acts. That Fort Pulaski has been or will be reinforced, admits of no doubt; and with regard to Fort Sumter, the Administration will do all in its power either to relieve Major Anderson, or to secure his evacuation of the post, if needs be, without dishonor, or committing the Government to the acknowledgment of any right claimed by the Confederate States, or in any way recognize the doctrine of secession. The proceedings in the future, beyond the relief of Fort Pickens, will be governed by circumstances.

"The above has been prepared from reliable sources, with a view to show, to some extent, the basis of the present military preparations."

This was the first semi-official announcement of "the policy of the Administration."

On the 11th of April, Fort Sumter was demanded by the South to surrender, which Major Anderson refused to do at that time; but was compelled two days after to give up the fort, which he had so gallantly defended.

On the 13th of April, in answer to the Virginia Commissioners, President Lincoln recommended to them a careful reading of his Inaugural, and added: "In that I expressed my policy, and with deep regret and mortification I now learn there is great and injurious uncertainty in the public mind as to what that policy is, and what course I intend to pursue. Not having yet seen occasion to change, it is now my purpose to pursue the course marked out in the Inaugural Address. I now repeat, that the power confided to me will be used to uphold, occupy, and possess the property and public buildings for the Government, and to collect the duties on imports, but beyond what is necessary for these objects, there will be no invasion, no using of force against and among the population anywhere." He also stated that he would carry out all the laws concerning the forts in the seceding States belonging to the Federal Government.

The Administration now began to act in earnest; and on the 15th of April called for seventy-five thousand volunteers to maintain the laws of the United States; and for an extra session of Congress on the 4th of July. The calls for additional volunteers were from time to time repeated, and met with a generous and patriotic response.

It is not a part of my plan, as I think I have already stated, to give a chronology of events, but merely allude to battles, in order to state something else in that connection.

The house of the President continued to be guarded, as it was apprehended he was in personal danger.

Early in the first year of the war, the Government, for the first time, took possession of the telegraph wires, and established a Censorship of the Press. This did not relate to despatches for distant newspapers only, but affected those in our own city.

The battle of Bull Run was fought on Sunday, the

21st of July, 1861. Toward nine o'clock, P. M., of that day, our army correspondent returned from near the front — he had travelled over a hard, dusty road, in very warm weather, and the only loss he sustained was his hat!

He was too much agitated and nervous to write out his own account of that day's events, and so I relieved him by preparing the despatch at his dictation. He paced up and down the room, with the stump of an unlit cigar in his mouth, communicating the desired information. The proprietor of the "National Republican" came into the office, and I made a bargain to give him a manifold copy of the narrative, for a specified amount of money. This turned out a better arrangement than I at that time imagined, as the sequel will show. The account was a long one — rapid movements of troops — flank performances — attacks, retreats, firing of guns — killed and wounded, so far as could be ascertained — and all the *et ceteras* to make the story interesting. The writing was completed by eleven or half-past eleven o'clock. Everything looked beautiful; we had conquered the rebels and won a splendid battle. And this, up to the hour the correspondent left the vicinity of the field, appeared to be true. The correspondent and myself then left the office, in search of persons later from the scene than himself. We were successful. A hack-load of passengers had just alighted at the Metropolitan — at that time called Brown's Hotel. One of them, in response to the inquiry for the latest news, commenced telling what he had seen and heard, describing, by the light of the moon, the movements of troops, with the aid of his cane. He had a large audience. We listened very attentively, for what he narrated was really news. Instead of our troops securing a victory, the fortune of the day turned, and they met with a defeat! Well loaded with gunpowder news, we repaired to the telegraph office, ordered it to be kept open, and then hastily supplied the operators with despatches. We commenced our second edition, or rather addition, with something like the following:

"At this point there was a sudden change in affairs; a stampede commenced;" and we went on, describing the subsequent disasters.

Judge of our disappointment. The papers which arrived here the next day, did not contain a single word of the "disaster;" but only the telegrams of the first part of the occurrences. The people of the North were rejoicing over a victory, not having been permitted to learn that we suffered a defeat. The telegraph censor, by official order, had "closed down" on us. He permitted the *good* news to go, but suppressed the *bad*. At that time the rule was, that we could copy what appeared in the Washington papers, and telegraph it — in other words, what was *printed* was legitimate; manuscript, suspicious, and always subject to erasure! I have already mentioned that I supplied the "National Republican" with the full Bull Run battle account, which was printed on the next Monday morning. Availing myself of the rule,

I clipped out the "disaster," filed it, and it went over the wires as swift as the lightning could carry it. Of course, you will believe the gladness of the readers of it was turned into sorrow. Editors did *not*, in their next editions, *praise* the wisdom of the censorship!

The rule was so severe that censors had to be very circumspect, for they feared arrest and imprisonment if they should, by inadvertence, suffer an obnoxious sentence to be telegraphed. Soft lead-pencils for some kinds of paper, and heavy pens with the blackest of ink for others, were essential to the performance of their grave functions. The censors were not all passably good scholars; owing to this, it not unfrequently happened that the marking out of one sentence, or less, left the remainder of the telegram a mass of nonsense, there being no proper connection of its parts. The censor was the sole, the supreme judge. If *he* did not like the despatch, he would assassinate it, or so maim it as to destroy its original features.

One of them would not permit me to telegraph a word about a battle having been fought at Fredericksburg; would not even permit a telegram to be sent, that wounded men had arrived from the Rappahannock; but was liberal enough to let me say, "a number of wounded men have arrived here." From where, and the circumstances under which they were wounded, was information to which the public had a right. But the rule was, we must not let the enemy know what was taking place, as if the enemy did not already know that he had fought a battle!

The censor was not always at his post. At an early hour he would become thirsty or hungry, and would leave his office to satisfy his appetite; or he would take a notion to patronize Canterbury Hall in the afternoon, and on more than one occasion, despatches would have to be sent to him at that unclassic place to be inspected and viséd, before being telegraphed for the afternoon papers. The changes in the censors were frequent, and the appointments, as already observed, were not always made as to fitness or competency.

I called one evening on Mr. Lincoln, to learn the latest news. It was ten o'clock, and he had just returned from the War Department, and therefore was duly advised of the condition of affairs in the South. He said his mind had been much relieved by ascertaining that, for the first time, Generals Grant and Banks (the former at Vicksburg, and the latter at Port Hudson) were now in communication. I made notes of his conversation, and mentioned to him that I intended to form them into a telegraphic despatch. "That 's right," he said; "the public ought to know good news." And we parted. I innocently thought at that time, while there was so much interest manifested in the army under Grant, at Vicksburg, that I had been peculiarly fortunate in getting an important item. Reaching my office, I prepared a despatch to the following effect:

Further Despatches from Gen. Grant — Gen. Joe Johnston concentrating Troops to operate against him — Grant able to protect himself Front and Rear.

Two despatches were received here Thursday night from Major-General Grant, addressed to different gentlemen in high official positions.

The despatches are dated Monday, 8th inst., — a much shorter time in obtaining advices from Vicksburg than heretofore.

An important fact, and one which obviates much anxiety, is derived from them, namely, — that General Grant was in communication with General Banks as late as the 4th inst., at which time Port Hudson was closely invested.

General Grant repeats what is already known or believed, that General Johnston is concentrating troops with which to operate against him, and mentions a report that three divisions are moving from General Bragg to reinforce Johnston. General Breckinridge is known to have joined him.

Vicksburg is still closely invested. The siege is progressing favorably.

The tone of the despatches is represented to be such as to show that Grant fears neither the enemy in his front nor in his rear. He will protect his lines at all hazards.

It is presumed that he did not know at the date of his telegram, whether or not he was to be reinforced.

The information inspires increased hope and confidence in the success of the siege.

This despatch had, like all others, to undergo censorship. The censor, at the time, was a very young man, who, appreciating the importance of his position, "put on airs," and assumed an undue degree of gravity. He had a small room in the National Hotel, high up, badly lighted stairs, and at first somewhat difficult to find. There he had on his table, scissors of various sizes, a full rack of pens, several inkstands, a dozen or more of lead-pencils, of different colors — black and blue, — a pot of mucilage, half a ream of paper, and other properties, thought by him to be essential to his *high* office. Well, I handed the despatch to the young man, Mr. Holland, in the office, directing him to give it to the censor, and to be particular in watching what the mighty little man did with it. When he returned, he informed me that the censor, without fully reading the despatch, stuck it into his capacious pocket, which answered the purpose of a waste-basket. I knew, from this verbal report, that my well-directed efforts had been vain, and, of course, was not in the best humor at the course of the aforesaid censor. There was no hope for me. I then dispatched these words to our agents: "If you fail to receive an interesting telegram from me to-night, it will not be *my* fault." This happened to slip through without the censorial *visé;* and when the censor heard of the *indiscretion* of the operator in sending the piece of information unapproved, he was not a little indignant, and for some reason vented his small vial of wrath upon me; and several of his officials at the War Department sustained him in the rejection of my item. When I heard that the censor had disposed of my labor by a "pocket veto," I manifolded the substance of the despatch, and mailed it; and this was published in the distant papers. "A council of war" was held, at which President Lincoln, the Secretary of War, and the censor, were present. So important was the matter considered, that the telegram which was offered to be filed, and the item, as printed, were carefully compared. The verdict was, that I was not phraseologically correct. The two did not agree in exact language, (although the facts stated were precisely the same;) and, therefore, I had made a "false issue," in saying that the censor had suppressed the despatch, as printed. The fact was, I wrote the second despatch with more care than I did the first; and, instead of leaving out prepositions and articles, in the way of condensation, I put them all in. The two despatches, I repeat, were substantially alike, for I wrote them from the same notes. Mr. Lincoln, at that council of war, closed the investigation by the recital of an anecdote about a little boy.

Another instance of censorial caution and astuteness: Passing up Pennsylvania Avenue, on a Saturday night, I happened to meet one of General Wool's staff. My friend had just arrived from Frederick, Maryland, and had in his pocket an official communication from his chief to the Secretary of War. He informed me that there was much alarm in Western Maryland, Lee and his army having invaded that State. He told me no more, because he had not yet ascertained the particulars. I immediately went to the telegraph office, to "send off" the fact of invasion — making not more than twenty lines. The censor — not the young man who had vetoed my former communication, but a man at that time well known to many persons in New York and elsewhere — looked at my despatch; then said, "*It can't go!*" "Why not?" "Because it gives information to the enemy." "Colonel, do you suppose the enemy does not know what he himself is doing? And, besides, is it not important that the people of Pennsylvania and New York should know of their danger? Should they be kept in ignorance on so vital a question?" I continued my interrogatories. Although the censor had not the reputation of being a very wise man, he was impressed a little with my arguments, and, by way of compromise, agreed to forward my despatch, with the qualification of the one which, he said, he had sent to his wife.—That qualification was, "*It is said* that," etc. Thus the positive announcement was turned into a mere rumor, which the public could believe or not. No better bargain could be made, and I, of course, was forced to submit.

When General McClellan was called to Washington, from Western Virginia, after the battle of Bull Run, and made General-in-Chief as the successor of Lieutenant-General Scott, he was then regarded as "the right man in the right place." One of his first acts was to invite the correspondents and reporters of the press to an interview, or conference, at which he stated that military operations were often thwarted by disclosures concerning them; therefore he appealed to them not to print anything which would give the enemy an advantage; or words to this effect. A telegraph-man, who was *not* connected with the press, had a good deal to say on that occasion. He was then, or some time afterward, a censor of the press, and expunged many a harmless paragraph from mere caprice. As I had no chance to make a suggestion to General McClellan, with whom I never exchanged a word, I in a low tone mentioned to this telegraph-man what it was; but, for reasons best known to himself, he neglected to repeat it to the General. It was, in substance, that letters containing war-news which was declared "contraband" by the censor, appeared in Northern papers, and thence telegraphed to Louisville, and from that city all the way to Richmond, by way of New Orleans! Now, I thought *that* leak ought to be stopped, and that the stringency ought not to be confined to Washington. It appeared to me that the Southern agent at Louisville ought to be subject to the same iron rule that was applied to the Washington correspondents. In the course of time, the lines of communication between Louisville and Richmond were cut by the events of the war.

Some of the newspaper offices in this city were oftentimes invaded by detectives, or other ignorant persons detailed for duty, and the proof-sheets inspected, and matter in the "form" ordered to be removed.

The Hon. Stephen A. Douglas died at Chicago, on the 3d of June, 1861. Mr. Lincoln had offered him an appointment as Brigadier-General in the Army.

CHAPTER XVII.

FLAG-RAISING — PRESIDENT LINCOLN'S SPEECH — CHEERS TO MY HAT — AN ORGAN-GRINDING SPY — HOW HE DECEIVED THE PRESIDENT — MR. LINCOLN AS A STORY-TELLER — ANECDOTES — HIS PARTICULARITY IN RELATING WAR NEWS — HIS INTERCOURSE WITH THE PRESS — A FALSE REPORT FROM VICKSBURG — HOW THE PRESIDENT LOOKED AND WHAT HE SAID ABOUT IT, ETC.

DURING the month of May, 1861, the President and all the members of the Cabinet attended the flag-raising at the Post-Office Department. Thousands of persons were present. As the colors ascended, a lull in the breeze caused them for a moment to hug the staff. In a few seconds, however, the breeze freshened, and caused the stars and stripes to float out for full fifty feet. The effect was electric. The host of spectators, together with the President and the Cabinet, all united in cheers. Mr. Lincoln, in the wildest enthusiasm of the mass, made a brief address, in which he said, a few months ago the stars and stripes hung as listless and still all over the Union as the flag just raised, but in a short time they were caught up by the coming breeze, and made to float over the whole loyal nation, and among millions who were now determined to keep the flag flying until the bitter end, or until the restoration of peace and unity.

Speeches were also made by Messrs. Blair, Seward, and Caleb B. Smith, of the Cabinet. The remarks of Mr. Seward were especially received with intense enthusiasm.

I myself, or rather my hat, was rapturously applauded on that occasion. It happened thus: I went there to report the proceedings. The crowd below could not see the window from which persons passed to the platform. Cries had been made for "Lincoln;" and, just about that time, I was on the point of stepping upon the platform, to take a seat, when, my hat only being seen by the crowd beneath, they evidently thought that the hat belonged to the President, and that it was on the President's own head! The applause was deafening. I made no bow of acknowledgment, but quietly stepped back into the room.

After the war had progressed about a year, an enterprising young man, who had been in his earlier years employed in an humble capacity in a State legislature, secured an interview with Mr. Lincoln. Possessed of much shrewdness, he proposed to visit Richmond, and obtain, for the use of the Government, drawings of the various works of defence in the neighborhood of that city, number of men, cannon, etc. He stated his plans so clearly and confidently, that the President was willing to trust him. He wanted to know how the young man was going to reach Richmond without detection or arrest. "As an organgrinder," the adventurer responded. The President thought that this was a good disguise, and, at the suggestion of the youngster, contributed a hundred and fifty dollars, or over, to buy a hand-organ and to pay necessary expenses.

The adventurer, after an absence of several weeks, made a report to the President, gave details of his cunning or adroitness on the way, and sent him full drawings of the fortified places, and the number of troops defending them. It was thought to be very valuable information. And the young man was regarded as a wonder, a most valuable friend of the Union.

Returning to Washington, he was duly honored. One of his patrons gave him a sword and a new military uniform, and about the same time he was nominated by the President to the Senate for confirmation as a second lieutenant. The little fellow made a fine-looking soldier.

Unfortunately for the future fame of the pretended organ-grinder, it was accidentally discovered, that, instead of going to Richmond in that humble capacity, he spent the money obtained from Mr. Lincoln in returning to his home, where he planned or invented the military information which was, for a time, appreciated for its supposed value.

The fact of deception becoming known to a Senator from his State, the latter waited on Mr. Lincoln and stated the circumstances of the fraud, when the President withdrew the appointment which he had so cheerfully made.

The following changes occurred in Mr. Lincoln's Cabinet.

Secretary Chase resigned September, 1864, and was succeeded by Hon. W. P. Fessenden as Secretary of the Treasury; Montgomery Blair's resignation was accepted in October, 1864, and William Dennison, of Ohio, was appointed Postmaster-General. Edward Bates resigned as Attorney-General, and was succeeded by James Speed, of Kentucky. Mr. E. M. Stanton was appointed Secretary of War in January, 1862, in the place of Mr. Cameron, resigned. Caleb B. Smith resigned his position of Secretary of the Interior in December, 1862, and was succeeded by John P. Usher. The Hon Caleb B. Smith, late Secretary of the Interior, and afterward United States district judge for the district of Indiana, died at his residence, early in July, 1864. The Executive Departments were draped in mourning in consequence of this event.

I pass over the intervening period of the war — the alternate defeats and victories — the many anxieties concerning the safety of Washington, and the continuous calls for troops. They are all narrated in Frank Moore's "Rebellion Record," and other works concerning the war.

A despatch was received at Philadelphia, and telegraphed to Washington, that our fleet had captured the city of Charleston. The two gentlemen who received the "good news," proceeded to the White House to communicate it to President Lincoln. It was about eleven o'clock at night, and Mr. Lincoln had gone to bed. The doorkeeper said the gentlemen could not, therefore, see him. Insisting upon an interview, and being satisfied, from the nature of their errand, that the President would excuse the interruption, they prevailed upon the doorkeeper to disturb him. He soon returned, saying they would see the President in a style of costume in which no other visitors had ever seen him, and this was true. Entering the room, there was Mr. Lincoln, with no clothing on excepting his shirt! He invited his guests to be seated, and he himself took a chair. He inquired as to the date of their news; and on being informed, said he had three days later intelligence, and that "the bombardment was then going on."

The visitors began to apologize for disturbing his slumbers. The President said it made no difference, and good-humoredly bade them good night, with a profound bow.

The gentlemen of the party, from whom I obtained this incident, described the President's appearance as not only novel, but ludicrous.

In 1864, five six-footers, accompanied by two representatives, called on the President and were introduced to him. These six-footers seemed to astonish the Chief Magistrate, who, after carefully surveying the tall specimens, exclaimed, "Are they all from your State?" "All," was the spontaneous response. "Why, it seems to me," said the President, glancing at the short representatives, "that your State always sends her *little* men to Congress." Of course, there was a general laugh.

In May a pleasant interview took place between the

President and the schoolmaster who taught him the rudiments of education, when the former was a little boy. Mr. Lincoln gave him a warm grasp of the hand that once wielded the birch or sceptre of authority over him. The jolly old pedagogue was delighted with the reception with which he met. He was ten years older than his former pupil.

Mr. Lincoln never would, if he could help it, permit anybody to tell a better story than himself. One day an elderly gentleman called to see him on business—to ask for an office. Before they parted, the President told him a "little story." It pleased the visitor very much; and their joint boisterous laughter was heard by all in the ante-rooms, and became contagious. The elderly gentleman thought he could tell a better story; and did so. Mr. Lincoln was delighted to hear it, and laughed immoderately at the narration. It was a good one, and he acknowledged that it "beat" his own. The next day he sent for his new friend, on purpose, as it was afterward found out, to tell him a story, a better one than the gentleman had related. The gentleman answered this by a still better than he had previously furnished, and was, thus far, the victor over Mr. Lincoln. From day to day, for at least a week, the President sent for the gentleman, and as often did the gentleman get the advantage of him. But he was loth to surrender, and finally the President told the visitor a story, which the latter acknowledged was the very best he had ever heard. The President thus got even with his friend. He never permitted anybody to excel him in those little jokes.

Mr. Lincoln extended the Executive clemency to a large number of persons, including those who had slept at their posts. The following cases, perhaps, have not heretofore been published.

A young Irishman, who was employed as a fireman on a railroad-train, had been, together with others, engaged in a riot, resulting from the draft; and his mother came to Washington to see Mr. Lincoln in his behalf. She called, and waited at the Executive Mansion during three or four hours, several days in succession. She was successful in procuring an interview. Mr. Lincoln told her to call the next day; when she said that she had lost much time already, and besides, the porter would not let her into his room. "No difficulty about that," he replied; and he sat down and wrote a ticket of admission; and giving it to her said, "Present this at the door to-morrow, and you will be admitted."

She accordingly called the next day, when Mr. Lincoln, touched by the earnestness and eloquence of the old lady, inquired into all the circumstances attending the imprisonment of her son. He took immediate measures to effect the release — to pardon the rioter, much to the joy, of course, of the parent. And he said to her, if she, on her return home, would prepare the proper papers, he would pardon the other rioters. The woman was absent from Washington several months, and when she made her reappearance, Mr. Lincoln recognized her. The petition being in proper form, accompanied by the facts in the case, Mr. Lincoln extended the Executive clemency to the extent he had promised; and the old lady went away happy, showering blessings upon the head of her distinguished friend.

Three young men were arrested and tried in Baltimore as rebel spies. One of them was from Kent Island, Maryland, but his friends being intensely "Southern," would or could not take the necessary oath to secure passage to that city in order to inquire into his condition. They, however, at the suggestion of a loyal resident of Washington, who happened to be on Kent Island, wrote a letter to a gentleman here, requesting him to see the President on the subject. This letter failed to reach its destination, the person to whom it was addressed being out of town. The citizen of Washington, to whom I have just alluded, procured a note of introduction to Mr. Lincoln, and proceeded to the White House with it. While there, a lawyer from Philadelphia came in, and, without much ceremony, began to speak to Mr. Lincoln like an attorney before a magistrate, and he mentioned that another of the young men, his client, was willing to swear that he acted as a rebel letter-carrier only for the purpose of getting away from the South. Mr. Lincoln said this was the first time in his life he had heard of a man's own oath being offered to save his neck. Mr. Lincoln then looked at my friend, recently returned from Kent Island, as much as to say, "What is your business, sir?" The gentleman remarked, he did not come there as an advocate, but having recently been in that part of Maryland, he found that the people there were intense rebels—thought the President was a tyrant, and utterly denied that the young man was a spy, which they would have been proud to avow if it had been true. My friend said to Mr. Lincoln, he believed the exercise of executive clemency would have a good effect upon the people on Kent Island. Mr. Lincoln replied: "They are hanging our men in Richmond, and there are no persons there interceding for them." The visitor rejoined, that he did not come there to intercede for the young Marylander; he did not even know him; but had come to tell what he believed to be true. Mr. Lincoln dismissed his visitors with the remark that he wanted to see the proceedings in the case, and could not act until he received them. These were, within a few days, produced. As there was nothing showing positively that the parties were spies, the President commuted their sentence from death to imprisonment in Fort McHenry.

It is related that a woman, whose husband died in the military service, wanted to be appointed sutler in the army, and went to the Secretary of War to secure his aid. The Secretary plainly told her that it was against the regulations to appoint a woman to such a place. Finding it of no avail to continue longer her importunity, she sought an interview with the President. He sympathized with her, but could do nothing for her, saying "Madam, the fact is, I have very little influence with this administration!"

While Mr. Lincoln was generally courteous to newspaper correspondents, it is not known that he gave to any of them his entire confidence.

Whenever he did impart any item of news, especially relating to events of the war, he was extremely cautious in his narration, so that the exact facts might be stated to the public. As a case in point: On one occasion an important telegram was received at the War Department, announcing a grand Union victory, but for some reason unexplained at the time, the Secretary was not disposed to communicate the particulars. Failing thus to obtain them at the Department, several of the correspondents hastened to the Executive Mansion in order to secure the desired information from the President. The Cabinet meeting had just adjourned, and several of the members were leaving the room. The representatives of the press had no sooner sent in their cards to him than he welcomed them in a loud voice. "Walk in, walk in; be seated; take seats." Before they had time to announce the object of their visit, he remarked: "I know what you have come for; you want to hear more about the good news. I know you do. You gentlemen are keen of scent, and always wide awake." One of them replied: "You have hit the matter precisely, Mr. President: that 's exactly what we want — the news."

He was more than ordinarily cheerful. As we had recently suffered a defeat in battle, this latest intelligence of which he was in possession evidently gave him much comfort. He was happy.

Leaning back in his chair and stretching his legs on the table, he took up a small piece of paper — memoranda — saying at the time: "I 've already told this story half a dozen times, but I'll tell it again, as you have n't heard it." He then prefaced his narrative with a few explanatory remarks, in order that we all might more clearly understand it. He next alluded to what the telegram said, and made his comments, being very careful in separating the announcement in the despatch from his own conclusions. The newspaper men, meanwhile, as is their custom, noted the words. They had made a profitable call. "Gentlemen," he said, "that 's all there is about it. The public will be glad to hear it." "We shall be very happy, Mr. President," replied one of the gentlemen, "to give the good news that direction." And, without unnecessary delay in bidding good morning, and thanking the President for his kindness, they hastened to the telegraph-office to flash over the wires the cheering intelligence.

At the time Vicksburg was invested, President Lincoln, in common with all Union men, felt intense interest on the subject. During both day and night he frequently visited the War Department to hear the latest news, and to ask questions, by telegraph, to the most accessible commander nearest to that interesting scene. This seeking after information was the last thing he did before retiring to bed. The writer of this article called to make inquiry about Vicksburg. "I have nothing new," said Mr. Lincoln. "I am much concerned about affairs; I can't sleep to-night without hearing something; come, go with me to the War Department, perhaps Stanton has something." So we went thither. We had no sooner ascended to the second story, than a messenger of the telegraph-office in that building handed him a despatch, reading as follows, dated somewhere in the Southwest: "A report has reached here that our troops at Vicksburg have been defeated, and our army dispersed." Mr. Lincoln read the telegram under the disadvantage of imperfect light. He was extremely nervous; his hands and legs shook violently; his face, upon which the gas shone, was ghastly. He again read the telegram, to fully satisfy himself of its purport. Turning to the writer of this article, he repeated, in faltering accents, the substance of the telegram. "Bad news, bad news," he added, in evident distress, articulating slowly and with mournful emphasis. Then turning to me, he said, in an admonitory tone: "*Don't say anything about this — don't mention it.*" "Mr. President, allow me to say one word." "Well, sir." "The despatch you have received mentions that the communication of disaster is founded on mere '*report.*' It does not come from an army officer, or from any known responsible party. It is given as rumor; probably uttered by some deserter as an excuse for leaving the field. At all events, the story lacks confirmation; and please believe, as we all know from observation, if not from experience, that more than one half of war rumors are false. And so it may be in this particular case."

The President was by these remarks somewhat relieved of his distress. He repeated, "But don't say anything about this." He was unwilling that such disheartening information should get into print.

The President then, with a few strides, reached the office of the Secretary of War. And I, at this point, left the Department.

As I predicted, the rumor was false; and, not long after this interview, news of an entirely different character — the fall of Vicksburg, — gladdened the President's heart.

Mr. Lincoln was sometimes distrustful of newspaper people, as the following will show. He had written a political letter to a Springfield (Illinois) Committee, to be read on the meeting of the State Convention. It was known that a copy of the letter was on its way to some other point, to be published when the original should be officially promulgated. The agent of the New York Associated Press at Washington was instructed, if possible, to obtain a copy and forward duplicates by mail. The request was accordingly made of Mr. Lincoln. "I can't do it," he said, "for I have found that documents given to the press in advance are always prematurely published." It was interposed that "the Associated Press had never thus promulgated documents before the proper time, and besides, the desire was to avoid mistakes in telegraphing." "I can't help that — I have always found what I say to be true." "Well, Mr. President, it is your own property, and you have a right to dispose of your letter as you choose. Good day." The next forenoon, a second application was made, but with no better success. In the afternoon of the same day, however, I received a telegram from Philadelphia, to the following effect: "The Springfield letter of Mr. Lincoln appears in a New York afternoon paper — do you want it?" "Yes," I responded, "send me all of it." At night the entire letter was received in Washington over the wires, and the next morning appeared exclusively in one of the Washington journals — the paper to which the President was in the habit of first turning his attention. It appeared as if coming from Chicago; but Mr. Lincoln had not noticed the date. He was sitting comfortably and calmly in his office, when he for the first time saw his letter in print, before it was read in the State Convention, — the same letter which he was so fearful of being published prematurely! and for which reason he had declined to furnish it to me.

Rushing into the acting private secretary's office, he hastily and impatiently inquired how the agent got the copy of his letter — "Who gave it to him?" etc. The questions were asked in such quick succession that the alarmed secretary could merely respond that he did n't know, but that it was certain he did not obtain it there. Mr. Lincoln returned to his office, wondering "how the thing got out!" He afterward made inquiry, and found that the "premature publication" was made by an enterprising editor, who spread it before his readers nearly a day in advance of its being read at the Springfield Convention. The President was in that case the victim of misplaced confidence; for it was said a copy of the letter had been sent to an editorial friend, not to be published until the proper time.

The President, throughout his administration, acted on the fear that his annual messages might, if supplied to the press in advance, find their way into print in advance of delivery; therefore they had to be telegraphed. And the private secretary would not give copies for this purpose, even to the responsible agent of the press, until he had delivered the manuscript documents to the Senate, and the clerk had commenced the reading of them.

Notwithstanding the President's caution, he was repeatedly astonished to find the keen-scented correspondents publishing important matters in advance of the time designated by himself.

On the 9th of March, 1864, Grant's commission as Lieutenant-General was formally presented to him by President Lincoln, at the Executive Mansion. The ceremony took place in the cabinet chamber, in the presence of the entire Cabinet, General Halleck, Hon. Owen Lovejoy, General Rawlins, and Colonel Comstock, of Grant's staff, the son of Grant, and Mr. Nicolay, the President's private secretary. On the twelfth of that month there was a grand military banquet at the White House in honor of the Lieutenant-General.

CHAPTER XVIII.

NOMINATION AND RE-ELECTION OF LINCOLN, AND THE ELECTION OF ANDREW JOHNSON TO THE VICE-PRESIDENCY — THE SECOND INAUGURATION — COLORED MEN FOR THE FIRST TIME IN THE PROCESSION — SERENADE SPEECHES — PUBLIC REJOICINGS — THE ASSASSINATION — THE PARTICULARS CONCERNING IT — A NIGHT OF HORRORS, ETC.

THE Republican National Convention renominated Mr. Lincoln for the Presidency on the 8th of June, 1864, at Baltimore, and Mr. Andrew Johnson, for the Vice-Presidency.

Despatches were sent to the President, announcing the fact, but he was absent from his official room in the Executive Mansion at the time, and therefore did not see them. Some two or three hours afterward, still ignorant of his own nomination, he called at the War Department, and there accidentally saw a despatch announcing the nomination of Andrew Johnson for Vice-President. He expressed his surprise at "the curious action of the Convention," as it seemed to him that the Convention "got the cart before the horse." He was asked by a telegraph operator whether he had seen a despatch announcing his own nomination for the Presidency. On saying he had not, he was informed that the despatch had been sent to him at the White House. He then explained that probably his absence from his office was the reason of his not having seen it. On his return to the Executive Mansion, he found the despatch.

The President, the next day, was serenaded in honor of his renomination; and in the course of the brief speech of thanks which he made, said: "What we want more than the Baltimore Convention, is success under Grant."

The election of November resulted in choosing him for a second term.

Abraham Lincoln, for President, and Andrew Johnson, for Vice-President, received two hundred and twelve electoral votes.

George B. McClellan, for President, and George H. Pendleton, for Vice-President, twenty-one electoral votes, namely, those of New Jersey, Delaware, and Kentucky.

In March, 1865, Hugh M'Culloch was appointed Secretary of the Treasury, vice Fessenden, resigned.

There was a fall of rain with hail on the 4th of March, 1865. As soon as the sun came out, the crowds on the principal thoroughfare began to thicken.

Mr. Lincoln did not occupy the position assigned him in the carriage, (third in the procession,) as he had been at the Capitol during the entire morning, engaged in signing bills. Mrs. Lincoln, accompanied by Senators Harlan and Anthony, was driven to the head of the line, and preceded the procession to the Capitol. A platoon of marshals pioneered the carriage of Mrs. Lincoln, the escort being composed of the

Union Light Guard. The crowd generally mistook the carriage of the President's wife for that of the President, and under this delusion cheered it all along the route.

The procession moved to the sound of cannon and the clangor of the bells.

First came artillery and cavalry, next the corporate authorities, civic societies; the Washington Fire Department escorted a deputation of their Philadelphia brethren; the fire-engines, trucks, and hose-carriages, being decorated with flags and wreaths of flowers. Prominent in the procession was a moving platform, bearing a structure representing the temple of Liberty, drawn by four horses, the several States typified by ladies. The model of a monitor was elevated on a platform, drawn by four white horses; sailors fired miniature cannon from the turrets. Following these were civic societies, the Republican Campaign Club, with insignia and banners; a company of veteran reserves; a printing-press in operation, mounted on a platform, and drawn by four bay-horses; two companies of colored troops, a lodge of colored Odd-Fellows in regalia, (this was the first appearance of colored men in a Presidential procession,) and the Giesboro Cavalry.

At all the street-corners, squads of horsemen were stationed, and a large police force kept the crowds in order.

In the Senate chamber were members of Congress, Vice-Admiral Farragut, Major-Generals Banks and

Hooker, the diplomatic corps, governors and ex-governors of States and Territories, the mayors of Washington and Georgetown, Heads of Departments, officers who had received the thanks of Congress, Judges of the Supreme Court, and many others of prominence.

When the procession reached the Capitol, President Lincoln was escorted into the Senate chamber, when Andrew Johnson took the oath of office, and delivered an address.

A procession was formed of those in the chamber, and it proceeded to the eastern portico, where President Lincoln delivered his second Inaugural Address, in which occurred these memorable words: "With malice toward none, with charity for all, — with firmness in the right as God gives us to see the right, let us finish the work we are in, to bind up the nation's wounds, to care for him who shall have borne the battle, and for his widow and his orphans; to do all which may achieve and cherish a just and lasting peace among ourselves and with all nations."

The oath of office was administered by Chief-Justice Chase.

At the conclusion of the ceremonies, a salute was fired, the band struck up "Hail to the Chief," and the thousands in attendance greeted the President with repeated huzzas.

The President was escorted back to the Executive Mansion, where he was welcomed by a multitude of friends.

On the Monday following there was a grand inauguration ball at the Patent Office, which was attended by the President and his wife.

President Lincoln, accompanied by Mrs. Lincoln, Senators Harlan and Sumner, and others, paid a visit to City Point early in April. While there, the President passed through the wards of the several hospitals, giving a word of comfort to the invalids. He looked feeble, and was, for this reason, met with a remonstrance from all the surgeons in charge for attempting the hand-shaking of several thousand of men; but, in answer, he said, "Gentlemen, the war seems about over, and I must shake the hand of and say a good word to every brave fellow who has aided in the glorious work."

Secretary Stanton, on the 9th of April, officially announced the surrender of General Lee; and, in accordance with his order, a salute of two hundred guns was fired at the head-quarters of every army department, and post and arsenal in the United States, and at the military academy, West Point, on the day of the receipt of the order.

President Lincoln, finding Petersburg evacuated, passed to that city, thence to Richmond in a row-boat, in company with Farragut and Porter. He met with a hearty greeting from his friends. After sitting for some minutes in the reception-room, which ten days before had been thronged with visitors to the fugitive Confederate President, he passed to other places of interest.

My readers will recollect the feelings of joy with

which they heard the good news, and with what demonstrations the dawn of peace was celebrated.

Mr. Lincoln returned to Washington on the 10th of April. A large crowd gathered at the White House, and called him out for a speech. When he appeared, he was greeted with repeated cheers. He stood at a hoisted window of the second story, clothed in a new suit of black. I had never before seen him so quietly happy, as he complacently surveyed the throng before him.

It seemed that his tall form had received an additional foot of stature. The band played "Hail to the Chief," the President deeply appreciative of the musical compliment thus bestowed. At last he said:

"I am very greatly rejoiced that an occasion has occurred, so pleasurable that the people can't restrain themselves. (Laughter and cheers.) I suppose arrangements are being made for a formal demonstration, to-night or to-morrow night. (Cries of "We can't wait.") I shall have to respond. I shall have nothing to say then, if I dribble it all out before. (Laughter.) I see you have a band of music with you. (A cry, "We have two bands.") I propose, for closing up, that you will have them play the air called "Dixie." ("Agreed.") I have always thought it was the best tune I ever heard. Our adversaries over the way have attempted to appropriate it as their own national air. I insisted, yesterday, that we had fairly captured it, and are entitled to it. I asked the opinion of the Attorney-General, and he states that we have lawfully captured it, and that it was therefore ours. I now request the band to play it." (Cheers.)

The band then played "Dixie." The President proposed "three good, rousing cheers for Lieutenant-General Grant and all under his command."

The proposition was responded to "with a will." The President then proposed three more cheers for our gallant navy. The crowd responded as heartily as before, when the President bowed and retired. The crowd dispersed, moving away in different directions, to call upon other officers of the Government.

General Butler made a speech near Willard's Hotel to a delighted crowd.

In the afternoon of the same day, between four and five o'clock, several hundred persons gathered before the Executive Mansion. Frequent calls were made for the President, who appeared merely to say, if the company had assembled by appointment, some mistake had crept into their understanding. He had appeared before a larger audience than this one to-day, and would now repeat what he then said, namely: he supposed that, owing to the good news, there would be some demonstration,—he would prefer to-morrow evening,—when he should be quite willing, and, he hoped, ready to say something. He desired to be particular, because everything he said got into print. (Laughter.) Occupying the position he did, a mistake would produce harm, and therefore he wanted to be careful not to make a mistake. (A voice: "You have not made any yet.")

The President, as he retired, was repeatedly cheered.

The next night an immense concourse of people gathered in front of the Executive Mansion, and he made them a speech, commencing by saying: —

"We meet this evening, not in sorrow, but in gladness of heart. The evacuation of Petersburg and Richmond, and the surrender of the principal insurgent army, give hopes of a righteous and speedy peace, when joyous expressions cannot be restrained. In the midst of this, however, 'He from whom all blessings flow,' must not be forgotten. A call for a national thanksgiving is being prepared, and will be duly proclaimed. Nor must those whose harder part gives us the occasion of rejoicing be overlooked. Their honor must not be parcelled out with others. I myself was near the front, and had the pleasure of transmitting much of the good news to you. But no part of this honor, for plan or execution, is mine. To Grant, his skilful officers and brave men, all belongs. The gallant navy stood ready, but was not in reach to take an active part."

He then proceeded to speak of the movement, already begun, to reorganize Louisiana, remarking in that connection, "Concede that the new government there is only to what it should be, as the egg is to the fowl — we should sooner have the fowl by hatching the egg, than by smashing it."

Senator Harlan was called for, and made a short speech, expressing the opinion that treason should be punished, and saying that he was willing to trust the future in the hands of the citizen elected to a second term, to see that the laws were faithfully executed.

The speech of Mr. Lincoln was read from his own manuscript — foolscap pages. It was written in a remarkably plain style, with a firm hand, and well punctuated. Only one word was misspelled, and that was "collateral," the President using only one *l* but two *t*'s.

Mr. Lincoln's little son, Thad., held a candle for him while he read. The members of his household occupied the adjacent windows to listen to him.

On the 13th of April there was a general illumination throughout the city, in commemoration of the Union victories, and the prospect of general peace.

This rejoicing, however, was soon turned to sorrow.

On the night of the 14th of April, I was sitting in my office alone, everything quiet: and having filed, as I thought, my last despatch, I picked up an afternoon paper, to see what especial news it contained. While looking over its columns, a hasty step was heard at the entrance of the door, and a gentleman addressed me, in a hurried and excited manner, informing me that the President had been assassinated, and telling me to come with him! I at first could scarcely believe the intelligence. But I obeyed the summons. He had been to the theatre with a lady, and directly after the tragedy at that place, had brought out the lady, placed her at his side in his carriage, and driven directly to me. I then first went to the telegraph office, sent a short "special," and promised soon to give the particulars. Taking a seat in the hack, we drove back to the theatre and alighted; the gentleman giving directions to the driver to convey the lady to her home.

The gentleman and myself procured an entrance to

the theatre, where we found everybody in great excitement. The wounded President had been removed to the house of Mr. Peterson, who lived nearly opposite to the theatre. When we reached the box, we saw the chair in which the President sat at the time of the assassination; and, although the gas had for the greater part been turned off, we discovered blood upon it. A man standing by picked up Booth's pistol from the floor, when I exclaimed to the crowd below that the weapon had been found and placed in my possession. An officer of the navy — whose name I do not now remember — demanded that I should give it to him; but this I refused to do, preferring to make Major Richards, the head of the police, the custodian of the weapon, which I did soon after my announcement. My friend having been present during the performance, and being a valuable source of news, I held him firmly by the arm, for fear that I might lose him in the crowd. After gathering all the points we could, we came out of the theatre, when we heard that Secretary Seward had also been assassinated. I recollect replying that this rumor probably was an echo from the theatre; but wishing to be satisfied as to its truth or falsity, I called a hack, and my companion and myself drove to the Secretary's residence. We found a guard at the door, but had little trouble in entering the house. Some of the neighbors were there, but they were so much excited that they could not tell an intelligent story, and the colored boy, by whom Paine was met when he insisted on going up to the Secretary's room, was scarcely able to talk. We did all we could to get at the truth of the story, and when we left the premises, had confused ideas of the events of the night. Next we went to the President's house. A military guard was at the door. It was then, for the first time, we learned that the President had not been brought home. Vague rumors were in circulation that attempts had been made on the lives of Vice-President Johnson and others, but they could not be traced to a reliable source. We returned to Mr. Peterson's house, but were not permitted to make our way through the military guard to inquire into the condition of the President. Nor at that time was it certainly known who was the assassin of President Lincoln. Some few persons said he resembled Booth, while others appeared to be confident as to the identity.

Returning to the office, I commenced writing a full account of that night's dread occurrences. While thus engaged, several gentlemen who had been at the theatre came in, and, by questioning them, I obtained additional particulars. Among my visitors was Speaker Colfax, and as he was going to see Mr. Lincoln, I asked him to give me a paragraph on that interesting branch of the subject. At a subsequent hour, he did so. Meanwhile I carefully wrote my despatch, though with trembling and nervous fingers, and, under all the exciting circumstances, I was afterward surprised that I had succeeded in approximating so closely to all the facts in those dark transactions. The telegram is as follows:

"WASHINGTON, April 14.

"President Lincoln and wife, with other friends, this evening visited Ford's Theatre, for the purpose of witnessing the performance of the 'American Cousin.'

"It was announced in the papers that General Grant would be present. But that gentleman took the late train of cars for New Jersey.

"The theatre was densely crowded, and everybody seemed delighted with the scene before them. During the third act, and while there was a temporary pause for one of the actors to enter, a sharp report of a pistol was heard, which merely attracted attention, but suggesting nothing serious, until a man rushed to the front of the President's box, waving a long dagger in his right hand, and exclaiming, '*Sic semper tyrannis,*' and immediately leaped from the box, which was in the second tier, to the stage beneath, and ran across to the opposite side, making his escape, amid the bewilderment of the audience, from the rear of the theatre, and mounting a horse, fled.

"The screams of Mrs. Lincoln first disclosed the fact to the audience that the President had been shot; when all present rose to their feet, rushed toward the stage, many exclaiming, 'Hang him! hang him!'

"The excitement was of the wildest possible description, and of course there was an abrupt termination of the theatrical performance.

"There was a rush toward the President's box, when cries were heard, 'Stand back and give him air!' 'Has any one stimulants?' On a hasty examination, it was found that the President had been shot through the head, above and back of the temporal bone, and that some of the brain was oozing out. He was removed to a private house opposite to the theatre, and the Surgeon-General of the Army, and other surgeons, were sent for to attend to his condition.

"On an examination of the private box, blood was discovered on the back of the cushioned chair in which the President had been sitting; also on the partition, and on the floor. A common single-barrelled pocket-pistol was found on the carpet.

"A military guard was placed in front of the private residence to which the President had been conveyed. An immense crowd was in front of it, all deeply anxious to learn the condition of the President. It had been previously announced that the wound was mortal, but all hoped otherwise. The shock to the community was terrible.

"At midnight the Cabinet went thither. Messrs. Sumner, Colfax, and Farnsworth; Judge Curtis, Governor Oglesby, General Meigs, Colonel Hay, and a few personal friends, with Surgeon-General Barnes and his immediate assistants were around his bedside. The President was in a state of syncope, totally insensible, and breathing slowly. The blood oozed from the wound at the back of his head.

"The surgeons exhausted every possible effort of medical skill, but all hope was gone!

"The parting of his family with the dying President is too sad for description. The President and Mrs. Lincoln did not start for the theatre until fifteen minutes after eight o'clock. Speaker Colfax was at the White House at the time, and the President stated to him that he was going, although Mrs. Lincoln had not been well, because the papers had announced that General Grant and they were to be present, and, as General Grant had gone North, he did not wish the audience to be disappointed.

"He went to the theatre with apparent reluctance, and urged Mr. Colfax to accompany him; but that gentleman had made other engagements, and with Mr. Ashmun, of Massachusetts, bade him good-bye.

"When the excitement at the theatre was at its wildest height, reports were circulated that Secretary Seward had also been assassinated."

"REPORTED ASSASSINATION OF MR. SEWARD.—On reaching this gentleman's residence, a crowd and military guard were found at the door, and on entering, it was ascertained that the reports were true.

"Everybody there was so excited, that scarcely an intelligible word could be gathered; but the facts are substantially as follows: —

"About ten o'clock, a man rang the bell, and the call having been answered by a colored servant, he said he had come from Doctor Verdi, Secretary Seward's family physician, with a prescription, at the same time holding in his hand a small piece of folded paper, and saying in answer to a refusal, that he must see the Secretary, as he was intrusted with particular directions concerning the medicine. He still insisted on going up, although repeatedly informed that no one could enter the chamber. The man pushed the servant aside, and walked heavily toward the Secretary's room, and was then met by Mr. Frederick W. Seward, of whom he demanded to see the Secretary, making the same representation which he did to the servant. What further passed in the way of colloquy is not known, but the man struck him on the head with a billy, severely injuring the skull, and felling him to the floor almost senseless. The assassin then rushed into the chamber and attacked Major Seward, Paymaster United States Army, and Mr. Hansell, a messenger of the State Department, and two male nurses, disabling them all. He then rushed upon the Secretary, who was lying in bed in the same room, and inflicted three stabs in the neck, but severing, it is thought and hoped, no arteries, though he bled profusely. The assassin then rushed down-stairs, mounted his horse at the door, and rode off before an alarm could be sounded, and in the same manner as the assassin of the President.

"It is believed that the injuries of the Secretary are not fatal, nor those of either of the others, although both the Secretary and the Assistant Secretary are very seriously injured.

"Secretaries Stanton and Welles, and other prominent officers of the Government, called at Secretary Seward's house, to inquire into his condition, and there, for the first time, heard of the assassination of the President. They then proceeded to the house where he was lying, exhibiting, of course, intense anxiety and solicitude. An immense crowd was gathered in front of the President's house, and a strong guard was also stationed there, many persons supposing that he would be brought to his home.

"The entire city to-night presents a scene of wild excitement accompanied by violent expressions of indignation and the profoundest sorrow. Many shed tears. The military authorities have dispatched mounted patrols in every direction, in order, if possible, to arrest the assassins. The whole metropolitan police are likewise vigilant for the same purpose.

"The attacks, both at the theatre and at Secretary Seward's house, took place at about the same hour, ten o'clock, thus showing a preconcerted plan to assassinate those gentlemen. Some evidences of the guilt of the party who attacked the President are in possession of the police. Vice-President Johnson is in this city, and his headquarters are guarded by troops."

It was subsequently ascertained that when the assassin (Booth) jumped from the theatre-box to the stage, his spur struck the frame of a portrait of Washington, used as a decoration beneath the balustrade of the box, and also tore the festooned national flag. Lower down, his spur scraped the ledge of the stage-box beneath.

I can never forget the alarm and horror of that night. The streets were crowded with persons, talking over the startling and shocking events. It was feared that a wide-extended conspiracy existed, and it was not known where the stroke would next fall. Thousands of persons feared to retire to their beds. Meantime, military guards were stationed throughout the city, and mounted patrols were rapidly in motion. Reports were constantly made to head-quarters, to keep the authorities fully advised of all movements.

Secretary Stanton addressed Major-General Dix, New York, a telegram, dated Washington, April 15, 1.30 A. M., in which he said:

"Last evening, about 9.30 P. M., at Ford's Theatre, the President, while sitting in a private box with Mrs. Lincoln, Mrs. Harris, and Major Rathbun, was shot by an assassin, who suddenly entered the box, and approached behind the President. The assassin then leaped upon the stage, brandishing a large dagger or knife, and made his escape in the rear of the theatre. The pistol-ball entered the back of the President's head, and penetrated nearly through. The wound is mortal. The President has been insensible ever since the wound was inflicted, and is now dying. About the same time — it is not known whether it was the same or not — an assassin entered Mr. Seward's apartments, and, under pretence of having a prescription, was shown to his chamber. The assassin immediately rushed to the bed, and inflicted two or three stabs on the throat and two or three on the face. It is hoped his wounds may not prove mortal. My apprehension is, that they will prove fatal. The noise alarmed Mr. Frederick Seward, who was in an adjoining room; he hastened to the door of his father's room, when he met the assassin, who inflicted upon him one or more dangerous wounds. The recovery of Frederick Seward is doubtful. It is not probable the President will live through the night. General Grant and wife were advertised to be at the theatre this evening, but he started for Burlington at six o'clock this evening. At a Cabinet meeting, at which General Grant was present, the subject of the state of the country, and prospect of a speedy peace, were discussed. The President was cheerful and hopeful, and spoke very kindly of Lee and others of the Confederacy, and of the establishment of the Government in Virginia. All the members of the Cabinet, except Seward, are now in attendance on the President. I have seen Mr. Seward, but he and Frederick are both unconscious."

Secretaries Stanton and Welles, and other prominent officers of the Government, called at Secretary Seward's, to inquire as to his condition.

At the time of the attempted assassination of Mr. Seward, he was an invalid, having met with an accident on the 5th of April, the particulars of which are as follows:—

He was about to start from his house for a drive, accompanied by his son Frederick, Miss Fanny, his daughter, and Miss Titus, of Auburn. The door of the carriage being open, Mr. Seward ordered the driver to close it. The driver dismounted from his box, and with the reins in one hand he slammed the door with the other. The horses became restive, and started as the driver resumed his seat. He again jumped off and attempted to hold them. Mr. Frederick W. Seward leaped from the carriage to assist the driver, but fell to the ground, and was unable to seize the reins. The horses ran round a corner swinging the driver, who still tightly held the reins. The horses went on madly, and before they "got to the top of their speed," the Secretary jumped from the carriage, evidently thinking that he could maintain his footing, but he violently fell to the ground upon his right side, breaking his arm close to the shoulder-joint, terribly bruising his face, and breaking his jaw-bone. He was insensible when carried to his home, where it was discovered that he was also injured internally. Meanwhile, the ladies, with remarkable presence of mind, remained in the carriage. Miss Seward had remonstrated against her father's getting out. The horses were forced into an alley and driven against a brick wall, when the ladies quickly alighted, and the horses, "brought to their senses," ran into a stable.

Secretary Seward was soon visited by the members of the Cabinet and other prominent gentlemen. Mr. Frederick Seward had but recently recovered from a broken arm, caused by a fall from a carriage.

On the morning of the 15th of April, at twenty-two minutes after seven o'clock, Secretary Stanton telegraphed to Major-General Dix that the President had just died, and that there was evidence to show that J. Wilkes Booth was the murderer.

During that forenoon, official notice was given to Vice-President Johnson by the Heads of the Departments, when he appeared before Chief-Justice Chase, took the oath of office, and assumed the functions of the Presidency.

CHAPTER XIX.

THE PRESIDENCY OF ANDREW JOHNSON — HIS ADDRESS ON ASSUMING THE OFFICE — HIS POLICY — PREPARATION FOR THE FUNERAL OF MR. LINCOLN — THE OBSEQUIES AT THE EXECUTIVE MANSION — THE JOURNEY WITH THE REMAINS TO OAK RIDGE CEMETERY, NEAR SPRINGFIELD, ILLINOIS — THE VOICE FROM THE TOMB, ETC.

AT twelve o'clock the President met the Heads of the Departments in Cabinet meeting, at the Treasury building. Among the business, the making of arrangements for the funeral of the late President was referred to the several Cabinet officers.

The President formally announced that he desired to retain the present Cabinet, and requested them to discharge their respective duties in the same manner as before the deplorable event that had changed the head of the Government.

All business in the Departments was suspended for the day.

President Johnson made a brief speech, saying, he was almost overwhelmed by the announcement of the sad event. He felt incompetent to perform the duties, so important and responsible as those which had been so unexpectedly thrown upon him. As an indication of any policy, which might be pursued by him in the administration of the Government, he had to say that must be left for development as the administration progressed. The message or declaration must be made by the acts as they appear. The course which he had taken in the past, in connection with the rebellion, must be regarded as a guarantee of the future.

He then received the good wishes of all who were present.

On the morning of the death of Mr. Lincoln, his remains were removed to the Executive Mansion. Very soon the columns of the portico were draped in black, as was also the exterior of all the public buildings. Carpenters and costumers were employed to arrange the East Room, and it was not until the next day that their work was completed. The decorations were tasteful; the dark hangings imparting the gloom of a vault, into which that splendid and capacious room had been converted for a brief season. The silver trimmings and white satin embellishments contrasted in good taste with the general design. As well as I can recollect, the catafalque was an open canopy of alpaca, lined with satin of a creamish hue, looped at the curving roof, and drooping to the four corners. Beneath the roof the dim light fell on a stage of fresh, fragrant flowers. The high coffin was covered with black, trimmed with pure silver lace. The plate, nails, hinges, and emblazonings were of silver. A cross of lilies stood at the head, and an anchor of roses at the foot. The lid of the coffin was thrown back to show the face and bosom of the deceased. On the coffin-top were precious flowers and sprigs of green. A view of the features of the honored dead was obtained by ascending the raised steps of the catafalque.

The watchers were several general army officers and staff captains.

On the morning of the funeral, thousands of persons resorted to the White House premises. In order to prevent confusion and overcrowding, tickets of admission were issued to the East Room. There assembled the new President and the Cabinet, (with the exception of Mr. Seward,) chiefs of bureaus, officers of the army and the navy, governors of States, foreign Ministers, members of Congress, and others of distinction. Mrs. Lincoln's relatives were present, namely: Dr. Lyman Beecher Todd, General John B. S. Todd, C. M. Smith, and N. W. Edwards, the late President's brother-in-law; also Captain Robert Lincoln and "little Tad" Lincoln, his sons. Mrs. Lincoln did not enter the East Room, or follow the remains.

It was a deeply interesting spectacle. Here was the murdered President, surrounded by the highest officers of our land and by the representatives of the principal nations of the world. All hearts were naturally bowed with sorrow, and stricken with grief.

Bishop Simpson made the prayer, a chapter from the Bible was read, and then the Rev. P. D. Gurley delivered the funeral address.

The solemn ceremonies concluded, a procession was formed and escorted the remains to the rotunda of the Capitol, bells meantime tolling. In the cortege was Mr. Lincoln's favorite horse, an athletic, spirited animal.

The houses on the line of Pennsylvania Avenue, and others throughout the city, were draped in mourning.

The next day we started on the journey to Springfield, with the remains of Mr. Lincoln, stopping at various cities on the route. Everywhere the people manifested their respect, not only by emblems of mourning, including shrouded flags and portraits, and appropriate inscriptions selected from Mr. Lincoln's addresses, but by funeral arches, and groupings of ladies to represent the States of the Union mourning for their loss.

There was not more generosity displayed in this than in the profuse hospitality of the citizens of the country through which we passed. The escort, in part, included Governor Oglesby and suite, and other governors, and prominent officers of the army and navy. The guard directly in charge of the corpse was composed of officers of the Invalid Corps. At cities where we stopped for a day, or a night, the coffin rested under magnificently festooned canopies, State and municipal authorities seeming to be in rivalry as to which should make the best outward demonstration.

Much of our travelling was at night, throughout which, no matter at what hour, crowds gathered on the roads to see the train on its onward progress; and whenever we halted, flowers were brought into the funeral car, and placed upon the coffin by the delicate hands which had culled them for this purpose. It would have been impossible to render greater honors to any mortal remains. The funeral was continuous from Washington to Oak Ridge Cemetery, near Springfield, Illinois. At places where we tarried for a day or a night, the coffin was always removed to its temporary resting-place under military arrangement, accompanied by funeral dirges. The face exposed to public view, countless thousands looked upon it, though but for a few moments in the passing throng. Those who had never seen Mr. Lincoln in life, now saw him in the stern and shuddering reality of death.

On the 26th of April, Secretary Stanton telegraphed to Major-General Dix that Booth and Harold were pursued into Maryland, chased into a swamp, from St. Mary's county to Garnett's farm. The barn in which they took refuge was fired. Booth endeavored to make his escape, but was shot, by Sergeant Boston Corbett, in the head, while holding in his hand a six-barrelled revolver, and died after lingering three hours. And the next day he telegraphed to the same gentleman, that Booth's body, and Harold who had surrendered, were both in Washington.

We were at Buffalo when we received this intelligence.

Arriving at Springfield, the corpse was placed in the Capitol, where, as at other places on the route, the greatest care was taken of it, and abundant hospitalities extended to those who had accompanied it from Washington.

It was here that the embalmer soldered on the lid, thus closing from scrutiny, forever, the features of one so familiar in that city. The face had considerably withered, the flesh adhering closely to the bones, and the skin had turned dark. This might have been owing, in part, to the exposure, as it was unprotected from the atmosphere on the way to Springfield.

A procession was formed in that city, and the remains escorted to the grave.

I had seen the President when he had just returned to Washington from Virginia, at the time of Lee's surrender; I had heard him make his speeches of rejoicing on the termination of the war; and now I was privileged to witness the final obsequies. I saw the coffin removed to the vault, near the door of which I stood, while the pall-bearers placed it in position — in that gloomy recess, which had been tastefully and appropriately decorated.

Bishop Simpson delivered the address; and there was solemn music, the words composed to accord with the occasion. Prayer followed, and the Rev. Mr. Hubbard, as a part of the programme, read Mr. Lincoln's last Inaugural Address, in clear and distinct tones, and with proper feeling and emphasis. The door of the vault stood open, and, while the reading was progressing, it seemed that the voice came from that tomb! This was one of the most impressive features of the day. A dirge and the benediction closed the ceremonies.

We had followed the remains of President Lincoln from Washington, the scene of the assassination, to Springfield, his former home, and now to be his final resting-place. He had been absent from that city ever since he left it in February, 1861, for the National

Capital, to be inaugurated as President of the United States. We had seen him lying in state, in the Executive Mansion, where the obsequies were attended by numerous mourners, some of them clothed with the highest public honors and responsibilities which our Republican institutions can bestow, and by the diplomatic representatives of foreign governments.

We had followed the remains from Washington, through Baltimore, Harrisburg, Philadelphia, New York, Albany, Buffalo, Cleveland, Columbus, Indianapolis, and Chicago, to Springfield, a distance, circuitously, of from fifteen hundred to eighteen hundred miles. On the route, millions of people had appeared to manifest, by every means of which they were capable, the deep sense of the public loss, and their appreciation of the many virtues which adorned the character of Abraham Lincoln. All classes, without distinction of politics, spontaneously united in the posthumous honors; all hearts seemed to beat as one at the bereavement. The funeral processions ended with our duty of escorting the mortal remains of Abraham Lincoln to Oak Ridge Cemetery. We saw them deposited in the tomb. The bereaved friends, with tearful eyes and grief-stricken hearts, turned their faces homeward, ever to remember the affecting and impressive scenes which they had witnessed. The injunction, so often repeated on the way, "Bear him gently to his rest," had been obeyed; and the great heart of the Nation throbbed heavily at the portal of the tomb.

CHAPTER XX.

PRESIDENT JOHNSON'S OFFICE TEMPORARILY IN THE TREASURY DEPARTMENT — REJECTION BY HIM OF A PRESENT — THE TRIAL OF THE CONSPIRATORS — THE TESTIMONY SHOWING WHAT TOOK PLACE IN THE STAGE BOX AT THE TIME OF THE ASSASSINATION, AND THE SCENE AT THE HOUSE OF SECRETARY SEWARD — RECOVERY OF THE SECRETARY AND HIS SON FREDERICK — DEATH OF MRS. SEWARD — TRIAL AND CONVICTION OF WIRZ, THE ANDERSONVILLE JAILER — JOHN H. SURRATT, ETC.

MRS. LINCOLN continuing in occupation of the White House, where she remained for some weeks, President Johnson transacted business and received visitors at his rooms in the Treasury Department.

To that place numerous delegations resorted to tender their regret at the event which had thrown the nation into mourning, and to express their best wishes for a prosperous and happy administration of affairs.

During the month of May, 1865, a number of prominent citizens of New York wrote President Johnson a letter, proposing to present to him a span of horses as a token of their appreciation of his fidelity to his country; but he declined to receive them, saying in reply, solely from conviction, that it was improper in those occupying high official position to receive presents. He nevertheless expressed his thanks to his kind and loyal friends for their good intentions.

On the 1st of May, 1866, the President issued an executive order, commencing with a recitation of the Attorney-General's opinion that the persons implicated in the murder of the late President Lincoln, and the attempted assassination of the Honorable William H. Seward, Secretary of State, and in an alleged conspiracy to assassinate other officers of the Federal Government at Washington, and their aiders and abettors, were subject to the jurisdiction of and lawfully triable before a military commission, and ordering the trial to take place.

The commission met at the Washington Arsenal on Monday the 8th of May.

The charge against David E. Harold, George A. Atzerodt, Lewis Paine, Michael O'Laughlin, Edward Spangler, Samuel Arnold, Mary E. Surratt, and Samuel A. Mudd, was as follows:

"*Charge.* — For maliciously, unlawfully, and traitorously, and in aid of the existing armed rebellion against the United States of America, on or before the 6th of March, A. D. 1865, combining, confederating, and conspiring together with one John H. Surratt, John Wilkes Booth, Jefferson Davis, George N. Sanders, Beverley Tucker, Jacob Thompson, William C. Cleary, Clement C. Clay, George Harper, George Young, and others unknown, to kill and murder, within the Military Department of Washington, and within the intrenched lines thereof, Abraham Lincoln, late, and at the time of said combining, confederating, and conspiring, President of the United States of America, and commander-in-chief of the army and navy thereof; Andrew Johnson, now Vice-President of the

United States aforesaid; William H. Seward, Secretary of State of the United States aforesaid, and Ulysses S. Grant, Lieutenant-General of the army of the United States aforesaid; then in command of the armies of the United States, under the direction of the said Abraham Lincoln; and in pursuance of and in prosecuting said malicious, unlawful, and traitorous conspiracy aforesaid, and in aid of said rebellion, afterward, to wit: On the 14th day of April, A. D. 1865, within the Military Department of Washington, aforesaid, and within the fortified and intrenched lines of said military department, together with said John Wilkes Booth, and John H. Surratt, maliciously, unlawfully, and traitorously murder the said Abraham Lincoln, the President of the United States and commander-in-chief of the army and navy of the United States as aforesaid; and maliciously, unlawfully, and traitorously assaulting, with intent to kill and murder, the said William H. Seward, then Secretary of State of the United States, as aforesaid; and lying in wait with intent maliciously, unlawfully, and traitorously to kill and murder the said Andrew Johnson, then being Vice-President of the United States; and the said Ulysses S. Grant, then being Lieutenant-General, and in command of the armies of the United States, as aforesaid."

Then followed the specifications—signed by order of the President of the United States, J. Holt, Judge-Advocate-General.

The accused were arraigned on the 12th of May, and severally pleaded "not guilty" to the charge and specification.

Three hundred and thirty-nine witnesses were examined on this trial.

Mr. Henry Clay Ford, the treasurer of Ford's Theatre, testified that he was the treasurer of the establishment. When he returned from breakfast, about half-past eleven o'clock on the 14th of April, his brother, James R. Ford, told him that the President had engaged a box for that night. John Wilkes Booth was at the theatre about half an hour afterward. He did not know that the fact of the President's going to the theatre that night was communicated to Booth, but he thought it was very likely he found it out while there.

Major Henry R. Rathbone gave the following testimony: "On the evening of the 14th of April last, at about twenty minutes past eight o'clock, I, in company with Miss Harris, left my residence, and joined the President and Mrs. Lincoln, and went with them in their carriage to Ford's Theatre. On reaching the theatre, when the presence of the President became known, the actors stopped playing, and the band struck up 'Hail to the Chief,' and the audience rose and received him with vociferous cheering. The party proceeded along in the rear of the dress-circle, and entered the box that had been set apart for their reception. On entering the box, there was a large arm-chair, that was placed nearest the audience, farthest from the stage, which the President took and occupied during the whole of the evening, with one exception, when he got up to put on his coat, and returned and sat down again. When the second scene of the third act was being performed, and while I was intently observing the proceedings upon the stage, with my back toward the door, I heard the discharge of a pistol behind me, and, looking round, saw through the smoke a man between the door and the President. The distance from the door to where the President sat was about four feet. At the same time I heard the man shout some word, which I thought was 'Freedom.' I instantly sprang toward him and seized him. He wrested himself from my grasp, and made a violent thrust at my breast with a large knife. I parried the blow by striking it up, and received a wound several inches deep in my left arm, between the elbow and the shoulder. The orifice of the wound was about an inch and a half in length, and extended upward toward the shoulder several inches. The man rushed to the front of the box, and I endeavored to seize him again, but only caught his clothes as he was leaping over the railing of the box. The clothes, as I believe, were torn in the attempt to hold him. As he went over upon the stage, I cried out, 'Stop that man.' I then turned to the President: his position was not changed, his head was slightly bent forward, and his eyes were closed. I saw that he was unconscious, and supposing him mortally wounded, rushed to the door for the purpose of calling medical aid. On reaching the outer door of the passage-way, I found it barred by a heavy piece of plank, one end of which was secured in the wall, and the other resting against the door. It had been so securely fastened that it required considerable force to remove it. This wedge or bar was about four feet from the floor. Persons upon the outside were beating against the door for the purpose of entering. I removed the bar, and the door was opened. Several persons, who represented themselves as surgeons, were allowed to enter. I saw there Colonel Crawford, and requested him to prevent other persons from entering the box. I then returned to the box and found the surgeons examining the President's person. They had not yet discovered the wound. As soon as it was discovered, it was determined to remove him from the theatre. He was carried out, and I then proceeded to assist Mrs. Lincoln, who was intensely excited, to leave the theatre. On reaching the head of the stairs, I requested Major Potter to aid me in assisting Mrs. Lincoln across the street to the house where the President was being conveyed. The wound which I had received had been bleeding very profusely, and on reaching the house, feeling very faint from the loss of blood, I seated myself in the hall, and soon after fainted away, and was laid upon the floor. Upon the return of consciousness, I was taken to my residence. In a review of the transactions it is my confident belief, that the time which elapsed between the discharge of the pistol and the time when the assassin leaped from the box, did not exceed thirty seconds. Neither Mrs. Lincoln nor Miss Harris had left their seats."

A bowie-knife, with a heavy seven-inch blade, was exhibited to the witness, stains of blood still being upon the blade. He said this knife might have made a wound similar to the one he received. "The assassin held the blade in a horizontal position, I think, and the nature of the wound would indicate it: it came down with a sweeping blow from above."

The following is from the testimony relative to the occurrences at Secretary Seward's house:

Sergeant George F. Robinson said: "On the 14th of April I was at the residence of Mr. Seward, Secretary of State, acting as attendant nurse to Mr. Seward, who was confined to his bed by injuries received from having been thrown from his carriage. One of his arms was broken, and his jaw fractured. That man (pointing to the accused, Lewis Payne) looks like the man that came to Mr. Seward's house on that Friday night. I heard a disturbance in the hall, and opened the door to see what the trouble was; and as I opened the door, this man stood up close to it. As soon as it was opened, he struck me with a knife in the forehead, knocked me partially down, and passed by me to the bed of Mr. Seward, and struck him, wounding him. As soon as I could get on my feet, I endeavored to haul him off the bed, and then he turned upon me. In the scuffle, some one (Major Seward) came into the room and clinched him. Between the two of us, we got him to the door, or by the door, and he, unclinching his hands from around my neck, struck me again, this time with his fist, knocking me down, and then broke away from Major Seward, and ran down-stairs. I saw him strike Mr. Seward with the same knife with which he cut my forehead. It was a large knife, and he held it with the blade down, below his hand. I saw him cut Mr. Seward twice — that I am sure of; the first time he struck him on the right cheek, and then he seemed to be cutting around his neck. I did not hear the man say anything during this time. I afterward examined the wounds, and found one cutting his face from the right cheek down to the neck, and a cut on his neck, which might have been made by the same blow, as Mr. Seward was partially sitting in bed at the time; and another on the left side of the neck. Those were all I noticed, but there may have been more, as it was all bloody when I saw it. Mr. Seward received all his stabs in bed; but after the man was gone, and I went back to the bed, I found that he had rolled out, and was lying on the floor. I did not see Mr. Frederick Seward down on the floor; the first I saw of him was after the man was gone; when I came back into the room, he was inside the door, standing up. The man went down-stairs immediately after he unwound his arm from round my neck, and struck me with his fist. I did not see him encounter Major Seward."

Major Augustus Seward testified: "I am the son of the Hon. William H. Seward, Secretary of State, and was at his home in this city on the night of the 14th of April. I saw that large man (pointing to Payne) with no coat on at my father's house that night. I retired to bed at half-past seven on the night of the 14th of April, with the understanding that I was to be called about eleven o'clock to sit up with my father. I very shortly fell asleep, and so remained until awakened by the screams of my sister, when I jumped out of bed and ran into my father's room in my shirt and drawers. The gas in the room was turned down rather low, and I saw what appeared to me to be two men, one trying to hold the other at the foot of my father's bed. I seized by the clothes on his breast the person who was held, supposing it was my father, delirious, but immediately on taking hold of him I knew, from his size and strength, it was not my father. The thought then struck me that the nurse had become delirious sitting up there, and was striking about the room at random. Knowing the delicate state of my father, I shoved the person, of whom I had hold, to the door, with the intention of getting him out of the room. While I was pushing him, he struck me five or six times on the forehead and top of the head, and once on the left hand, with what I supposed to be a bottle or decanter that he had seized from the table. During this time, he repeated, in an intense but strong voice, the words, 'I'm mad, I'm mad!' On reaching the hall, he gave a sudden turn and sprang away from me, and disappeared down stairs. When near the door of my father's room, as I was pushing him out, and he came opposite where the light of the hall shone on him, I saw that he was a very large man, dark, straight hair, smooth face, no beard, and I had a view of the expression of his countenance. I then went into my room and got my pistol. It may have possibly taken me a minute, as it was in the bottom of my carpet-bag, to find it. I then ran down to the front door, intending to shoot the person, if he attempted to return. While standing at the door, the servant boy came back and said the man had ridden off on a horse, and that he had attacked the persons in the house with a knife. I then realized, for the first time, that the man was an assassin, who had entered the house for the purpose of murdering my father. I suppose it was five minutes before I went back to my father's room. Quite a large crowd came around the door. I sent for the doctors, and got somebody to keep the crowd off before I went to his room. It might not have been five minutes, but certainly three, before I got back, I think near five. I was injured pretty badly myself, I found when I got up-stairs again. After my father's wounds were dressed, I suppose about an hour, and after my own head had been bandaged, I went in and saw my father, and found that he had one very large gash on his right cheek, near the neck, besides a cut on his throat on the right-hand side, and one under the left ear. I did not examine my brother's wounds; in fact, I went into his room but for a short time that night. I did not know how badly hurt he was. The next day he was insensible and so remained, and it was four or five days before I saw what his wounds were. I found then that he had two wounds, one on the scalp, that was open to the brain, and another one over the ear. After the pieces of fractured skull were taken out, it left the covering of the brain open. It was such a wound that I should have supposed could have been made with a knife, but the surgeons seemed to think it was made by the hammer of a pistol. I heard that a pistol was picked up in the house, but I did not see it. I saw the hat that was found, and I think I should recognize it. [A slouch felt hat was exhibited to the witness.] I am quite certain that is the hat. I did not see it the night it was picked up, but the next day it was taken out of the bureau drawer, where it had been put the night before, and shown to me. The surgeons think it was a knife with which I was struck, and after the servant-boy told me what the man had been doing, I supposed so myself, though at the time I thought I was being struck with a bottle or a decanter. Not having any idea that it was a man with a knife, I did not think anything about it. I feel entirely satisfied that the prisoner at the bar, Payne, is the same man that made the attack on that night."

Doctor T. S. Verdi, testified: "I am a physician. On Friday night, the 14th of April, about half-past ten o'clock, perhaps a little sooner, I was summoned to the house of Mr. Seward. I saw the Hon. William H. Seward, Mr. Frederick Seward, Major Augustus H. Seward, Sergeant Robinson, and Mr. Hansell, all wounded, and their wounds bleeding. I had left Mr. Seward about nine o'clock that evening, very comfortable, in his room, and when I saw him next he was in bed, covered with blood, with blood all around him, blood under his bed, and blood on the handles of the door. I found Mr. Emrick W. Hansell on the same floor with Mr. Seward, lying on a bed. He said he was wounded. I undressed him, and found a stab over the sixth rib, from the spine obliquely toward the right side. I put my fingers into the wound, to see whether it had penetrated the lungs. I found that it had not, but I could put my fingers probably two and a half inches or three inches deep. Apparently, there was no internal bleeding. The wound seemed to be an inch wide, so that the finger could be put in very easily and moved all around. It was bleeding then very fresh to all appearances, probably it was not fifteen or twenty minutes since the stab had occurred."

In the cross-examination, he said: "I saw terror in the expression of all Mr. Secretary Seward's family, evidently expecting that his wounds were mortal. I examined the wounds, and immediately turned round to the family, and said: 'I congratulate you all that the wounds are not mortal;' upon which Mr. Seward stretched out his hands, and received his family, and there was a mutual congratulation."

The entire story is too long to be told in this book, but it appeared from the testimony of Samuel K. Chester, an actor, that on the Friday previous to the assassination, he saw Booth in New York. Booth exclaimed to him, "What an excellent chance I had to kill the President, if I had wished, on Inauguration day!" Booth spoke of the plot to capture the President, not to assassinate him, and to take him to Richmond. The affair, he said, failed, owing to some parties backing out.

The testimony clearly showed this fact. There were abundant opportunities for making a capture, as President Lincoln sometimes passed alone through the grounds of the White House, and frequently rode to the Soldiers' Home, several miles in the country, without a sufficient escort.

It appeared to me, while listening to the evidence, that the plan to assassinate the President, though long meditated by Booth, was matured on the morning that Booth heard that the President was to be at the theatre. Atzerodt was to take the life of Vice-President Johnson, at the Kirkwood House; Payne was to assassinate Secretary Seward, and Booth undertook to dispatch both the President and General Grant. Harold was nothing more than a lacquey for his patron, Booth, and the others were adjudged to be implicated in the conspiracy.

The damaging testimony against Mrs. Surratt was given by Weichman and Lloyd; and besides, her house had been a resort for blockade-runners, and the parties implicated in the abduction and conspiracy plots.

The prisoners were ranged in the following order, in the dock, namely: Mrs. Surratt, Harold, Atzerodt, Payne, O'Laughlin, Mudd, Spangler, and Arnold. Whether by accident or design, the four first-named were sentenced to death, and the others to imprisonment.

On the 5th of July, 1865, the President issued the following order:

"The foregoing sentences (of the Commission) in the cases of David E. Harold, G. A. Atzerodt, Lewis Payne, Michael O'Laughlin, Edward Spangler, Samuel Arnold, Mary E. Surratt, and Samuel A. Mudd, are hereby approved, and it is ordered that the sentences of said David E. Harold, G. A. Atzerodt, Lewis Payne, and Mary E. Surratt, be carried into execution by the proper military authority, under the direction of the Secretary of War, on the 7th day of July, between the hours of ten o'clock A. M., and two P. M. of that day. It is further ordered that the prisoners, Samuel Arnold, Samuel A. Mudd, Edward Spangler, and Michael O'Laughlin be confined at hard labor in the Penitentiary at Albany, New York, during the period designated in their respective sentences."

The four first mentioned were accordingly hung on the day named, and the place of confinement, as to the four last mentioned, was changed to "the military prison at Dry Tortugas, Florida." Spangler was sentenced for six years, the others for life. O'Laughlin died at that prison during the present year.

The bodies of Booth, Atzerodt, Payne, Harold, and Mrs. Surratt, were buried on the arsenal grounds.

On the 24th of May, during the trial of the conspirators, there was a grand review of Sherman's army. They had just reached here from the South, since their hundred days' tramp from "Chattanooga to the sea." The war-worn veterans, as they passed through our streets, were repeatedly cheered, and their officers loaded down with bouquets and wreaths of flowers, presented to them by the admiring ladies.

On the 23d of August, 1865, a special military commission was appointed for the trial of Henry Wirz, charged with maliciously, wilfully, and traitorously, and in aid of the then existing armed rebellion against the United States of America, on or about the first day of March, 1864, and on divers other days between that day and the 10th of April, 1865, combining, confederating, and conspiring together with

John H. Winder, Richard B. Winder, Joseph White, W. S. Winder, R. R. Stevenson, and others unknown, to injure the health and destroy the lives of soldiers in the military service of the United States, then held and being prisoners of war within the lines of the so-called Confederate States, and in the military prisons thereof, to the end that the armies of the United States might be weakened and impaired. 2. Murder in violation of the laws and customs of war.

The prisoner put in a plea in abatement as to jurisdiction.

This trial exhibited the details of the shocking condition of the Andersonville prison, of which Captain Wirz was in charge.

He was found guilty on the charges and specifications, with some modifications. The first was amended, so as to include Jefferson Davis, James A. Seddon, Howell Cobb, John H. Winder, Richard B. Winder, Isaiah H. White, W. S. Winder, W. Shelby Reed, R. R. Stevenson, S. P. Moore, —— Kerr, late hospital steward at Andersonville, James Duncan, Wesley W. Turner, Benjamin Harris, and others unknown, in the design to injure the health and destroy the lives of soldiers in the military service of the United States.

Mr. Henry G. Hayes, the reporter, prepared Captain Wirz's defence, at the instance of the prisoner. Wirz claimed, as a self-evident proposition that he, a subaltern, merely obeyed the legal orders of his superiors in the discharge of his official duties, and could not be held responsible for the motives which dictated such orders; and, if he overstepped them, violating the laws of war, and outraging humanity, he should be tried and punished according to the measure of his offence. He concluded as follows:

"The statement, which I now close, will probably survive me and you alike. It will stand as a complete answer to all the mass of misrepresentation heaped upon me. May God so direct and enlighten you in your deliberations that your reputation for impartiality and justice may be upheld, my character vindicated, and the few years of my natural life spared to my helpless family."

Judge-Advocate-General Holt, in a review of the trial, said, the proof under the second charge showed that some of our soldiers, for mere attempts to escape from their oppressors, were given to ferocious dogs to be torn to pieces; that others were confined in stocks and chains till life yielded to the torture, and that others were wantonly shot down at Wirz's bidding or by his own hand. The Andersonville prison records contain a roster of over thirteen thousand dead, buried—naked, maimed, and putrid—in one vast sepulchre. Of these, a surgeon of the rebel army, who was on duty at this prison, testified that at least three fourths died of the treatment inflicted on them while in confinement; and a surgeon of our own army, who was a prisoner there, stated that four fifths died from this cause.

The President of the United States approved the findings and sentence of the Commission.

Captain Wirz, in accordance with them, was hung in the Old Capitol prison-yard, on the 10th day of

November, 1865. His body was buried in the arsenal grounds, beside that of George A. Atzerodt.

John H. Surratt left this country directly after the assassination of President Lincoln, for Canada, thence for England, and Rome, in which city he enlisted in the Pope's service, joining the Zouaves. He made his escape from arrest and took passage for Egypt, where he was apprehended, and brought to Washington, arriving here in January, 1867. He was tried at the June term of the Criminal Court, in the same year, for killing, and for aiding and abetting in the death of President Lincoln. The jury failed to agree. A new indictment for conspiracy, etc., was made out; but before he was brought to a second trial, on the 21st day of September, 1868, he was finally discharged by Judge Wylie under the statute of limitations.

On the 25th of May, Mr. Seward, for the first time since the attempt to assassinate him, visited the White House. He was accompanied by his daughter and supported by two servants. His face was necessarily bandaged, so much so as to prevent him from speaking to the friends who gathered around him. President Johnson gave him an audience in the East Room. Though the Secretary was severely injured by the carriage accident, he did not remit his official labors. Suffering as he was, he managed, though in faint and imperfect whispering sentences, to dictate to his son Frederick what to write for him.

It was a marvel to everybody that he recovered at all, considering the ferocity with which Payne, on the

14th of April, attacked and lacerated him with a large knife. The Secretary, when Paine came into his room, was dozing, but, somewhat aroused by his footsteps, opened his eyes, and (as he related to friends) saw, without alarm, the man come near his bed, as if to take a seat upon it. He was in a very weak and dreamy condition. He heard his daughter, Fanny, who was in the room, scream. And this was all he recollected. Two of the watchers were also injured by Paine's knife, one of them, Mr. Hansell, attached to the State Department, receiving a severe stab in his shoulder. The Secretary entirely recovered from his injuries. Mr. Frederick W. Seward suffered for a much longer time than his father. A piece of his skull-bone had to be removed. A voyage to the West Indies evidently improved his physical condition. The father and son, who were brought so near the grave by the hand of the ruffian, are, at the time of the writing of this notice, (the 20th of November, 1868,) now actively engaged in the transaction of official business, with as much cheerfulness and apparent good health as at any time before the attempted assassination.

In June, Mrs. Seward, the wife of the Secretary of State, died in this city. Her remains were conveyed to Auburn, New York. The shock to her nerves, by the terrible events of the 14th of April, doubtless hastened her death.

CHAPTER XXI.

THE FIRST ACTS OF PRESIDENT JOHNSON — PROCLAMATIONS AND ORDERS — THE WAR BETWEEN HIM AND CONGRESS — HIS POLICY—PROVISIONAL GOVERNMENT — IMPEACHMENT — AD INTERIM THOMAS — AND OTHER THINGS IN CONNECTION.

AMONG the first acts of President Johnson's Administration, were: An order from him relieving "all loyal citizens and well-disposed persons residing in insurrectionary States from unnecessary commercial restrictions, and to encourage them to return to peaceful pursuits; to re-establish the authority of the United States, and execute the laws within the limits known as the State of Virginia; a proclamation declaring equality of rights with all maritime nations; proclamations of amnesty, with fourteen exceptional classes; the rescinding of the blockade; annulling the suspension of the habeas corpus; an order that in appointments to office in the several Executive Departments of the General Government, and the various branches of the public service connected with the departments, "preference should be given to such meritorious and honorably discharged soldiers and sailors, particularly those who had been disabled by wounds received or diseases contracted in the line of duty, as might possess the proper qualifications;" an order, that hereafter, whenever offences committed by civilians were to be tried where civil tribunals were in existence which could try them, their cases were not authorized to be and would not be brought before courts-martial or commissions; a proclamation (April 2, 1866,) announcing that the rebellion had ended, and in September, 1867, extending full pardon, with a few exceptions, to those who had been engaged in it.

On the 9th of May, 1865, the President inaugurated his policy of reconstruction by appointing William W. Holden Provisional Governor of North Carolina, with power to prescribe rules and regulations for "convening a convention," for the purpose of altering or amending the Constitution of that State, and in June he appointed like Provisional Governors for Mississippi, Georgia, Texas, Alabama, and South Carolina, and (in July) Florida, for similar purposes. The Provisional Governors at once commenced the duties prescribed. Delegations from those States, or the Governors themselves, came to Washington for consultation. They appeared to be happy in view of the practical restoration of their respective States to the Union. Congress, soon after the assembling in December, 1865, expressed their dissent from the President's policy and plan, and appointed a joint Committee on Reconstruction. The Committee examined many witnesses. The result of their labors is comprised in a volume of seven hundred and seventy-five printed octavo pages.

This report shows that the Southern States, at the

close of the rebellion, were in a state of utter exhaustion and complete anarchy, without governments and without the power to frame governments, excepting by "the permission of those who had been successful in the war." The President, in the proclamations under which he appointed Provisional Governors, and in his various communications to them, had, the Committee said, recognized the fact, that the people of those States were, when the rebellion was crushed, deprived of all civil government, and must proceed to organize anew. As President of the United States, he had no power, except to execute the laws of the land as Chief Magistrate. The conclusion of the Committee was, that "the so-called Confederate States are not, at present, entitled to representation in the Congress of the United States; that, before allowing such representation, adequate security for future peace and safety should be required; that this can only be found in such changes of the organization as shall determine the civil rights and privileges of all citizens in all parts of the Republic, shall place representation on an equitable basis, shall fix a stigma upon treason, and protect the loyal people against future claims for the expenses incurred in support of the rebellion and for the manumitted slaves, together with an express grant of power in Congress to enforce those provisions.

The President, in his first annual message, gave his reasons for appointing Provisional Governors, and his opinion, that "the States attempting to secede placed themselves in a condition where their vitality was impaired, but not extinguished — their functions suspended, but not destroyed." He concluded by saying, "from the sufferings which have attended them, (the Southern States,) during our late struggle, let us look away to the future, which is sure to be laden for them with greater prosperity than has ever before been known. The removal of the monopoly of slave labor is a pledge that those regions will be peopled by a numerous and enterprising population, which will vie with any in the Union in compactness, inventive genius, wealth, and industry."

In the same month, the President sent to Congress the report of General Grant, who said, "I am satisfied that the mass of thinking men of the South accept the present situation of affairs in good faith;" and further on, "My observations lead me to the conclusion, that the citizens of the Southern States are anxious to return to self-government within the Union, as soon as possible; that while reconstructing, they want and require protection from the Government; that they are in earnest in wishing to do what they think is required by the Government, not humiliating to them as citizens, and that if such a course were pointed out, they would pursue it in good faith. It is to be regretted that there cannot be a greater commingling at this time between the citizens of the two sections, and particularly of those intrusted with the law-making power."

The President soon found that the party which elected him did not like his "policy," and hence they vigorously assailed him. He maintained that he had *not* proved recreant to his trust, and that those who were now foremost in assailing him, were themselves the violators of the Constitution. He said, in reply to the committee who presented him with an account of the proceedings of the Philadelphia (conservative) Convention of the 14th of August, 1866, "We have seen Congress gradually encroach step by step upon constitutional rights, and violate day after day, and month after month, fundamental principles of the Government," and this was repeated, in substance, and elaborated, in his subsequent speeches. In his oration at the New York banquet, he remarked, "I have helped my distinguished friend on my right, General Grant, to fight the rebels South, . . . and when we whipped them at one end of the line, I want to say to you, that I am for whipping them at the other end of the line."

Congress engaged in the work of passing Freedmen's Bureau, District of Columbia Negro Suffrage, Tenure-of-Office, and Reconstruction Bills, all of which the President, from time to time, vetoed, and which Congress finally passed over his objections, "to the contrary notwithstanding." Thus the war commenced and continued.

The following changes in the Cabinet took place: May 1865, James Harlan, of Iowa, to be Secretary of the Interior, in the place of Mr. Usher, resigned; O. H. Browning, of Illinois, succeeded Mr. Harlan, resigned, in July, 1866; Henry Stanbery in place of

James Speed, resigned, as Attorney-General, and A. W. Randall, of Wisconsin, vice William Dennison, resigned, in July, 1866, as Postmaster-General.

On the 5th of August, 1867, the President informed Mr. Stanton, that "public considerations of a high character constrained" him to say, that his resignation as Secretary of War would be accepted; but Mr. Stanton, from like "considerations," said he would *not* resign the office before the next meeting of Congress. On the 12th of the same month the President suspended him, and "authorized and empowered" General Grant to act as Secretary of War *ad interim.* General Grant, in notifying Mr. Stanton of his acceptance, said: "I cannot let the opportunity pass without expressing to you my appreciation of the zeal, patriotism, firmness, and ability, with which you have ever discharged the duties of Secretary of War."

Mr. Stanton then wrote a letter to the President, denied his right, under the Constitution and laws, without the advice and consent of the Senate, and without legal cause, to suspend him from office: but, inasmuch as the general commanding the armies had been appointed *ad interim,* and had notified him that he had accepted the appointment, he had no alternative "but to submit, under protest, to superior force."

Mr. Stanton, in his letter to General Grant, said: "You will please accept my acknowledgment of the kind terms in which you have notified me of your acceptance of the President's appointment, and my cordial reciprocation of the sentiments expressed."

The Senate, in January following, engaged in debate, continuing several days, and passed a resolution declaring they did not concur in the suspension of Mr. Stanton from office. This was on the 13th of that month.

Copies of the resolution were sent, respectively, to the President, General Grant, and Secretary Stanton.

General Grant wrote a note to the President, informing him that his functions as Secretary of War *ad interim* ceased from the moment he received the resolution of the Senate. He accordingly retired from the office, and Mr. Stanton resumed his duties.

On the 21st of February, the President informed the Senate that, "by virtue of the power and authority vested" in him "by the Constitution and laws," he had removed Mr. Stanton from the office of Secretary of War, and designated General Lorenzo Thomas as Secretary *ad interim*. The Senate debated the subject, as before, in secret session, and passed a resolution — "that under the Constitution and laws of the United States, the President has no power to remove the Secretary of War, and designate any other officer to perform the duties of that office *ad interim*."

A resolution proposing to impeach the President, "for high crimes and misdemeanors," was reported by the House Committee on the Judiciary, November 25, 1867, but it was disagreed to by the House.

On the 10th of February, 1868, the evidence taken on Impeachment by the Committee on the Judiciary, was, on motion of Mr. Thaddeus Stevens, referred to the

Committee on Reconstruction; and the correspondence between General Grant and President Johnson relative to the retirement of the former from the War Department, and other papers, were also referred to the same Committee, which on the 22d of February reported a resolution that the President be impeached.

A similar resolution, which was rejected in the previous November, by a vote of—yeas 57, nays 108, was, on the 24th of February, adopted by a vote of—yeas 128, nays 47. And on the 2d of March, 1868, the quarrel between the President and Congress culminated in Articles of Impeachment, "exhibited by the House of Representatives of the United States, in the name of themselves and all the people of the United States, against Andrew Johnson, President of the United States, in maintenance and support of their Impeachment against him for high crimes and misdemeanors in office." There were nine articles, with specifications. His conduct toward Secretary Stanton was first set forth, and he was accused of conspiring with *ad interim* Thomas, and others, to perpetrate acts of great enormity, and to usurp power not conferred by the Constitution and laws; and two additional articles charged him with making and delivering, on divers days and times, with a loud voice, certain intemperate, inflammatory, and scandalous harangues; and did therein utter loud threats and bitter menaces, as well against Congress as the laws of the United States duly enacted thereby, amid the cries, jeers, and laughter of the multitudes then assembled and in hearing," which were set forth in the several specifications, "which utterances, and declarations, threats, and harangues, highly censurable in any, are peculiarly indecent and unbecoming in the Chief Magistrate of the United States, by means whereof said Andrew Johnson has brought the high office of the President of the United States into contempt, ridicule, and disgrace, to the great scandal of all good citizens, whereby said Andrew Johnson, President of the United States, did commit, and was then and there guilty of a high misdemeanor in office."

The Articles of Impeachment were agreed to in the House.

Messrs. John A. Bingham, George S. Boutwell, James F. Wilson, Benjamin F. Butler, Thomas Williams, John A. Logan, and Thaddeus Stevens, were elected managers to conduct the Impeachment.

On the 4th of March, the articles were read to the Senate by the managers. On the 5th and 6th, Chief-Justice Chase administered the oath to the various Senators, when an order was adopted, directing a summons on Andrew Johnson, to file answer to the articles, returnable on the 13th instant.

The President entered an appearance by his counsel, Henry Stanbery, Benjamin R. Curtis, William S. Groesbeck, William M. Evarts, and Thomas A. R. Nelson. The President asked for forty days as necessary for the preparation of his answer; but the Senate adopted an order that the President file answer on or before the 23d of March. At that time Mr. Curtis read the answer to the charges and specifications, in which the President claimed his Constitutional rights, and denied the premises of his accusers.

On the 24th of March, the managers presented in the House the replication to the answer of the President — which was adopted. It was quite brief. They denied each and every averment, and were "ready to prove that he was guilty of high crimes and misdemeanors."

On the same day an order was adopted by the Senate that the trial should commence on the 30th, and proceed with all convenient dispatch. So, on that day the opening argument was made by Manager Butler, and then the testimony for the prosecution commenced, and continued till, and including the 4th of April, when an adjournment took place until the 9th of that month, at the request of the President's counsel. April 9th and 10th were occupied by Judge Curtis's opening argument for the defence, and in presenting testimony. And the proceedings were continued until the 16th of May, when a vote was taken on the last article — guilty 35; not guilty 19; and on the 26th of May the second and third articles were voted upon, with the same result as on the eleventh.

[The last, or eleventh article, charged the President with a high misdemeanor for declaring, in substance, during his speech in Washington, on the 18th of August, 1866, that the thirty-ninth Congress was not a congress authorized by the Constitution to exercise legislative power under the same, but, on the contrary, was a congress of only part of the States, thereby denying and intending to deny, that the legislation of Congress was valid or obligatory upon him, except in so far as he saw fit to approve the same; and, in pursuance of such declaration, he attempted to obstruct the execution of the Tenure-of-Office Act by contriving means to prevent Mr. Stanton from resuming the functions of Secretary of War, notwithstanding the refusal of the Senate to concur in his suspension. Also, with contriving means to prevent the execution of the act making appropriations for the support of the army for the year ending June 30, 1868, and for other purposes, and also to prevent the execution of the Reconstruction Acts.

The second article charged high misdemeanors, in this: that, contrary to the provisions of the Tenure-of-Office Act, and with intent to violate the Constitution of the United States, the President authorized and empowered General Lorenzo Thomas to act as Secretary of War *ad interim*, there being no vacancy in the office at the time; and the third article charged that, without authority of law, while the Senate was in session, he appointed General Thomas Secretary *ad interim*, without the advice and consent of the Senate, no vacancy having happened during the recess of the Senate, and no vacancy existing in the office at the time.]

The yeas declaring the President guilty, were Messrs. Anthony, Cameron, Cattell, Chandler, Cole, Conkling, Conness, Corbett, Cragin, Drake, Edmonds, Ferry, Frelinghuysen, Harlan, Howard, Howe, Morgan, Morrill, of Maine, Morrill, of Vermont, Morton, Nye, Patterson, of New Hampshire, Pomeroy, Ramsey, Sherman, Sprague, Stewart, Sumner, Thayer, Tipton, Wade, Willey, Williams, Wilson, Yates — 35.

Not guilty — Messrs. *Bayard*, *Buckalew*, *Davis*, *Dixon*, *Doolittle*, Fessenden, Fowler, Grimes, Henderson, *Hendricks*, *Johnson*, *McCreery*, *Norton*, *Patterson*, of Tennessee, Ross, *Saulsbury*, Trumbull, Van Winkle, *Vickers* — 19. (Democrats in *Italics*.)

So the President was not convicted — a two third vote being requisite in cases of impeachment.

A motion was made and carried — yeas 34, nays 16, that the Court adjourn *sine die*.

Judgment of acquittal was then entered by the Chief-Justice on the three articles voted upon, and the Senate, sitting as a Court for the trial of Andrew Johnson, President of the United States, upon Articles of Impeachment exhibited by the House of Representatives, was declared adjourned without day.

As incidental to this trial, it may be stated that humorous accounts were given in the newspapers as to the manner in which Adjutant-General Thomas endeavored to obtain possession of the War Department, when the "eyes of all Delaware were upon him!" General Thomas testified that, in his interview with Secretary Stanton, "Mr. Stanton turned to me and got talking in a familiar manner. I said, 'the next time you have me arrested, please do not do it before I get something to eat.' I said I had had nothing to eat or drink that day. He put his hand around my neck, as he sometimes does, and ran his hand through my hair, and turned around to General Schriver and said, 'Schriver you have got a bottle there, bring it out.' (Laughter.) Schriver unlocked his case, and brought out a small vial, containing, I suppose, about a spoonful of whiskey, and stated at the same time that he occasionally took a little for dyspepsia. (Laughter.) Mr. Stanton took that and poured it into a tumbler and divided it equally, and we drank it together."

Question. — A fair division?

Answer. — A fair division, because he held up the glasses to the light, and I saw that each had about the same, and we each drank. (Laughter.) Presently a messenger came in with a bottle of whiskey, a full bottle; the cork was drawn, and he and I took a drink together. "Now," said he, "this, at least, is neutral ground." (Laughter.)

Question. Was that all the force exhibited that day?

Answer. That was all.

On the day the final vote had been taken on Impeachment, Mr. Stanton addressed the President a letter, saying: "The resolution of the Senate of the United States, of the 21st of February last, declaring that the President has no power to remove the Secretary of War, and designate any other officer to perform the duties of that office *ad interim*, having this day failed to be supported by two thirds of the senators present and voting on the Articles of Impeachment preferred against you by the House of Representatives, I have relinquished charge of the War Department, and have left the same, and the books, archives, papers, and property, heretofore in my custody as Secretary of War, in care of Brevet Major-General Townsend, the senior Assistant Adjutant-General, subject to your direction."

The President, on the 23d of April, had nominated General John M. Schofield to be Secretary of War, in place of Edwin M. Stanton, removed. This nomination rested in the Senate during the Impeachment. On the 29th of May, the Senate took up the subject in secret session, and after a long debate, adopted the following preamble and resolution:—

"Whereas, on the 23d of April, 1868, the President nominated John M. Schofield to be Secretary of War, in place of Edwin M. Stanton removed; and whereas, in the opinion of the Senate, the said Stanton has not been legally removed from his office, but inasmuch as the said Stanton has relinquished his place as Secretary of War, for cause stated in his note to the President, therefore,

"*Resolved*, That the Senate advise and consent to the appointment of John M. Schofield to be Secretary of War."

The Impeachment created much interest, and full accounts of the proceedings of the trial were telegraphed throughout the country. The Senate chamber was crowded with spectators. To prevent disorder, tickets of admission were distributed every day, through members of Congress. Of course they were in great demand. As to the President, it was said by those who were nearest to his person, that from the time he was impeached up to the moment of his acquittal, he never had any doubt of a favorable result.

Some indeed, very many of his political opponents — including men of eminence and influence — insisted upon the conviction of the President, as a State necessity. They considered him as standing in the way of Southern reconstruction, and hence sought to remove the alleged impediment. Besides, it was claimed by not a few, that the Republican party, as they had undertaken Impeachment, would be seriously damaged by a failure. The Republican Senators who voted "not guilty," were the subjects of stern condemnation, but they openly placed their conduct on grounds other than those of party. The predictions that the Republican organization would suffer by an acquittal of the President were not verified. The election of its candidates for the Presidency and Vice-Presidency, was secured by two hundred and fourteen, while the opposing candidates — Seymour and Blair — received only eighty electoral votes.

Not only did the Republicans seek to impeach the President, but they sheared him of much of the power hitherto exercised by his predecessors in the Presidential chair. He was greatly embarrassed, particularly by the Tenure-of-Office Act, and the restrictions in relation to the army. The fight still continued. He changed none of his opinions, and continued to veto bills, which the dominant party as promptly passed, notwithstanding his objections.

Hon. Henry Stanbery resigned his office of Attorney-General on the 12th of March, in order to defend the President on the Impeachment trial, Mr. Secretary Browning having been the same day appointed acting Attorney-General. Mr. Stanbery was nominated for re-appointment, after the trial; but the Senate rejected him. Hon. William M. Evarts was afterward confirmed as Attorney-General.

The events of the present Administration are too recent to require mention, beyond what has been already stated: and, besides, the intention of the author, when he commenced this work, was more especially to deal with occurrences under past Administrations. But it may be added, that the President, in his last annual message, 8th of December, 1868, said it again became his duty to call attention to the state of the Union, and to its continued disorganized condition under the various laws which had been passed upon the subject of reconstruction. "It may safely be assumed," he said, "as an axiom in the government of

States, that the greatest wrongs inflicted upon a people are caused by unjust and arbitrary legislation, or by the unrelenting decrees of despotic rulers, and that the timely revocation of injurious and oppressive measures is the greatest good that can be conferred upon a nation. The legislator or ruler who has the wisdom and magnanimity to retrace his steps, when convinced of error, will sooner or later be rewarded with the respect and gratitude of an intelligent and patriotic people.

"Our own history—although embracing a period less than a century — affords abundant proof that most, if not all of our domestic troubles, are directly traceable to violations of the organic law and excessive legislation. The most striking illustrations of this fact are furnished by the enactments of the past three years upon the question of reconstruction. After a fair trial, they have substantially failed and proved pernicious in their results, and there seems to be no good reason why they should longer remain upon the statute-book."

He concluded his message by saying: "In Congress are vested all legislative powers, and upon them devolves the responsibility as well as for framing unwise and excessive laws, as for neglecting to devise and adopt measures absolutely demanded by the wants of the country. Let us earnestly hope that before the expiration of our respective terms of service, now rapidly drawing to a close, an All-wise Providence will so guide our counsels as to strengthen and preserve the Federal Union, inspire reverence for the Constitution, restore prosperity and happiness to our whole people, and promote "on earth peace, good-will toward men."

Christmas day, the President issued a proclamation of general pardon and amnesty, including all political offenders.

On the 4th of March, 1869, Andrew Johnson will retire from the Presidential office, which he has filled for nearly a full term. One whose name will always illumine the pages of heroism, and by whose concurrent efforts the rebellion was crushed, will succeed him.

Forty years ago, a large and powerful party in this country deprecated the election of "a military chieftain" as fraught with evil to the Republic; but now, in 1868, another large and powerful party look to the President elect of their choice as a man to pacify discordant elements, and by a firm, yet conciliatory policy, encourage the restoration of prosperity throughout the section not long ago desolated by war. The great public already await his Inaugural Address, and are impatient to hear his official announcement as President of the principles by which he will be governed.

The future must decide whether the course of administration will be of pleasantness and peace.

The present incumbent, no longer harassed with the cares of State and the bitterness of party warfare, will retire to private life, and soon cease to be the object of invective and complaint. Time, one of our best friends, softens all asperities; and Andrew Johnson will, in his own person, realize this truth; for when freed from the position of President, he will be permitted to enjoy the calm which will succeed the storms of passion, by which his Administration was attended.

CHAPTER XXII.

THE NEWSPAPER PRESS — CORRESPONDENTS — ODDS AND ENDS.

IF any one have an opportunity, he will see by looking over the newspapers printed a third of a century ago, that they contain no telegrams. The New York papers, which were regarded, even at that time, as enterprising, rarely contained more than half a column of Washington news, Congressional proceedings included; and this was the complexion of all journals outside of Washington. The number of Washington correspondents was small, and even these were poorly paid. I recollect that, even twenty-two years ago, I was, for six weeks, the only newspaper correspondent in Washington. It was the fashion for almost every newspaper man to follow the example of the members of Congress, and leave the city at the same time they did. The influx of strangers, which imparted to the Metropolis the gayety and enterprise of a city, left it, on their exodus, a mere country town of scattered habitations. The meeting of Congress was always regarded as a source of new life to the almost dying city.

There was no deficiency of reporters for the "Register of Debates," and the "Congressional Globe," — men of fine education and critically expert in their profession. Joseph Gales, of the "National Intelligencer," was the pioneer in verbatim reporting in Washington. Although he wrote what is now considered to be a clumsy system, — Gurney's, — he was wonderfully rapid and accurate. Arthur J. Stansbury and John Agg were not stenographers, but they did an amazingly large quantity of work with their contractions of long-hand, and a set of uncouth arbitrary characters. They would turn from their pens column after column of legislative matter, which would read much better than the awkwardly expressed sentences of such honorable gentlemen as acquired what reputation they possessed from their published speeches. Then came short-hand writers, increasing in number from time to time, as the newspaper business demanded.

I might, if it were of sufficient interest, relate a large number of anecdotes connected with reporting. Several only may suffice. —

During a night-session, one of the reporters of the "National Intelligencer," over-fatigued with his labors, fell asleep at his desk, some member being at the time engaged in making a speech. Having refreshed himself with a half-hour's unconsciousness, he awoke, by which time another honorable gentleman was expressing his views. The reporter did not individualize, but resumed his work. The neglect of his making the proper distinction of speakers, led to a very provoking error, namely, parts of two speeches, different in their character, having been published as emanating from the same gentleman!

In the winter of 1839–40, I commenced as one of

the "Globe" corps of reporters. Lund Washington and William W. Curran were my associate reporters in the House of Representatives. At that time they were engaged in a controversy with Waddy Thompson, a member of Congress from South Carolina. He had made a gross attack upon them, and perhaps threatened them with personal chastisement; the result was, Curran armed himself with a knife and Washington with a big stick. They regularly took their seats—it was in the old hall—and in their leisure moments watched the movements of Waddy Thompson, whose *physique* was alarming, and whose spirit was thought to be like that of the fiery Hotspur.

Thus things went on for several weeks. The reporters, almost every day, published cards, or notes to the proceedings, about the quarrel. This, fortunately, came to an honorable conclusion. Mr. Thompson, finding that they left out his name from print, and failed to notice him in the Congressional proceedings, no more than if he were not a member of the House, sought an opportunity to make the *amende honorable,* by publicly apologizing, in his place, for his conduct toward these gentlemen. The long knife and the big stick were then left at home, for the war was at an end.

Numerous instances might be cited of "contempt" of the privileges of the House: one will be sufficient. Early in January, 1857, a committee was appointed to investigate the charge that a corrupt combination existed among members of the House, for the purpose of passing or preventing legislation. The inquest was predicated upon a Washington letter and accompanying editorial article, in the New York "Times," supported in the House by Mr. Paine, of North Carolina, who certified that a corrupt proposition had been made to him by a fellow-member, in connection with one of the very measures named in the "Times" letter.

The first report from the "Corruption Committee" was made by Mr. Orr, who, without referring to the attendant circumstances, simply announced that during the progress of the investigation, they had summoned as a witness Mr. James W. Simonton, the "Times" correspondent, and propounded to him the question: "You stated that certain members had approached you and desired to know if they could not, through you, procure money for their votes on certain bills: will you state who these members were?"

Mr. Simonton replied: "I cannot, without a violation of confidence, than which I would rather suffer anything. I do not decline in order to screen any member: my declination is based upon my own conviction of duty."

The Committee urged that Mr. Simonton was a material witness; though they failed to state what fully appeared subsequently, to wit: that he disclaimed, at the outset, any personal knowledge of corruption, but justified the "moral convictions" which had inspired his charges, by directing the Committee to witnesses who *did* testify from personal knowledge of corrupt transactions.

Upon motion of Mr. Orr, a resolution was adopted directing the Sergeant-at-arms to take Mr. Simonton into custody, and bring him to the bar of the House, to answer for contempt. Mr. Simonton, being present on the floor, instantly surrendered himself, and was brought "to the bar," taking a position in the main aisle, claiming to be heard in his own defence, and declaring his readiness to respond at once to the charge of contempt. An exciting debate having resulted in a vote granting him permission to speak, Mr. Simonton proceeded, in a clear tone of voice, calmly and firmly, but respectfully, to vindicate his course. He cited the debate on ordering the investigation to prove that it was upon Mr. Paine's statement, and not upon the scouted letter of the "Times" correspondent, that the House had acted in ordering an investigation. He denied the right of the House to deprive him of his liberty for refusing to violate his honorable obligations,—claiming that he had infracted no statute in accepting the confidence that he now presented, and that he stood protected by the constitutional provision guaranteeing the citizen against deprivation of liberty, except by "due process of law." He urged that it was in the direct line of his professional duty to receive communications confidentially; that he had the right, in the absence of a law forbidding it, to pledge secrecy in regard to statements *to be* made to him, and that the House could not, by *ex post facto* legislation, deprive him of that right, or force him to break the seal. He denied that he had *volun-*

teered any reference to the confidential interviews in question, or that he had made charges against individual members which rendered it incumbent upon him to violate his plighted faith. Being morally convinced that corruption existed in the House, he had denounced it, in discharge of his duty as a member of the press. While he had stated to the Committee, under oath, that he had no personal knowledge of corruption, (which would have made him *particeps criminis*,) he had named to them witnesses who *had* personal knowledge, and whose evidence, when disclosed to the House, would justify his "moral convictions." He further urged that even if he would disclose the names demanded, he had no corroborative proof regarding the conversations, and that the only effect of the disclosure would be to cover with suspicion where it would be impossible to convict. While he had no desire to stand in antagonism to the House, he declared that he must judge for himself what duty demanded of him, and that he should pursue the path of duty, according to the convictions of his own conscience, to the end.

An exciting debate followed. It was soon understood among members, that evidence had already been elicited, tending to disgrace several of their number, and a sort of panic seized a majority of the House, each man seeming to fear that he might be suspected of trying to cover up corruptions, if he should fail to vote for whatever the "Corruption Committee" might ask. Under this pressure, the House adopted a resolution, ordering Mr. Simonton again into custody, there to remain until purged of his "contempt." A joint resolution was also rushed through, making the refusal to answer interrogatories of an Investigating Committee a misdemeanor, punishable by a year's imprisonment, and a fine of one thousand dollars. In the Senate, an effort was made to check this hasty legislation. Senator Hale, of New Hampshire, earnestly opposed this scheme as unwise, irregular, and sure to fail. Mr. Seward, of New York, and others, doubted its policy. But the power of Mr. Orr's Committee was dominating, and the Joint Resolution became a law.

Mr. Simonton, when brought up for re-examination under the new law, promptly announced that he would never answer the suspended question, and firmly maintained his position. Many of his friends, including his counsel, Hon. Reverdy Johnson — all of whom feared that the penalty of imprisonment would be visited upon him if he persisted — urged him to answer the question, assuring him that he was entitled to throw upon Congress the responsibility of such answer, and its consequences. He replied, "that it was a question of personal honor, in regard to which no one could judge so well as himself, and he resolutely refused to deviate from his convictions of duty." After being held three weeks in custody of the Sergeant-at-arms, Mr. Simonton was liberated under an order of the House, the Committee reporting that they had "no further questions to put to the witness," but omitting to state that the witness had not purged himself of the "contempt" for which he was arrested.

The result of the investigation was, that three members of the House — in consequence chiefly of testimony to which Mr. Simonton had directed the Committee — were allowed to resign their seats, when the vote was about to be taken on resolutions reported for their expulsion. The House, in view of their discoveries, passed "a bill to protect the people against corrupt and secret influence in matters of legislation."

I have already said, that a quarter of a century ago but few persons were employed as professional correspondents; and the same might be said up to a later period.

We began to see glimpses of the electric telegraph in the newspapers, in the year 1844, and not many months elapsed, before the lines extended far Northward. Correspondents increased; but it was not till 1860 that they were numerous enough to be seen everywhere. And when the rebellion commenced, this city became a headquarters for the war-news. Correspondents "sent off" much of their matter from the Washington telegraph offices. Ever since, the press has here been efficiently and respectably represented. Even distant newspapers have their established places of business, with their signs exhibited; and "Newspaper Row," where so many have their offices, is one of the permanent institutions of the Metropolis.

The best comment on journalistic enterprise and the uses of the electric telegraph, is seen in the newspapers themselves — in the number of columns which sometimes appear, supplied by that means of intercommunication; and besides, the journals have doubled their proportions within the last fourth of a century.

In December, 1863, the Hon. Schuyler Colfax was elected Speaker of the House of Representatives. As he was the first journalist ever elected to that position, the newspaper correspondents of all parties signalized the event by a dinner in his honor, and as indicative of the high esteem in which they held his character as a man. He made an appropriate response to the toast in which he was complimented. The majority of the House, at the next two Congresses, re-elected him to that office.

On the last occasion, the Hon. William E. Robinson, though of the opposite political party, voted for him, as a mark of respect for a brother journalist. The higher honor of Vice-President will soon be enjoyed by the popular Speaker.

Before the introduction of illuminating gas into the Capitol, the old hall of the House of Representatives (as well as that of the Senate,) was lighted with oil, from a mammoth chandelier, suspended from the ceiling. About half-past eleven o'clock, one morning, before the meeting of the House, the rope broke, and down came the chandelier, which was shivered considerably. Several members were at their desks near by at the time, but none hurt. They were, however, much frightened.

Hon. James A. Pearce, of Maryland, while sitting in his place, in the Senate, was injured by the accidental falling of a parasol upon his head, point downward.

The lady to whom it belonged occupied a seat directly over the honorable gentleman. Considerable commotion was caused by the occurrence. The proceedings of the body were for a time interrupted, and the Senator bled profusely.

I have only an indistinct recollection of an interesting colloquy between Webster and Calhoun, which took place a good while ago. I wish I knew where I could readily find the report. But this I recollect: Mr. Calhoun had vaunted himself on the support which he had given to the late war between the United States and Great Britain,— usually known as the war of 1812,—and he charged Daniel Webster with a want of patriotism in that contest. Mr. Webster asked for "the proofs." Mr. Calhoun said he *could* produce them—but "NOT NOW." It was then that Mr. Webster rose from his seat, like a lion in his strength, and proceeding to the nearest passage-way between the desks, walked several steps. He stood there a few moments—the grand central figure of the scene; and then broke the silence, in slow and measured tones, by alluding to the charge of the opposing giant. He was unwilling this contest should remain unsettled. He desired the issue should be decided without delay. "Not now," repeated the South Carolinian. "Yes," exclaimed Webster, in his loudest voice, and in a grand, defiant manner, extending his hand toward Mr. Calhoun, "now's the day, and now's the hour. Let the Senator make good his accusation." The South Carolinian was not, however, ready to do so.

Mr. Webster was always a bright object of attack from the party opposed to him. I remember that the Democrats were savagely severe on him, for saying that rather than the Constitution of the United States should be violated, he would prefer seeing the British battering at the gates of the Capitol.

One day, the Hon. Joshua R. Giddings, under his privilege as a member, brought two men with him into the hall of the House of Representatives. They were respectable in appearance; and one of them had a clergymanic look. Suspicion was at once excited. More than one Southern man thought that the visitors had a dash of black blood in their veins, and besides, it was discovered that their hair was a little wiry. Such an introduction into the hall had never before been made, nor since. The doorkeeper undertook to enforce the rules, called Mr. Giddings aside, and whispered to him something on the subject, whereupon Mr. Giddings, answering the little doorkeeper with a smile, conducted his friends from the hall.

The greatest nuisance connected with the House of Representatives is the time set apart "for debate only." It simply means that members may read speeches, which they often do, in low and monotonous tones, and not unfrequently so inaudibly that the reporters in the galleries cannot even hear what are the subjects of their discourse. Such an arrangement does not rise even to the respectability of a moot-court.

The Hon. Thomas H. Benton did not always make use of elegant language. During the bank discussion, he spoke of circulating notes as "rags and lampblack," and of gold coin as "yellow boys," which he wanted to be seen shining through the interstices of every poor man's purse. He was very tenacious of his words, using those only which he thought to be the most expressive. I recollect that after he had made use of the word "bamboozle," a brother Senator took exception to it as not being appropriate, or obsolete, or vulgar. The Colonel did not reply at that time, but the next morning, when he came into the chamber, he was followed by several pages, with armfuls of books, which they piled on Benton's table. As soon as an opportunity occurred, he called attention to the fact, that the word "bamboozle," as employed by himself, had been attacked. "It was a good word, sir, and very expressive." He then opened one of the mammoth books, at the place turned down, and told what Webster had said of the word, namely, "Bamboozle, *v. t.*, to confound, to deceive, to play low tricks upon. — *Arbuthnot.*" And here was what Worcester said: "Bamboozle, *v. a.*, (from *bam*, a cheat,) to deceive, to impose on, to confound. 'Babbled, absurd, bamboozled.' — *Addison.*" 'Bamboozler, *n.*, a tricky fellow. 'A set they call banterers and bamboozlers.' — *Arbuthnot.*" And then the Colonel told Senators what Richardson, Johnson, Walker, and many other philologists said about this word "bamboozle." The Senator stooped down to read from the books, with the aid of his eye-glass. He occupied at least half an hour in vindicating his use of this word "bamboozle."

For the first time in the history of Congress, when the House of Representatives met on the 4th of July, 1861, pursuant to the proclamation of President Lincoln, they found National flags festooned over the Speaker's chair. Colonel John W. Forney, Clerk of the House, directed this to be done. He was at that session elected Secretary of the Senate. Soon, thereafter, he called the clerks and employes together, made them a brief speech, and proposed they all take the oath of loyalty. Several refused to do so, and went South, in aid of the rebellion.

Several years before the death of Henry Clay, an artist, whose name I do not remember, painted his portrait, at the National Hotel, in this city. I was invited to see it — not because I was an art-critic, but for the reason that I was connected with the press. The limner had just laid down his pencil, having given the picture the finishing touch, and "old Harry" had just completed his last sitting. When I went into the room, the artist was congratulating himself on his success; — "I think, Mr. Clay, I have you, sure enough." Mr. Clay was not yet ready to pronounce judgment on the work, so he turned to me, and asked what I thought of it. "I'll have to compare it with yourself," I replied, "therefore you'll excuse me for examining your features so minutely, in order that I may make the comparison." "Certainly, certainly," said Mr. Clay, in the most generous manner. Really, I thought I had seen better pictures of Mr. Clay, as well as worse; and regulated my "criticism," if it could be so called, accordingly, when I responded to Mr. Clay's question. "Now," I asked in turn, "Mr. Clay, what do *you* think of the portrait?" "Oh, my dear sir, it's not for *me* to say. I am too much of an interested party. I may remark, however, without giving offence, it is a fair picture, *but the artist has given me too much shirt-collar. It comes up too high, sir.*" I could not agree with Mr. Clay in this; for while the painter had actually reduced Mr. Clay's shirt-collar, so that it did not come up to the tip of the ear by one inch, at that very time Mr Clay wore a collar at least two inches higher, that seemed to be sawing his ears!

Clay was a great man for large shirt-collars.

On the 31st of October, 1861, Lieutenant-General Scott retired from the command of the army. He said in his letter to the President, that for more than three years he had been unable, from a hurt, to mount a horse, and could walk only a few paces. These, and symptoms of dropsy and vertigo, admonished him that repose of mind and body, with medicine, were necessary to add a little more to a life already protracted beyond the usual span of man. In conclusion, he expressed the hope that "the unnatural and unjust rebellion against a good government" would soon be suppressed.

The President, in reply, paid a high compliment to his bravery and valuable services, in behalf of his country; accepted his resignation, and ordered him to be placed on the list of retired officers.

The scene at the Cabinet meeting was very affecting. The correspondence between Secretary-of-War Cameron and General Scott was read; and the latter wept, when the President, in a brief address, alluded to that part of it relating to his retirement; the terms being so kind as to touch deeply the old hero's heart.

The President and Cabinet shook him warmly by the hand on that memorable occasion.

Secretary Cameron accompanied Lieutenant-General Scott to New York.

On the breaking out of the rebellion, the Virginia Convention appointed a committee to wait upon Lieutenant-General Scott, and tender him the command of the military forces of Virginia in the struggle.

General Scott received the chairman of the committee kindly, listened to him patiently, and then said to him, "I have served my country under the flag of the Union for more than fifty years, and, as long as God permits me to live, I will defend the flag with my sword, even if my native State shall assail it."

Major-General McClellan was appointed to command the armies, and issued an order announcing this fact. He also alluded to the distinguished chief, in words of admiration and profound respect.

Many persons, including army officers, called upon him in the way of congratulation.

During the contest for the speakership, which resulted in the election of Mr. Pennington, Mr. Stevens, of Pennsylvania, gravely rose to "a personal matter." "It is well known," he said, "that I departed from the general rule of obeying party decrees, and voted for an honorable gentleman from North Carolina, (Mr. Gilmer.) This may require some explanation, as I see from the paper I send to the Clerk's desk to be read.

The presiding officer said, after looking at it, the paper is printed in German, and the Clerk cannot read it. (Great laughter.)

Mr. Stevens then remarked, "I will postpone my remarks until the Clerk *can* read it." (Laughter.)

When, in 1860, Mr. Burlingame, of Massachusetts, was a member of the House, he offered a preamble and resolution, as follows:

"Whereas, the kingdom of Sardinia, by reason of accessions, has been raised to a first-class power, extending from the Alps to the Adriatic, and embracing within it the richest and most populous portion of Italy, over which extensive dominion a constitutional representative government has been established, order maintained, and freedom of the press and religion secured, therefore,

"*Resolved*, That the Committee on Foreign Affairs be instructed to inquire into the expediency of raising the mission to Sardinia to a first-class mission."

Objection having been made to the preamble, Mr. Burlingame withdrew it, and the resolution was agreed to by the House.

Mr. Burlingame, owing to his advocacy of Sardinia, rendered himself unpopular with the Austrian Government, which was disinclined to receive him as Minister to Vienna, after the President had appointed him. The mission to China was then given to Mr.

Burlingame, who, in the summer of 1868, came to Washington in company with two Chinese princes, and a full suite, as Envoy-Extraordinary and Minister-Plenipotentiary from the Celestial Kingdom, duly accredited to all the treaty powers. Austria's opposition to him threw him into the channel which bore him to his present high position.

On the 14th of May, 1860, three Japanese ambassadors arrived here, and were received with due honors. They were under the escort of Commodore Dupont and Captains D. D. Porter and Sydney Smith Lee, of the navy, with Dr. C. F. Macdonald (now the chief of the Money-Order Bureau of the Post-Office Department) as Secretary, and Mr. Portman Interpreter. These gentlemen were very courteous to "the press," and gave every facility to obtain information concerning the Japanese. I mention this as an instance of due appreciation of reporters and correspondents.

I presume that all Japanese doctors have their heads shaved, for, when a Methodist preacher, whose pate was hairless, was introduced to the physicians of the Japanese embassy, they shouted out "Doctor! doctor!" and rushed forward to shake him by the hand. Congress voted fifty thousand dollars to pay their expenses as the guests of the Government. Secretary Seward, as with the Chinese embassy, gave the Japanese a splendid entertainment. This gentleman never failed, on such occasions, to make a good impression on distinguished foreign visitors in the extension of his hospitalities.

The distinguished princes brought with them the treaty negotiated with the Japanese Government by Commodore Perry. It was a large document, in a heavy case, and was carried to their lodgings on the top of an omnibus. Our Government paid all the expenses of the embassy.

Ford's Theatre, in which President Lincoln was assassinated, was formerly a church. After the assassination, Secretary Stanton made a preliminary arrangement for its purchase, for one hundred thousand dollars, which sum Congress appropriated. The building was then remodelled, and is now occupied as the Government Army Medical Museum.

Hon. Thaddeus Stevens died at about midnight on the 12th of August, 1868, at his residence on Capitol Hill, in this city. His nephews, Simon Stevens and Thaddeus Stevens, Jr.; his housekeeper, Mrs. Smith; Mr. J. Scott Patterson, of the Interior Department; Sisters Loretta and Geneviève, of Providence Hospital, and the servants of his household, were at his bedside during his last moments. He passed away calmly and quietly, without a struggle. He always announced his views with boldness, and fearlessly invited the consequences.

Hon. Silas Wright, Senator from New York, was distinguished as much for his courteous and gentle manners, as for his great intellectual powers in debate. During an exciting discussion, Hon. Benjamin Watkins Leigh, of Virginia, who was opposed to Mr. Wright in politics, undertook to annoy him, supposing that he would bear the unprovoked ill-treatment with silence. Mr. Wright quieted the gentleman by deliberately informing him that he would not enter into a personal quarrel in the Senate, but would, outside the chamber, give him any satisfaction he desired.

In 1842, Mr. Joshua R. Giddings, of Ohio, after having been expelled from the House for an expression of his views on the subject of slavery, was promptly returned to his seat by his constituents. In a subsequent speech, he said: "I will not speak of the time when Dawson, of Louisiana, drew a bowie-knife for my assassination. I was afterward speaking with regard to a certain transaction in which negroes were concerned in Georgia, when Mr. Black, of Georgia, raising his bludgeon, and standing in front of my seat, said to me, 'If you repeat that language again, I will knock you down.' It was a solemn moment for me. I had never been knocked down, and having some curiosity upon that subject, I repeated the language. Then Mr. Dawson, of Louisiana, the same who had drawn the bowie-knife, placed his hand on his pocket, and said, with an oath, which I will not repeat, that he would shoot me, at the same time cocking the pistol, so that all around me could hear the click."

In April, 1844, John Quincy Adams presented to the House the camp-chest of General George Washington, used by him during the Revolutionary war, and bequeathed to Congress by the late William S. Winder. An equally interesting event was the presentation of the sword of Washington, and the staff of Franklin, which was made through the late Hon. George W. Summers, of Virginia, whose entire speech was, on motion of Mr. Adams, recorded on the Journal of the House. This act was as indicative of the appreciation of the oration, as of the sword of the hero, and the staff of the philosopher.

Preston S. Brooks made his personal assault upon Senator Sumner in May, 1856. Mr. Brooks died in this city, at Brown's Hotel, on the 27th of January, 1857. He had been in bed for a day or two, suffering severely from the effects of a severe cold. He was assuring his friends that he had passed the crisis of his illness, and felt improved in health, when he was seized with a violent croup, and died about ten minutes afterward. He expired in intense pain, an event so sudden as to cause much surpise and sympathy throughout the city.

A good pun was made by the Hon. Joseph R. Chandler, of Philadelphia. During a debate in the House on a bill to prescribe punishments in the navy, Mr. Chandler inquired of Mr. Bocock, who had spoken of "keelhauling," what it was. Mr. Bocock replied: "Tying ropes to a sailor, throwing him overboard, and then hauling him under the keel to the other side of the vessel." Mr. Chandler thanked him for the explanation, and said that was making a man *undergo a hard-ship.*

While the addition to the Capitol was in course of construction, several Southern members of Congress (including Keitt and Miles, of South Carolina) sought to have sport with two Irish laborers, who were hauling a small cart of building-material. "They make horses of you," said one of the members. "That's true, gentlemen," was the response, "but we are not quite as bad as them jackasses in yonder Capitol." The Congressmen were silenced, and passed on to the Hall of Representatives.

The "Bird of Liberty" was formerly a favorite theme with members of Congress. The eagle, so poetically described by Mr. Bedinger, from the Harper's Ferry district, was characterized by a western member as a turkey-buzzard, which Mr. Bedinger indignantly denied. There was no way of settling the dispute. The eagle of Mr. Williamson R. W. Cobb, of Alabama, was of wonderful dimensions. He said that it rested its feet on the highest peak of the Rocky Mountains, drank from the Pacific Ocean, and, at the same time, laid the egg of annexation in the island of Cuba!

www.ingramcontent.com/pod-product-compliance
Lightning Source LLC
LaVergne TN
LVHW011153110826
845150LV00006B/1220

* 9 7 8 1 4 2 5 5 4 6 1 7 5 *